CLIO

CLIO

The Autobiography of Martha Fowke Sansom (1689–1736)

Edited with an Introduction and Notes by
Phyllis J. Guskin

Newark: University of Delaware Press
London: Associated University Presses

© 1997 by Associated University Presses, Inc.

All rights reserved. Authorization to photocopy items for internal or personal use, or the internal or personal use of specific clients, is granted by the copyright owner, provided that a base fee of $10.00, plus eight cents per page, per copy is paid directly to the Copyright Clearance Center, 222 Rosewood Drive, Danvers, Massachusetts 01923. [0-87413-607-5/97 $10.00+8¢ pp, pc.]

Associated University Presses
440 Forsgate Drive
Cranbury, NJ 08512

Associated University Presses
16 Barter Street
London WC1A 2AH, England

Associated University Presses
P.O. Box 338, Port Credit
Mississauga, Ontario
Canada L5G 4L8

The paper used in this publication meets the requirements of the American National Standard for Permanence of Paper for Printed Library Materials Z39.48–1984.

Library of Congress Cataloging-in-Publication Data

Sansom, Martha Fowke, 1689–1736.
  Clio : the autobiography of Martha Fowke Sansom, 1689–1736 / edited with an introduction and notes by Phyllis J. Guskin.
    p. cm.
  Includes bibliographical references and index.
  IBSN 0-87413-607-5 (alk. paper)
  1. Sansom, Martha Fowke, 1689–1736—Biography. 2. Women authors, English—18th century—Biography. 3. Authors, English—18th century—Biography. I. Guskin, Phyllis J., 1934– . II. Title.
PR3461.F665Z474 1997
821'.5—dc20
                                          96-19029
                                            CIP

PRINTED IN THE UNITED STATES OF AMERICA

Contents

List of Illustrations	7
Preface	9
Introduction	15
Family and Upbringing	19
Fowke and Her Social Context	22
Fowke and Sexuality	25
Fowke and Eliza Haywood	28
Fowke and Aaron Hill	31
Fowke as Mrs. Sansom	37
Clio as Text	40
Textual Note	51
Clio: Or, A Secret History of the Life and Amours of the Late celebrated Mrs. S——N——M	53
Explanatory Notes	149
Appendix A: Letters and Poems of Aaron Hill to Martha Fowke Sansom	168
Appendix B: Eliza Haywood's Attack on Martha Fowke in *Memoirs of a Certain Island Adjacent to the Kingdom of Utopia*	191
Bibliography	198
Index	205

Illustrations

1. "The Female Lover," from *The Cupid,* 2d ed. London, 1739 — 16
2. Dedication to Aaron Hill, from *Clio* — 33
3. Title page of *Clio* (1752) — 41
4. Aaron Hill. Frontispiece to *A Full and Just Account of the Ottoman Empire,* 2d ed. London, 1710 — 59
5. Page 1 of Fowke's Life, from *Clio* — 61
6. View of St. James's Park and Palace, from John Stow's *Survey of London,* ed. Strype (1720) — 68
7. Map of Fulham, detail from John Rocque's *New and Accurate Survey of London* (1748) — 80
8. Eliza Haywood. Frontispiece to Vol. 1 of *Secret Histories, Novels, and Poems.* London, 1732 — 83
9. Detail of map of St. James's parish from John Stow's *Survey of London,* ed. Strype (1720) — 95
10. Early eighteenth-century watercolor sketch of the Paper Buildings in the Inner Temple — 118
11. The Temple, from John Stow's *Survey of London,* ed. Strype (1720) — 130

Preface

I first came across Martha Fowke's name over a decade ago when I was exploring early eighteenth-century periodicals looking for unknown women writers. Sitting in the Newberry Library, Chicago, and leafing through the little-read *Delights for the Ingenious* (1711), I found several poems by Martha Fowke. They were competent and confident, written in a fresh and lively style, and explicitly attributed to her. My interest was piqued by this open claiming of authorship, particularly uncommon for a young woman at that period, and I looked for more. The Newberry had a copy of *Clio and Strephon,* her exchange of letters about poetry and feelings with the writer William Bond, published in 1720. Reading it, I became even more intrigued by Fowke's ambition and range. I discovered that her long autobiographical letter to Aaron Hill, published under the title *Clio* in 1752 after the death of the recipient, was sometimes referred to in footnotes to biographies of male writers, but the work itself was almost never discussed. On the rare occasions when it was characterized, it was dismissed as either transparent prevarication, a bowdlerized piece of pornography, or the product of a hysterical woman.

When I finally read *Clio* I was struck by Fowke's perceptive analyses of both her own motives and those of others, by her fresh and lively style, and by her intriguing depiction of the social life of a member of English literary circles in the early years of the eighteenth century. I have been unable to find a portrait of Martha Fowke but she seemed vivid to me as I read her account of her life.

During a parallel investigation of poems by women published in the *Gentleman's Magazine,* I came across a remarkable poem called "Written at Midnight," which I eventually tracked back to its first publication as one of a group of almost forty poems first published in the *Barbados Gazette* in the 1730s. As I tried to discover who had written those poems, I gradually became convinced that they too were works by Fowke. Again they were open, emotionally expressive, and unconventional in many ways. The extent and coherence of this body of work is of great interest to anyone studying the functioning of the woman writer at that period of great change in social and political assumptions, and I felt that all of it needed to be made available to scholars of the period. But I was convinced that Martha Fowke's autobiography in particular is valuable in its own right, because it makes us vividly aware of what writing could (and still can) mean to an individual. For many women, then and now, writing seems to provide a lifeline, a pathway to self-awareness through the labyrinth of social values that militate against achievement.

Martha Fowke was ambitious for her voice to be heard; she craved publication, publicity, recognition. She consciously and explicitly placed herself in a tradition of women poets, from Sappho to Lady Chudleigh. Psychologically and socially, however, the recognition of her own achievement came through men. When she was just beginning to write, her father's encouragement took the seductive form of inviting her to write his own love letters to potential mistresses; later, she responded to the praise of the circle of literary figures in the London of the 1720s, ranging from Richard Steele to Richard Savage, from Giles Jacob to Aaron Hill.

Many of Fowke's relationships still pose puzzles. Her relationship with Hill is cryptic, although we have a fair amount of evidence from *Clio* and from Hill's own letters and poems. Fowke writes to demonstrate both her sincerity and her emotional attachment to Hill, but she seems to become more despondent as she comes to the end of the bound blank book in which she inscribes her life. Hill's surviving letters show a Clio insisting on decorous friendship; the text of *Clio* shows a woman voicing a desperate love. Did Hill tire of the game, before or after consummation? We can never know, and perhaps it is mere prurience to think we should. Similarly, Fowke's relations with her erstwhile friend and fellow writer Eliza Haywood are not easy to untangle. Rivalry of some kind seems to have incited Haywood to pour out a torrent of abuse upon Fowke, charging her with offenses that range from bad writing to incest! Are Haywood's motives personal, mercenary, political, or mixed?

The research for this edition has been in many ways a kind of detective story. The referential truth of Fowke's account posed, and poses, interesting questions. Some figures were comparatively easy to identify, but I had considerable difficulty when I tried to find the Mr. R. described very specifically as a judge in Ireland. As reference book after reference book provided no possible identification, I began to wonder. Then one day I consulted the British Library's copy of *Clio,* with manuscript identifications and notes. The puzzle was solved. The contemporary annotator had corrected the cryptic initial R. to K.—an easy mistake in eighteenth-century handwriting—and identified the judge as Mr. Keightley. My confidence that Martha Fowke's allusions did have accurate referents enabled me to identify many of the other people in her life, although there are still blanks, and I hope other scholars may be able to contribute to the picture.

The value of such detective work, it seems to me, lies in its evocation of a literary and social context that was particularly complex in the early period of the spread of print. The social circle was still small in the London of the *Tatler* and the *Spectator*, but it was less simple and unitary than we often assume. The prescriptive middle-class morality of Addison and Steele has to be played against the continuing values of personal freedom and experimentation so salient in the Restoration. The importance of the holdover can be seen in Fowke's relationship with her libertine father.

In the course of this investigation I have drawn upon the resources of a number of libraries, in the United States and in Britain. Most important, not only has the Lilly Library of Indiana University provided a good part of the primary material that I have used, including the copy text of *Clio,* but the staff there have been unfailingly helpful and friendly. I would especially like to thank Lilly Librarian William Cagle, Joel Silver, Sue Presnell, and Helen Walsh. Lisa Killion transcribed the text for me with patient good humor. The British Library produced essential materials for me (and luckily delayed its move to the new building so that I have had the pleasure of using the great domed Reading Room and the North Library with all their associations). The Newberry Library gave me the initial impetus for this quest. Working in the Bodleian Library is always a nostalgic experience; there I came across the valuable manuscript genealogy of the Fowke family. I am grateful to the Keeper of Western Manuscripts of the Bodleian Library for permission to quote from this. I had efficient responses from the staff at the Public Record Offices of Hertfordshire, Leicestershire, and Staffordshire in my search for archival material. Librarians at Westminster Public Library and Hammersmith and Fulham Libraries and the Archivist of the Inner Temple were also helpful in my quest.

As important as libraries have been the many friends and colleagues who have listened, questioned, sympathized, encouraged, and generally supported me in many different ways. Particular thanks go to Sean Shesgreen, who read the manuscript at a critical time, and to Linda David, who has been consistently supportive and whose critical intelligence and sensitivity has, I hope, saved me from too many errors.

My daughters, Karen and Jane, have put up with their mother's enthusiasms for many years, and I am grateful for their love and understanding. My largest debt, however, is to the patience, love, and support of my husband, Sam Guskin.

I wish to dedicate this book to the memory of three influential teachers in my life: my father, Alfred Duffy; my Oxford tutor, Kathleen Lea; and my advisor and mentor at Vanderbilt University, John M. Aden.

CLIO

Introduction

In October 1723 Martha Fowke Sansom finished *Clio,* a long autobiographical letter to the writer Aaron Hill, which gives an account of her life to that date, intermingled with passionate declarations of her love for him. She was then in her early thirties, married, and the proud possessor of a considerable reputation as a writer.[1]

Fowke's major work, *Clio and Strephon,* a poetic correspondence with William Bond, had been published in 1720; it was accompanied by a glowing critical discussion by John Porter, which placed the work firmly in the epistolary tradition and praised the wit, humor, and delicacy of Fowke's contribution to the volume. Porter's dedication to Sir Richard Steele comments that Steele had often expressed "the singular Value and Esteem" he had for Fowke's "extraordinary Wit."[2] In 1720 Martha Fowke was described by Giles Jacob in his *Poetical Register* as "an accomplish'd Young Lady" with "a genius that would let her be Britain's Dacier."[3] When Fowke was only twenty-one she had boldly put her name to published poems in such periodicals as *Delights for the Ingenious* (1711), and subsequently her poems had featured in various miscellanies.[4] One large group of her poems seems to have made its way to Barbados, probably with the addressee, and was printed some years later in the *Barbados Gazette.*[5] In spite of this early visibility, Fowke's work has not received the reevaluation that is her due. Not only is she a poet of remarkable freshness, but her autobiography is a remarkable document of the formation of a unconventional woman writer at a key moment in the development of the world of print.

Fowke was often compared to Sappho, as was her poetic precursor and model Aphra Behn; Fowke reinforced the association by taking the poetic name Clio, the name of Sappho's daughter.[6] Fowke herself showed little reluctance in claiming the legacy of both female and male poetic forebears. She wrote elegies on the death of the writer Mary, Lady Chudleigh; she linked herself to other earlier women writers; she imitated Sappho, Donne, and Shakespeare. In her poem "The Interview," the evocation of her self-image as poet that ends *Clio and Strephon* (1720), she aligns

15

The Female Lover

Chartelain inv.   I. Sotin sculp.

*Plays Poems & Romances melt ỹ Heart,
And Love finds easy entrance for his Dart.*

Like Martha Fowke, this early eighteenth-century woman sits with poems and letters and thinks about her lover. "The Female Lover," from *The Cupid* (London, 1739).

herself with the women's tradition of Katherine Philips and Aphra Behn and then expands her vision. Explicitly ambitious for fame, she invokes Shakespeare: "I ask not *Life,* nor *Fortune,* but the *Art,* / As HE does *mine,* to *Touch* the READER's *Heart.*" The poem ends with a final cry of aspiration: *"But on the Wings of Verse I wish to Rise."* As Ros Ballaster has argued for Aphra Behn, so Fowke too sought "to win power through language over her reader/lover."[7] She laid claim to the natural language of the heart as a way of projecting an image of herself as a woman of passion, frankness, and genius.

However, by the time she died in poverty a decade later, Martha Fowke had essentially lost her standing as both writer and woman. Her name had been scandalized in a number of attacks by Eliza Haywood, an erstwhile friend. Married to a quarrelsome drunkard, Arnold Sansom, Fowke felt crushed by domestic worries and it seems that she had stopped writing. Later, Samuel Johnson spoke sneeringly of her as "once too well known," and a nineteenth-century critic remarked that "a list of her admirers might be mistaken for the index of names to Pope's 'Dunciad'."[8] More recently, Clarence Tracy in his account of Richard Savage saw only the work of "an over-sexed and neurotic woman, whose assertion that all her love affairs were Platonic only a simpleton would accept."[9] Although Fowke's verse is now represented in Roger Lonsdale's anthology, *Eighteenth-Century Women Poets,* and she appears in several recent dictionaries of women writers, her autobiography has not received the reevaluation that is her due.[10]

One possible reason for her eclipse may lie in the timing of publication of this work. Her manuscript, dated in the text as 1723, was not published until thirty years later, when it appeared at the same time as the flourishing of the scandal memoirs discussed by Felicity Nussbaum in *The Autobiographical Subject: Gender and Ideology in Eighteenth-Century England* (1989). The title page, presumably added by the publisher, seems to assimilate the work to the genre of the "secret history," stressing the "amours" as well as the life. However, such "fallen" women as Laetitia Pilkington, Teresa Constantia Phillips, and Lady Vane, whose autobiographical self-justifications appeared within six years of the publication of *Clio* in 1752, were engaged in a very different and more public confrontation with gender expectations and moral constraints, both of which had also changed dramatically over the course of a half century. In contrast, Fowke's "little book" was composed as a personal account and justification of her life at the request of her friend and "lover," Aaron Hill. Fowke uses the term "lover" for a spectrum of relationships, from casual admirer through serious suitor to intimate emotional, and possibly sexual, partner. How far her affair with Hill went is difficult to evaluate, but that topic is taken up later in this introduction. The personal origin of Fowke's autobiography in the complex social and literary circles of early eighteenth-century London shapes it as a very different work from later, more traditional public self-justifications.[11.]

Clio is both autobiography and love letter. It provides us with a detailed account of the author's background, upbringing, adventures, attitudes, and relationships, while exploring the psychological condition of being in love. It is also a conscious presentation and self-justification of the self as writer, and it has clear analogies with fictional strategies.[12] In some ways it can be compared to the mixture of autobiography and fiction in Delariviere Manley's *The Adventures of Rivella* (1714), but, unlike Manley, who uses a male narrator, Fowke speaks in her own voice. The personal narrative is both breached and reinforced by the immediacy of her direct appeals to Hill, the "onlie begetter" of her account.

Fowke's account of her life is also unusual in that it is the work of a comparatively young woman, although one already conscious of the passing of time and the fading of youth. In her early thirties, Fowke reflects upon the formative influences of her life with a passion and immediacy different from the more meditative retrospect of old age. Both Lady Halkett and Lady Fanshawe, for example, wrote their autobiographies late in life, apparently intending them as legacies for their children, preservations of family history. No such altruistic motive stirred Martha Fowke.[13]

Fowke was a woman who gloried in her literary achievements, in her social independence, and in a sense of her difference. The autobiography describes in detail her childhood and her relationship to her parents, her developing interest in reading and her growing sense of her own abilities as a writer. She also discusses with considerable psychological insight her various social and emotional relationships with a wide group of diverse men ranging from a blind merchant to the aging dramatist William Wycherley, from peers to commoners, from father to husband. Fowke presents herself as the constant object of desire, although she analyzes carefully gradations of feeling in her own responses, from friendship to gratitude to passion. Fowke's analysis is perceptive about gender roles, and in many ways remarkably frank, even though this frankness clearly serves as a strategy of intimacy in the overarching relationship with the primary reader, Aaron Hill.

Family and Upbringing

Martha Fowke was born in 1689, the first child of a couple that might have sprung from the pages of Restoration comedy.[14] Her father was a dark, handsome army officer, of a well-established family in Staffordshire, who made a practice of marrying wealthy widows. The Bodleian Library has a detailed manuscript genealogy from about 1677 by Gerard Fowke, which gives a description of Thomas Fowke, fourth son of John Fowke and Joyce, daughter and heir of Richard Marche of Limehouse, Stepney. Gerard Fowke observes that Thomas spent three or four years in France and is now at court: "A proper hansom Blacke Gent[le]man most of ye Fowkes of Gunston are Blacke, this Thomas is a very hopefull young Gent[le]man." Gerard Fowke notes that Thomas is married to Anne, oldest daughter of Sir James Austen and widow of Sir Anthony Vincent. The Fowke family connections range from gentry and minor aristocracy to the professions and wealthy merchants: one of Thomas's brothers was a clergyman who married into the family of physician Thomas Sydenham, another was a secretary to a bishop, and a sister married a Danish merchant living in London.[15]

Martha's mother, Mrs. Mary Chandler, was Thomas's third wife; she was less socially prestigious than the first two wives had been.[16] The marriage was loveless though publicly decent by the standards of the day. Thomas Fowke led a life of libertine dalliance, and his daughter comments that the "Chains of Marriage pressed him to death." Martha was a particular joy to her father, not even to be supplanted by the brother born a year later. She apparently took after her father, even in looks, as one of the "black" Fowkes. In a poetic picture of herself prefixed to her autobiography, she mentions her "olive" skin, and her nemesis Eliza Haywood more prosaically called her "a big-bone'd, buxom, brown Woman."[17]

The daughter idolized her libertine father, while her beautiful, well-educated, virtuous, and pious mother is described with coolness. Fowke saw her mother as influenced by prudential concerns in evaluating possible suitors for her daughter, whereas her father "studied my Happiness in a more refined Manner." When Fowke was about sixteen, her mother died; she remarks very objectively that her first responses to the death were to the practical consequences, such as the loss of her mother's jointure and the consequent breakup of the household, the lack of stability in domestic arrangements, and the separation from her beloved father.

Far more traumatic for Fowke than the early death of her mother was the murder of her father in 1708. Thomas Fowke was apparently murdered by one of his servants; the *London Gazette* of 20–24 May 1708 made an appeal for information:

> Whereas the Honourable Thomas Fowke Esq: Major, in the Right Honourable the Lord Mordaunt's Regiment of Foot, upon Saturday the 15th Day of this Instant May, was found barbarously murther'd in his Bed, at his Quarters in the Talbot in Sowerbridge in the County of Worcester, and that one Charles. . . . , Servant of the said Major, is violently suspected to have committed the said Murther, and was last in the Chamber with the said Major, and hath rode away with the Horse, and several other Goods of the said Major, and is describ'd to be a short, slender, strait Fellow, about 20 Years of Age, with short Hair of a very light pale Colour, round faced, and pale Colour'd, with a white colour'd Coat trim'd with black; rode away on a brown Gelding, about 14 Hands and a half high, with a longish Star down the Face, Paces fine, and hath a good Forehand, and is about 6 Years old. If any Person shall seize and Apprehend the said Servant, they shall be very well rewarded; and any Person who knows the said Servant's Name, or place of his last Service or Residence, or can give any further Description of him, is desir'd forthwith to cause the said Description to be inserted in the Gazette, or give notice to Matt. Wotton at the Three Daggers in Fleet Street.

We may speculate on the motives behind this murder of master by young servant; I have found no account of the trial. However, for orphaned Martha Fowke, at the age of nineteen, the loss was shattering: now she felt not just the practical consequences, as with her mother, but the deprivation of a basic source of her self-esteem as a woman and as a writer.[18]

Martha's close relationship with her father was bound up with her sense of herself as a writer; encouraged by her father's praise for her wit and precocity, she came to associate writing with the Restoration world of his social and sexual proclivities. The identification was further strengthened by the fact that she honed her literary skills at an early age by writing her father's love letters for him, an act of imaginative fictional identification that may well be the basis for her later awareness of the intricate networks between the sexual and the literary self. The praise she received from her father in many ways foreshadowed much of Fowke's personal and literary achievement, although she perceptively recognized some of its detrimental consequences: "it wakened a Vanity in me, which I have hardly yet been able to suppress, and which has led me into many Mistakes: The Homage I received then gave me a

Passion for it, which will never entirely dye." Certainly it is possible to see the remainder of her life as demonstrating a powerful urge to use her poetic abilities to win "Homage," or male esteem, an urge that may well have been reinforced by the traumatic murder of her father when she was nineteen. Her poems are filled with ambitious claims for "fame," and her most important relationships seem to have been with men who responded to her as writer as well as woman, such men as Richard Savage, John Dyer, and Aaron Hill. Martha Fowke has no anxiety about authorship, no qualms about writing and circulating letters and verses. In fact, this seems to have been one of the points that infuriated Eliza Haywood, after the friendship between the two women turned to enmity, for Haywood constantly alludes to Fowke's shameless behavior in openly writing to men.[19]

Fowke's education followed the pattern of girls of her class. She was primarily educated at home, with specialized tutors for languages, music, and dance. She knew French but not Latin; although she claimed to have been interested in learning the latter with her brother, she was not considered strong enough! Her reading began with romances, such as La Calprenède's lengthy *Cassandra* and *Cleopatra,* which opened for her delicious visions of female power: "I read there with Pleasure the Empire of Women, and doubted not of finding an *Orondates.* I could think of nothing below a King or a Prince." She continues, "This gave my Heart too exalted Notions, and has since occasioned a Thousand Disappointments." She also mentions becoming deeply involved in the love poetry of Ovid and Cowley, until rebuked by her religious mentor, a Jesuit priest, who encouraged her to read more serious moral works. Shakespeare became a passion later, possibly when Rowe's edition of 1709 made his work more easily accessible and even fashionable.

In the eighteenth century, writing was a separate skill, learned later than reading. Fowke states that she indulged herself in it so much that she alarmed her mother, who considered it dangerous. This response was not uncommon in the early part of the century when some fathers encouraged their daughters in literary and intellectual matters, while mothers, perhaps more realistically, tried to lower expectations and mandate conformity to social values. Laetitia Pilkington faced a similar clash of values when she was praised by her father and beaten by her mother for reading.[20] Fowke's mother took steps to replace such indulgence in reading and writing with a more appropriate female education in needlework: "She locked up her Books, my Pens were burned, and I bound down a

Prisoner to my Needle. Never did romantick Lady deplore her self more than Miss *Patty* [Martha]. I looked upon this as the highest Affront. . . . I secretly lamented the Loss of my dear Pen and Ink, as if I had lamented a Lover." Writing and sexual relationships consistently merged for Fowke, but always with considerable comic and ironic self-awareness.

Fowke and her social context

Fowke's autobiography derives much of its energy from the interaction of her sense of herself as a writer with her sharp observation of the social world around her. Her account of her early life focuses primarily on the development of her skills as a writer; later events in her life are often described with the shaping awareness and skills of a novelist. One example describes an evening at a dance where she has met a charming Mr. S. (not the Mr. Sansom she later married). He had bribed the servants not to hear her when they return to the friend's house where she is spending the night:

> I danced on as securely as if my Guardian Angel had led me along; but at last the Company prepared to be gone; I looked round, but my Friend, who was to conduct me, was slipped away with the Hours. I grew a little concern'd at this; but the Person who had danced with me offer'd his Service very gravely. It was late, and I alone, and a Stranger to the rest of the Company. I saw it was the Custom of the Place to see the Ladies home; I therefore gave my Hand to my Partner, who led me into a Hackney-Coach, that waited, and which he told me my Friend had left on Purpose. I knew not why, but my Heart began to tremble as if some Danger was near it. I sighed to myself, and now wished to be safe at home, though my Lover behaved as I could wish. The Coach drove to the Back-Door, as directed; but how was I surprized! we called, we beat at the Door enough to raise the Dead, but no Light appear'd, nor Servant; we stay'd above an Hour to no Purpose. It was extream dark, late, cold, and rainy. I knew it was impossible to get Entrance into my Lodgings, for there I left word that I would lye in the————. The Gentleman seem'd concern'd as much as I, and acted his Part very well. He spread his Cloak over me, and we walked and stood at the cruel adamantine Door till I was starv'd to Death. At length Mr. *S.* implor'd me to mount the Coach to defend us from the Weather.—The Wind blew, the Spouts pour'd, the Coachman grumbled, the Horses groan'd, and I sigh'd. Never were such deplorable Objects.

The vivid specificity of details (the rain, the cold, the pouring downspouts, and the grumbling coachman), the sense of colloquial speech combined with crisp rhythms and decisive syntax, the touches of parody ("the cruel adamantine Door"), the alertness to emotions—all combine to create a scene fully delineated, and convincingly real. Fowke's writing is in many places strikingly different from the flowing "warm" style of such earlier women writers as Behn and Manley.

The fictional flavor does not invalidate Fowke's account. Where her facts can be checked, they are remarkably accurate. Her cottage in Fulham featured in poems by herself and her friends. Her landlord, Mr. Cenny, is well documented; he also was Steele's landlord.[21] Fowke gives precise details about where she lived and whom she met; the very unglamorous nature of some of the details bear their own authenticity with them. The cousins who borrowed her clothes, the details about where people sat in a room, the specificity of addresses, all seem unlikely material to invent.

Social interaction is crucial in Fowke's autobiography. She defines herself as primarily formed by contacts with people in intimate domestic settings. Although Fowke was Catholic, at least in her youth, and may have had Jacobite sympathies, like her father, her contacts were not limited to partisan circles. She seems to display no interest in politics. The larger events of the first decades of the eighteenth century pass unnoticed in this account. Wars with Spain, the coming of the Hanoverians, the Jacobite Rebellion of 1715, the South Sea Bubble, all are absent from her pages. Even allusions to literature or the theater are linked to personal experience. Southerne's dramatic adaptation of Aphra Behn's novel, *Oronooko,* for example, was a favorite of hers, but its importance in her autobiography arises from the social implications of playgoing. Because she enjoyed the play, she consented to go to it unchaperoned; when the escapade is discovered, the male relative who had persuaded her to go incurs her father's wrath and is forced to leave the house. This unnamed relative then changes his intention to leave his fortune to Martha and bequeathes it to strangers. Thus Fowke presents herself almost as a martyr to the combination of her love of literature and the theater and her quest for freedom and independence.

Money is a subtle but pervasive subtext in Fowke's account of her life. For all her claims to despise it, she is always alert to those who borrow it from her and to the power and independence it gives. She asserts that one prime motive in marrying was to achieve the power to dispense more charity. One of the frequent themes in her account of her rejected lovers is the consequent loss of their financial well-being, as if, when they lose her, everything else of value disappears. She notes with considerable satisfaction that she has personally given charity to one suitor now destitute.

Fowke is not particularly explicit about her own financial situation but enough information is provided to indicate that she had a settlement that gave her independence. Her gentry family had connections both at court and with wealthy merchants trading in Turkey and Virginia. There are constant reminders of the importance of money in enabling Fowke to live the life she does. After the deaths of her parents she lives alone, sometimes as a guest with family or friends but often as an independent woman in lodgings in London, Fulham, or Bath. New developments in building town houses had made this a viable option for women at the turn of the century. She presents herself as someone who is essentially above money, who can lend acquaintances a lottery ticket worth two hundred pounds and scorn to dun her debtors, but she is clearly aware of the value of the debt. She scorns the relatives who borrow the clothes she herself cannot wear when she is in mourning, but she also comments on their theft of her belongings.

Her family standing and her settlement clearly made her an interesting marital prospect, but her appeal was obviously not just financial. Some of the literary and personal tributes to her may be simply part of the coterie games popular in literary circles, but Lewis Theobald, John Dyer, Richard Savage, and Aaron Hill all wrote enthusiastically of her. She was one of a convivial group of literary men and women that met at the house of the blind seer Duncan Campbell around 1720; the group included Anthony Hammond, Richardson Pack, Philip Horneck, William Bond, George Sewell, John Philips, Susanna Centlivre, and Eliza Haywood.[22] Although many of these were connected with the publisher Edmund Curll, notorious for issuing works of obscenity and scandal, they were certainly not of the lower class of hacks. It is particularly interesting to note the presence of women in such gatherings.

Fowke's social contacts extended widely, as we see not just from the evidence in her autobiography but also from allusions in her poems. She mixed with the nobility and gentry, for her family connections were extensive. Through her husband, Arnold Sansom, she became involved in the world associated with the Temple, which had the reputation of being a center for young men about town and aspiring writers as well as learned lawyers. Drama and music were also important activities for her. Richard Savage, who knew her well in the early 1720s, described her life at that time thus:

INTRODUCTION

> Crown'd with the Palm, Bays, Myrtle, and the Vine;
> Love, Pity, Friendship, Music, Wit, and Wine,
> In social Spirits, lead thy Hours along,
> Thou Life of Loveliness, thou Soul of Song![23]

The social circle drew in John Dyer, who arrived in London at that time ready to abandon the study of law for either poetry or painting. He painted a portrait of Martha Fowke, as we know from a poem by Savage, and also exchanged verse with her. Even when he went to Italy to study, in 1724, Dyer did not forget Clio, and his lines from Rome convey far more genuine feeling than the turgid praise of Savage:

> Alas, dear Clio, every day
> Some sweet idea dies away!
> Echoes of songs, and dreams of joys,
> Inhuman Absence all destroys.[24]

Certainly Fowke's warm friendship for Dyer allowed her to confess some of her ambivalence about her sense of self and the limitations of gender constraints. In a poem addressed to Dyer, published in 1726, she writes frankly of the problems of combining her domestic responsibilities with her poetic ambitions:

> My humbler lot was in low distance laid;
> I was, oh, hated thought! a woman made;
> For household Cares, and empty Trifles meant,
> The *Name* does Immortality prevent.
> Yet, let me stretch, beyond my *Sex,* my *Mind,*
> And rising, leave the flutt'ring train behind;
> Nor Art, nor Learning, wish'd Assistance lends,
> But Nature, Love, and Musick are my friends.[25]

Dyer is the "valued Friend" who represents her final bequest to Hill, in the poetic last will and testament that closes this autobiography: "No more, what have I else intitled mine, / My Life, my Soul, my Muse, my Friend, are thine."

FOWKE AND SEXUALITY

Interpreting Fowke's accounts of her relationships is not an easy task. She is clearly fascinated by men's responses to her, listing in considerable detail every man who fell in love with her, young, old, married, single, honorable or illicit. Her analysis of her own responses is complex. She is aware of how often she gets locked into a relationship by pity, as with the blind Sir William Maynard, or by habit, as with Sansom. She acknowledges the mixed motives that infuse her feelings and also the very different attitudes that she finds in men, from jealousy to naïveté, from misogyny to jealous despair. She is certainly aware that she seems fickle, writing to Savage in 1722 a poem called "The Inconstant," in which she justifies her change as a search for true intellectual compatibility and a flight from the "lumber" of "heavy Earth":

> I search—but rarely meet an equal Taste,
> Then I grow weary, and I change in haste:
> Where I discern, that heavy Earth prevails,
> I leave the Lumber, and I shift the Sails.[26]

Fowke's attempt to distance herself from "heavy Earth" and build relationships based on a platonic equality of souls was not exclusive to her. The Catholic circles in which she seems to have moved were particularly attracted to this tradition of aristocratic love, which often involved extensive correspondence between men and women, under such romantic and pastoral pseudonyms as Damon, Orinda, Philander, and Celia. As Valerie Rumbold has shown, Pope's close friends the Blount sisters were part of just such a circle.[27]

However, this indulgence in social flirtation could easily pass into more sexually charged relationships. Fowke is at no point explicit about her sexual relationships, but she gives an account of her relationship with her future husband that seems implicitly to substantiate the allegation of sexual freedom. It is perhaps indicative of Fowke's tendency to merge sexual feeling and literary creativity that she suggests premarital consummation in lines describing the "soft" and amorous scenes painted on the walls and ceiling of a house where she visited Sansom:

> He had a little retired House near *Windsor,* where I used to pass many very happy Moments. Nothing could be more romantickly sweet than this Place; it seemed formed for Love, far from Noise or Business. The Gentleman it had belonged to was a fine Painter, he had spread the Ceilings and Wainscot with *Cupids;* every Room had some soft Device. . . .
>
> > The artful Pencil kindles soft Desire,
> > And warms the Wishes with a dangerous Fire.

> Th'attending Lover sees the Passion rise,
> Watches the heaving Breast and streaming Eyes;
> Pours in his Sighs, when the dissolving Heart
> Gives way; and no Reserve to take its Part.[28]

Fowke's verse evocation of "the dissolving Heart" and the absence of "Reserve" seems an implicit acknowledgment of her sexual commitment to Sansom.

The Restoration world of wits and libertines into which Fowke was born in 1690 was gradually dying in the first decades of the eighteenth century, but it still retained its power in certain subgroups. James Turner has discussed the concept of "baroque sexuality": "In a significant and potentially unstable synthesis, a wholly unromantic cult of frank physicality and sexual freedom was grafted onto its apparent opposite—the heroic love-code of Romance, infinitely elaborated in the salon culture of mid-century France."[29] One can see the instability of this complex synthesis in Fowke, as her father's libertine values of the last part of the seventeenth century clashed with newer perspectives.

The newer perspectives were themselves complex, involving adjustments between the claims of the feeling heart and the claims of middle-class rational morality, both inculcated by such works as the periodical papers of Addison and Steele and the novels of Samuel Richardson.[30] Certainly there were negative aspects to the libertine social culture at the end of the seventeenth century, but it also released certain constraints and suggested opportunities later to be closed. As Lawrence Stone has noted, the decades embracing the turn of the century saw widespread "violence, perjury, rape, and obsessive promiscuous sexuality"; but they also saw new aspirations of women for personal liberty and the pursuit of happiness. This "period of conflicting values [which] led to extremes of behaviour patterns" acted to provide the matrix for a major shift in gender relations, perhaps not unfamiliar to us today.[31] Bishop South lamented "the mode, the gallantry and the genteel freedom of the present age," especially as it encouraged free behavior for women:

> Persons of that sex, whose proper ornament should be bashfulness and modesty, are grown so bold and forward, offer themselves into company, and even invite those addresses which the severity of former times would have scorned to admit. From the retirement of the closet, they are come to brave it in theatres and taverns; where virtue and modesty are drunk down, and honour left behind to pay the reckoning.[32]

FOWKE AND ELIZA HAYWOOD

Whether Fowke herself lived up to her platonic ideals or emulated her libertine father in the quest for pleasure, we are unlikely to know with certainty; nevertheless, her life illustrates the ways in which these conflicts showed themselves in the day-to-day interaction of men and women.

Fowke's fellow writer Eliza Haywood was explicit in accusing her onetime friend of a wide range of sexual transgressions, including fornication, adultery, and incest. The vituperative flurry of Haywood's attacks began in late 1720 or 1721 with the hitherto unnoticed character of a "wit" who initiates correspondence with men in *Letters from a Lady of Quality*.[33] The storm gathered force in *A Spy upon the Conjurer* (1724) and *Memoirs of a Certain Island Adjacent to the Kingdom of Utopia* (1725–26), suggesting a violent breakdown in an established friendship between the women. Fowke and Haywood were approximately the same age, had family connections in the same part of Staffordshire, and moved in the same theatrical and literary circles in the 1720s.[34] In *A Spy upon the Conjurer,* Haywood describes a visit that she and Fowke ("the famous Mrs. F——") made some years before to the blind fortune-teller, Duncan Campbell: Campbell tells Fowke that although she is virtuous at that moment, she will soon lose all reputation, but she will eventually manage to marry a gentleman. As a consequence of Haywood's presence at this fortune-telling, Haywood says Fowke has developed such a hatred "that I believe she neither eat nor slept in Peace the Day she did not do me some Injury."[35] However, while there is no evidence for Fowke's injuring Haywood, the latter's attacks are both vicious and disturbingly well informed about aspects of Fowke's life.

In *Memoirs of a Certain Island* Haywood purported to describe Fowke's life in salacious detail, beginning by implying incest with her father: "Some say it was from him she learn'd those deluding Arts, she has since practis'd, to the Ruin of as many Women as she could get acquainted with their Lovers or their Husbands.— Whether this Report be true, I will not pretend to determine, for my pure and hallow'd Fires would sicken at a sight so horrible, so shocking as an Act of Incest: but this is certain, that they scrupled not to be seen in the same Bed together, and the old Goat would run into luscious Encomiums on the Beauties of her Limbs to all the young *Chevaliers* who came to his Levee." She comments that

Fowke had a son by a duke "who never was over-nice in his Choice," but that he dismissed her after finding her *in flagrante delicto* with "the most dirty and disagreeable of his Footmen." She then, says Haywood, "rang'd the Town for a miserable Maintenance, was common even to the meanest Rank of Men, and [was] at last despis'd by the vilest, and most profligate." She claims that Fowke's relationship with Sansom began with a period as his mistress, on an allowance of four hundred crowns (one hundred pounds), which enabled her to figure in society. Eventually, Haywood alleges, Fowke's brother forced Sansom into marriage. Since then Fowke "does what she pleases, goes where she pleases," and lives in comfort:

> The best Wine, and Conversation with the handsomest Men, are all the Heaven she wishes, and having an absolute command of the unhappy *Rutho*'s [Sansom's] Purse, is resolv'd to want nothing that she thinks essential to her happiness;—from one scene of Debauchery she hurries to another, and scarce a Day passes, without being witness of some new Crime as extravagant as shameless.—Of all the Gods there is none she acknowledges but *Phoebus,* him she frequently implores for assistance to charm her Lovers with the Spirit of Poetry. (1:43–48; reprinted in appendix B).

Although Haywood's *Memoirs of a Certain Island* was not published until 1725, it may have circulated in manuscript earlier, since it seems to have been started just after the South Sea crash, which figures in its opening pages as the enchanted well destroying established patterns of wealth. Alternatively, Haywood may have talked about her plans, for Fowke in *Clio* in 1723 responds with anguish to having heard that the "Scorpion Haywood" has directed "the Poison of her Pen" on her dead father: "I hear she even violates the Dead, who never had the Misfortune to see her, and has committed no crimes against her but in giving me Life; she taxes him with Follies he never heard of, my Soul knows him innocent of every Charge." If Fowke had been aware of the specific accusation of incest, "follies" seems a remarkably inadequate description of the charge, and she does not seem to directly respond to the other accusations, although in some sense *Clio* is a self-justification of events in her life that could be misinterpreted.

It is difficult at this remove to clarify the relationship between Haywood and Fowke and determine the grounds of the accusations. Haywood was involved in theatrical activity from around 1715, both as actress and as writer.[36] Her marital status is uncertain, although it has recently been proved that the long-standing story of her repudiation by a clergyman husband is inaccurate.[37] In 1719 she had written a best-selling novel, *Love in Excess,* but although this may have made her notorious, it is unlikely that it made her financially secure. If, as she claimed, Haywood had gentry connections, the fact that she appeared in breeches roles on the stage and published popular fiction might well have imperiled her social standing; maybe Fowke, who seems to have maintained her own position in society throughout her life, refused to support Haywood at a critical juncture. Haywood also asserts that Savage's vicious behavior to her was instigated by Fowke. It is possible she is thinking of Savage's juxtaposition of portraits of the two women in one of his poems, printed in 1724. Haywood is painted as a "cast-off Dame": "Flush'd with Success, for Stage-Renown she pants, / And melts, and swells, and pens luxurious Rants," while Fowke is invoked as "Thou Life of Loveliness, thou Soul of Song!"[38]

Additionally, Haywood may have been incensed by the disparity in their financial status, as she saw Fowke financially secure, married, praised for her writing, while she herself struggled to survive, desperately churning out volume after volume of novels, memoirs, secret histories, plays, and translations. "Who that sees her now," writes Haywood of Fowke, "dress'd in her rich Brocade, Diamonds in her Hair and Breast, and a handsome Equipage to attend her, would believe that she has been accustom'd to trudge the Streets with scarce a Shoe, and been transported at the Invitation of a Blue-apron Gallant, who charitably feasted her on the Remnants of those Treats, made for more fortunate Ladies of the same Vocation?" Financial envy and literary rivalry may have been complicated by sexual jealousy. Haywood wrote effusive love verses to Aaron Hill, and on the evidence of her novel *The Injur'd Husband* (1723), which contains another fictionalized attack on Fowke, Haywood felt that Fowke had deprived her of Hill's love. (The Haywood figure in the novel is called "Montamour," that is, "Love Hill"!) Haywood's choice of "Gloatitia" as Fowke's pseudonym in *Memoirs* suggests that Fowke's gloating on her good fortune might well have infuriated her struggling rival.

Haywood's account of Fowke's marriage in *Memoirs* presents the malicious interpretation of the facts of the situation as Fowke herself acknowledges them: there apparently was a premarital relationship, and Fowke states that her brother pressured her to marry, in spite of her aversion to the loss of her liberty. Financial considerations were also clearly involved, though Fowke claimed to be motivated by the wish to be more generous in her charities. No record of the marriage has been traced, but Haywood in 1725 observes that a child had recently been born to the couple.[39] It is tempting to speculate that Fowke may have written her autobiography while she was pregnant. Fowke herself never directly mentions any children, merely alluding in various poems and sections of the autobiography to "household cares," but her view of the marital relationship is vividly evoked in one of the poems at the end of *Clio,* when she describes herself as lying "dully contented in cold lawful arms." Ultimately we must leave the matter open. Haywood may have known details of Fowke's life that the latter wished to keep secret, or she may have embroidered undoubted fact with vicious insinuations. We should note that Haywood also attacks Martha Blount, the friend of Pope, and there may well have been political motives at work.

Fowke and Aaron Hill

Fowke's autobiography is structured by constant allusions to the difference between all other relationships and her response to Hill, the friend for whom this account of her life and emotions is written. Fowke describes all her previous feelings as mere shadows of the love she now has for Hill; in fact, the last section of the book disintegrates into fragments of passionate verse and prose addressed to him. The tone of the work changes to some extent here, for once Fowke is no longer talking about her own life, she becomes more anxious and dependent, seeing Hill's response as increasingly doubtful. The certainty of some of the earlier narrative episodes gives way to increasing despair and darkness, and the last poem in the work takes the form of a last will and testament:

> Oh! if you sorrow, let it not be much,
> Pain not my Ashes, which thy Tears would touch,
> Nor hasten to me, let my Passion wait,
> No Hour at Death's cold Mansion is too late.
> When Age has gaz'd thy shining Beauties o'er,
> And ravish'd some from the luxuriant Store,
> Then let it give thee to my faithful Arms,
> And bless my Grave with thy remaining Charms.

The echoes of Shakespearean sonnets that pervade the last pages of the book testify not only to the fusion of love and loss in Fowke's relationship with Hill, but also at the same time to her sense of being involved in a literary enterprise. This combination of intense emotionality and self-conscious artifice is characteristic of Fowke's writing.

The awareness of the act of writing is not merely abstract for Fowke, but immediate and physical. Although the original manuscript has vanished, it seems clear that Fowke was writing in a bound volume, her "little book," possibly a gift from Hill that was intended to help her start to write again after a period of depression. Fowke seems to have written her manuscript in the form of a printed work, providing it with an elaborate dedication to Aaron Hill, as the "onlie begetter" of this account of her life, another Shakespearean echo. The poem "Clio's Picture" that opens *Clio* stands in the place of a portrait frontispiece, as it did in the second edition of *Clio and Strephon*. It was the most famous single work of Fowke's, appearing first in Hammond's *Miscellany* of 1720. Hill knew the poem, quoting from it in some of his poems to Fowke; the version in *Clio* has authorial variants, suggesting it derives from Fowke's manuscript. She may have added it as a reminder of both her physical presence and her poetical reputation.

The blank volume presented a challenge to Fowke—a physical book-shaped space in which she could use her skill with words to present herself both as a confident writer and a woman in love. Her constructed narrative and wryly ironic depiction of scenes and characters are combined with the offering of a frank and generous revelation of her deepest feelings: both the literary skill and the spontaneous bursts of emotional intimacy are meant as a double claim on Hill's heart. Thus, although on the one hand she is writing a private letter, on the other clearly Fowke is alert to aspects of public print, arranging the dedication to look as it would if set in type and alluding to publication practices even where she refuses them:

> No gaudy Title shall my Life defend,
> Nor shall it but to great Hillarius bend.
> Oh! bright Protector, to thy Arms receive
> My Life and me, then we, indeed, shall live.

Although Aaron Hill has been called "absurd and a bore of the first water," who displayed a sanguine interest in such projects as producing oil from beech mast, nevertheless he was an innovator in a number of cultural areas: he was a periodical writer, a theatrical promoter, an enthusiast for Shakespeare, an early promoter of English opera, a historian and dramatist, and a patron.[40] His charm

(v)

The *Dedication* of my Heart and Life.

TO

The Monarch of all my soft Desires;
The End of all my Wishes;
The Inspirer of my Heart;
The Adoration of my Soul;
The Elevater of my Thoughts;
The Immortalizer of my Songs;
The Charmer of my Bosom;
The Life of my Soul;
The Heaven of my Repose;

This is most fondly, most passionately, most respectfully addressed, by

His devoted, adoring

CLIO.

Dedication to Aaron Hill, from *Clio*. (Courtesy of the Lilly Library, Indiana University, Bloomington, Indiana.)

is suggested in the description by Theophilus Cibber, whose father, Colley Cibber, knew him well:

> His person was (in youth) extremely fair and handsome; his eyes were a dark blue, both bright and penetrating, hair brown and visage oval; which was enlivened by a smile the most agreeable in conversation, where his address was affably engaging; to which was joined a dignity which rendered him at once respected and admired by those (of either sex) who were acquainted with him. He was tall, genteelly made, and not thin. His voice was sweet, his conversation elegant, and capable of entertaining upon various subjects.[41]

The circle of his and Fowke's associates was drawn wide; one can trace connections with George Sewell, Benjamin Victor, Eliza Haywood, Duncan Campbell, and Richardson Pack as well as better-known figures like Steele, Thomson, Pope, and Handel. Hill's periodical, *The Plain Dealer* (1724–25), written in conjunction with William Bond, Fowke's "Strephon," is particularly interesting in its engagement with issues of women's writing. One issue prints a memorial elegy to Mrs. Manley by "Cleora," which it is tempting to assign to Fowke.[42] Hill was obviously an engaging and sympathetic presence who shared many of Fowke's interests.

Writing bound them together; it provided an initial point of contact when Hill wrote praising Fowke's work, and their friendship grew through an exchange of letters and poems as well as personal contact. (See appendix A for Hill's letters and poems to Fowke.) Writing legitimized the expression of feeling. Hill was an enthusiast for the type of platonic rapture that appealed to Fowke. In his poem "The Picture of Love," he speaks of "that Fire! That kindles *Body* into *Soul*." Fowke's account of her life was intended as a "faithful Picture of my Soul," and the completion of the book became an emblem of her heart, full of her love for him.

Although the relationship with Aaron Hill is the genesis and goal of this work, it is also problematic. Fowke's constant appeals to her "charmer," her comments on his "beauty" and his "soul," her poetic effusions, all may strike the modern reader as strange, sentimentally cloying or emotionally unbalanced. A more balanced view acknowledges that Hill's letters and poems to his "Clio" were in many ways just as effusive. Although Hill was married at the time, and from considerable evidence the marriage was a happy one, yet even quite early in the relationship he writes to Fowke as a besotted lover:

Receive me there, ever yours,—or, be so generous to save me from this growth of your attraction.—Condemn me never to behold you more; or let me never be depriv'd of seeing you.—All repetitions of such pleasures, as my heart is filled with, when I sit and listen to your sweetness, are succeeded by new pains, which you can never rightly judge of, because there is no man as worthy of your esteem, as you are of mankind's in general.—I carry with me, from your gentle conversation, a thousand inexpressible remembrances, of words, looks, movements, softnesses and graces;—which, compared with the gay female world, make all things tasteless in it, but the image of that single loveliness, where all those excellencies center.[43]

Hill's romantic enthusiasm, like Fowke's, oscillated between the theatrical and the sincere. Leon Guilhamet has discussed the circle around Hill and its concern with sincerity and defining greatness.[44] Hill's love letters to his wife survive, as do letters and poems to Martha Fowke; other women were also the recipients of his glowing tributes. These women were praised for their feelings and their sensitivity but also for their literary achievements.[45] Thus, in writing to Hill, Fowke can freely express both literary ambition and artless emotion, the thrust to independence and the longing for love.

Fowke's autobiography springs from a world of fused literary and emotional communication. Poised between the older coterie traditions of manuscript and the developing world of print, it is suffused with sensitivity to the social implications of literary acts and awareness of the complexity of both writing and reading. Fowke's consciousness of herself as writer ensures that her account of her life is a deliberate creation, controlled and constructed with a sense of narrative shaping and stylistic expressiveness.[46] Her emotional involvement ensures that it is also presented as a spontaneous overflowing of the heart, a love letter, with frequent direct appeals to her "charmer" Hillarius, transforming the relationship of writer and reader into imagined speech. At one point she describes a pause in her writing as "recover[ing] Breath." Fowke clearly wants Hill to know the quality of her mind and to admire her abilities as a writer as well as the strength and sensitivity of her emotions.

The shifts from prose to verse mirror complex movements of emotional tone: on the one hand, verse is more emotionally charged, and on the other, prose is more sincere and direct. Thus the mixed genres reflect a more inclusive commitment. Fowke does not conceive of her written life as a published document, with consequent generic constraints, but neither is it a purely personal letter. Rather it is a reflection of her self-image, a middle ground between the purely personal and the public. The rhetorical strategy of Fowke's continual self-conscious appeals to Hill, the direct address, her comments on the time and place of her writing, all have a strong psychological component; as do the novelistic elements of her writing, for the more vividly she describes and analyzes her past relationships with men, the more strongly she can specify the essential difference and uniqueness of her present feelings for Hill. There is a sense of the "presentation of self," as Irving Goffman calls it; this does not invalidate the account, since all accounts of our selves partake of an element of dramatic shaping, but it evokes something of the quality of the best eighteenth-century fiction.[47]

Fowke is conscious of the physicality of writing, noting at one point in her discussion of her education, that she learned to write "such a hand as you [Hill] now see." Her comments on her handwriting, the physical activity of writing and the actuality of pen on paper, are part of her creation of immediacy as an essential component of the letter form. The identity of writer and inscribed text is suggested in lines toward the end of the work:

> Oh! let the Fulness of this Book impart
> A little Emblem of my crowded Heart;
> Where thy immortal Beauties press as near,
> As Love has plac'd the tender Letters here,
> 'Tis all writ o'er by thy transporting Eyes,
> No Blank appears, all full of thee it lies.
>
> (140)

The work is emotionally structured by a constant interplay between the past of her experiences and the present of her relationship to Hill, between the awareness of self and the awareness of the other. Episodes are constantly measured against the emotional touchstone of her current feelings, but their specificity is not thereby diminished. Her autobiography is filled with the immediacy of the writing situation and the awareness of the self as writer, forming a clear model of the sort of writing later described by Richardson as "writing to the moment."[48]

The detailed evocation of the past has a double seductive pleasure for Fowke, testifying to the powerful passion she has inspired in men, as well as to the satisfaction of controlling her story. In this way the whole work becomes suffused with an erotic tone, for in the act of delineating the details of her life she constantly evokes her bodily presence. Thus giving Hill her "Life" is seen as an equivalent for giving him her "self." The work, however, is not explicitly erotic, and the theory that at some time erotic material was excised is unsubstantiated.⁴⁹

Fowke as Mrs. Sansom

Whether the frankness of Fowke's account frightened Hill, or whether her husband intervened, or whether the birth of a child and domestic responsibilities diminished Fowke's creative energy, cannot be determined. A fragment of manuscript from John Dyer dated around 1727 suggests that he felt increasingly uneasy about the platonic world of love that she was attempting to sustain and the challenge to traditional values of domestic patriarchy:

> The subject is too delicate. Had custom made us all free to unrestrained love, had law exacted no vows, I could then disturb the confidence of no man; I could then see and hear my Charmer, without doing an injury, real or imaginary. O Clio, I have often sate down with desire to do universal good, in the purest love, to be true to all. I have put myself in the place of the injured, and grieved at many things. For the future I am bent to do nothing that, were it known to all the world, would be thought unjust to any one. O Clio, forgive me, and still believe [me] your faithful, &c.⁵⁰

From the internal evidence of *Clio* we perceive a shift in Fowke's attitudes from enthusiasm and optimism to a pessimistic sense of rejection. Among the last lines she wrote were those prefixed to the second edition of Thomson's *Winter* (1726), which seem shadowed with a sense that her winter too is approaching:

> In thee, sad Winter, I a Kindred find,
> Far more related to poor human Kind;
> In Thee my gently-drooping Head I bend,
> Thy Sigh my Sister, and thy Tear my Friend:
> On Thee I muse, and in thy hastening Sun,
> See Life expiring e'er 'tis well begun.⁵¹

Certainly from about 1726 Fowke slides from the literary scene.⁵² No writing after that date has been identified, although there was some talk of a collected volume in 1731.⁵³ Her marriage clearly was unsatisfactory, although this is hardly surprising, given her negative attitudes toward it and the mixed motives involved in her decision to marry. Sansom was older, and although he was apparently a comparatively wealthy attorney and servant of the crown, his financial position was less secure than it seemed.[54]

Fowke describes his education as being "good, but not noble" and observes:

> His Days had been sacrificed to the morose God of Business, and his Nights to the wanton God of unrefin'd Pleasure, which had not given his Mind that Delicacy of Taste as I wish: 'tis this I lament even now, and is the sad Occasion of many unhappy Hours.

She clearly delineates the process by which she felt bound to Sansom by his assiduity and pressure from friends to marry, but she always uses the imagery of shipwreck or disaster. "At last I leapt down this precipice." She laments to Hill that Sansom could not keep love alive, that he took her for granted: "I have a thousand Obligations to Mr. S——but I would receive them as marks of his Tender Affection, not as Badges of Slavery, to bind me down to mean Servitude, such as he expects." Marriage had never seemed a joyful state to Fowke. The loveless marriage of her parents and her father's clear preference for affairs rather than the claims of matrimony had established her values early. She also had absorbed some of the imagery of earlier women's verse and prose, which repeatedly depicted marriage as slavery, chains, victimization.[55] Loss of liberty was terrifying to Fowke: she felt it in the boarding school where she stayed for a few months, but how much more onerous were the chains she assumed once committed to matrimony and motherhood.

Her marriage was even more disastrous than she initially feared. It seems likely that their income was diminished by the South Sea Bubble of 1720, and the records of the Inner Temple show that Sansom had difficulty paying his dues there. In 1730 he received the post of customs officer at Harwich, through the interest of Sir Robert Walpole, but his conduct was increasingly outrageous, as the Earl of Egmont reports:

> he [Sansom] is grown a perfect sot, being drunk every night, and then quarrelling with every body for the least word spoken, throwing glasses and challenging them to sword and pistol. That he was very poor, had indebted himself to several, and had no authority, being despised by all. . . . but I pitied him, and his father had been one of the honestest men I knew.[56]

Sansom finally died in January 1734, heavily in debt, just two years before Fowke herself died. We know nothing of her last years, except that she was buried in Leicester, close to where her brother lived. The affectionate epitaph Thomas Fowke provided for his talented but unhappy sister stresses the closely intricated themes of her life as a writer and her personality as a woman:

> Underneath lies the body of Mrs. Martha Sansom, relict of Arnold Sansom, Esq. and only sister to Lieut. Col. Fowke, born at Hartenford Bury Park, the 1st of May 1690. She was lineally descended from the Fowkes of Staffordshire.
> This stone can only tell, in a few words, what would require a history to relate, of her charity, good-nature, and excellent parts. She had by Nature what others scarce attain by art and application; and from the age of 16 composed several pieces of poetry, on different subjects; which, for their beautiful turn of thought and strength of imagination, have not only met with approbation, but the admiration of the good, the learned and the witty.
> Friend, whoe'er thou art, wish *her* soul at rest, who when living, wished well to the whole world. Obiit 17 February 1735/6.[57]

Fowke's life had been comparatively short, and her moment of personal freedom was brief, and even illusory. We do not know when or how her close relationship with Hill came to an end. When Hill belatedly heard from Savage of her death in 1736, he penned a characteristically cryptic comment:

> Poor C——o! It is long since I met with an affliction more sensible than the information you sent me concerning her! If half what her enemies have said of her is true, she was a proof that vanity overcomes nature in women, which it could never yet do in men: for desire of glory wants power to expel the pusillanimity natural to some ambitious princes and generals; while in that amiable pursuer of conquests, it [desire of glory] prevailed, not only against the finest reflection, but impelled an assumed lightness over every constitutional modesty.[58]

Fowke's gift of her "life" may well have disconcerted Hill by its frankness and lack of traditional female restraint. Fowke's assertiveness in emotional relationships was seen as a violation of both reason and nature. It is interesting that one of the characteristics of Hill's own wife, which he noted when lamenting her death in 1731, was that she was "*sincere* without *indecency* [that is, lack of decorum]."[59] Possibly Mrs. Haywood's attacks on Fowke finally came to seem convincing, or the widowed Hill now looked back on his past with regret. As he described an elaborate projected garden to Lady Walpole in 1734, did he think back to the days of wine and roses?

> They [the alleys] lead through the grotto of LOVE, 'till he ascends into a thicket of roses, jessamines, and honeysuckles, which end gradually in a little wilderness of briars, thistles, and furze bushes; in the center of which, appears the rock of REPENTANCE, covered over with moss, out of which water drops, weeping and melancholy.[60]

Hill, like Fowke, was a victim of time and changing moral values. Through the turgid prose one glimpses his ambivalence. Afflicted at the news of her death but vividly aware of the gossip and slander surrounding her, he denigrates her desire for glory in favor of her "reflection," her considered rationality. Her gaiety and freedom, her "lightness," now are at odds with the modesty that should be inherent in all women. She may have been lovable, but she was "unnaturally" vain. He remembers her as a "pursuer of conquests," not as the writer she aspired to be. Even her pseudonym, with its aura of classical authority, is reduced to a cipher. Poor C——o! In her mid-forties, with her name besmirched, her works uncollected, her writings scattered often anonymously in anthologies and periodicals, Martha Fowke Sansom died. She may have found death less dreadful than the thought of the oblivion that has since enshrouded her.

CLIO AS TEXT

When *Clio* was published, in 1752, thirty years after it was written, a reviewer made scathing observations about its extravagance, its blasphemy, and the madness of its writer:

> We have not been able to discover who this celebrated lady was; for she appears to have had a real, though insignificant existence. Her memoirs are dated in 1723. There is nothing interesting in them. They consist merely of unentertaining intrigues, interspersed with scraps of extravagantly amorous poetry; for which the author apparently had no contemptible genius; but her verses are so enthusiastically loose, as to run into downright prophaneness as well as immorality; and cannot but shock the mind of a reader who has any regard for decency. She is continually invoking God, heaven, every thing sacred to witness, or assist, a wanton woman in the practice or pursuit of the most unbounded sensual gratification. If the writer of this book was not crazy, which in charity we are inclined to suspect she was, what are we to think of the editors of it? In respect to the public it ought not to have appeared in print.[61]

CLIO:
OR, A
SECRET HISTORY
OF THE
LIFE and AMOURS
Of the Late celebrated
Mrs. S---N---M.

Written by HERSELF, *in a Letter to* HILLARIUS.

LONDON:
Printed for M. COOPER, in *Pater-noster-Row*, 1752.

Title page of *Clio* (1752). (Courtesy of the Lilly Library, Indiana University, Bloomington, Indiana.)

Reflecting the consolidation of assumptions about decorum and morality in women's role and voice in the second half of the eighteenth century, the reviewer voices a persisting unease. Even now, the extravagant claims for Hill as the God of her soul, the light of her life, the meaning of her existence, are difficult to accept in print, however tolerant we might be of such effusions in personal love letters. The circumstances of publication of *Clio* are unclear; it may have been an attempt by Hill's children to make some money while they were accumulating subscriptions for the four-volume edition of his works, which appeared the following year with some fifteen hundred subscribers. We do not know if either Fowke or Hill would have contemplated publishing the work, or whether they might have circulated the work in manuscript. Hill certainly assured Fowke in poems and in letters of his intention to keep her letters private, and none of her other letters survive.

Martha Fowke would not have thought of herself as writing an autobiography; she would have seen her action as writing her life.[62] We might call her work "pre-autobiographical," but it is more complex than that.[63] Some forms of life-writing by women would have been unlikely to enter into Fowke's frame of reference, such as the religiously motivated autobigraphies of religious activists in the seventeenth century.[64] The models that Fowke would have had in mind were of three kinds: the basic biographical introduction to a written work, conventionally appended only once the writer had died; the fictional or semifactual account of life incidents in early novels or scandal narratives; and the letter itself.[65] These forms were somewhat permeable. For example, Mrs. Manley's account of her life, written primarily to preempt an unfavorable biography of her planned by the publisher Curll, was presented with a fictional frame and a male narrator.[66] Experiences of Fowke's own relatives and friends appeared in a fictionalized context in Manley's *Memoirs of the New Atalantis;* she notes in *Clio* the identification of her cousin with Manley's "Louisa." The letter form was an extremely fluid one, ranging from the personal communication to the use of a letter frame for political pamphlets. Additionally, many writers, such as Behn, Abel Boyer, John Dennis, Pope, Swift, Elizabeth Thomas, used their personal correspondence as a basis for published work. Love letters were a specific subgenre, defined by its appeal to "nature," its lack of rules: True love, Behn wrote, is "all unthinking artless speaking, incorrect disorder, and without method as 'tis without bonds or rules."[67] Behn's works were clearly influential in developing the mixed genre of epistolary love letters; she mixed fact, political satire, and romantic and erotic fiction in

Love-Letters between a Nobleman and his Sister, and she mixed poetry and prose in an epistolary frame in her free adaptation from the French original, *La Montre, or The Lover's Watch.*

Fowke selects with care among these generic possibilities in order to embody chosen aspects of her self. She utilizes traditional strategies for the shaping of a life story, opening with the formal placement of herself in the lineal descents of genealogy, then carefully situating herself in the social and spatial geography of early-eighteenth-century London. She also draws upon narrative techniques of fiction, developing incidents at length with dialogue and descriptive detail. All these facets are held together within the flexible form of the personal letter.

In the end, we have to take Martha Fowke to some extent as she wished to be viewed. We cannot know whether she did or did not sleep with her lovers; we do know that she wanted Hill to be convinced that she was both desirable and discriminating, frank and perceptive, and that she constructed the apparently artless informality of her account of her life to that end. What clearly emerges is that, at least in her youth, Fowke was a confident writer—confident of her creativity and her individuality, of her social attractiveness, and of her ability to write spontaneously and fluently. Her account of her life reveals her chosen self-image with a strong sense of narrative structure and a fresh lively style. Finally, Fowke was not afraid—she risked exposing her personal feelings, both in prose and in verse, and she risked the dangers of living life as she chose to live it, not succumbing to the social, moral, and religious decorums of her time. This gives the work a different kind of authenticity, closer in many ways to more modern writings; Vita Sackville-West's memoir of her relationship with Violet Trefusis comes to mind.

Many established assumptions about eighteenth-century women, such as alienation, fear of antagonizing male readers, timidity about self-dramatization, dread of the patriarchal authority of art, and anxiety about impropriety seem qualified by Fowke's life and writing.[68] Fowke is assertive, confident, sexually aware, emotionally expressive. Her voice enriches our sense of women's lives: "for there are Charms in Truth which Falsehood cannot wear, and Art is but a Shadow of its godlike Beauty."

Notes

1. When Martha Fowke married Arnold Sansom, sometime in the early 1720s, she had already established her poetic reputation under her maiden name. I have

referred to her throughout as Fowke (pronounced "Foke"). The honorific "Mrs." was used for all mature women at this time; thus she is often confusingly alluded to as Mrs. Martha Fowke.

2. Martha Fowke and William Bond, *The Epistles of Clio and Strephon, being a Collection of Letters that passed between an English Lady, and an English Gentleman in France* (London: Printed for J. Hooke, F. Gyles, and W. Boreham, 1720), xxiv. There was a second edition with the same title (London: Printed for J. Hooke, 1729), and a third, which was actually a reissue of the 1729 edition with a new title page, *The Platonic Lovers, consisting of Original Letters, that pass'd between an English Lady, and an English Gentleman in France* (London: Printed for John Wilford; and Richard Chandler, 1732). A reprint edition is titled *A Critical Essay, Containing some Remarks upon the Nature of Epistolary and Elegiac Poetry*, by John Porter (New York: Garland, 1971). Edmund Curll, who seems to have been involved in some way with the original 1720 publication, issued a 36-page follow-up volume, *Epistles and Poems by Clio and Strephon* (London: E. Curll, 1729), reissued in 1732 as *Clio and Strephon: being, the Second and Last Part of The Platonic Lovers. Consisting of Love Epistles, &c. By William Bond, Esq.;... And Mrs. Martha Fowke* (London: Printed for E. Curll, 1732). *To Sylvia, a poem. Occasion'd by her Commending the Epistles of the Platonic Lovers, Clio and Strephon* (London: Printed in the year, 1738) may be a further attempt to market the remaining copies.

3. Giles Jacob, *The Poetical Register: or, The Lives and Characters of the English Dramatick Poets*, 2 vols. (London: Printed for E. Curll, 1719–20), 2:326. The comparison with Madame Dacier, the French scholarly critic of the classics, seems inappropriate but is indicative of Fowke's level of visibility and aspiration.

4. Anthony Hammond, ed., *A New Miscellany of Original Poems, Translations and Imitations* (London: Printed for T. Jauncey, 1720) contains five poems by Fowke: "Clio's Picture," "Thoughts to a Friend, on the Masquerades," "To CLEON's Eyes," "On CLEON's Letters, darlings of my Eyes," and "To these soft Lines what Name shall I impart." Richard Savage's collection, *Miscellaneous Poems and Translations* (London, 1726) contained a large number of poems from the Hill/Fowke circle, including nine identified as by "Clio": "The Innocent Inconstant," "To Lady E——H——," "The Invitation from a Country Cottage," "On Lady Chudleigh," "To Mr. John Dyer," "To Mr. Savage by Clio," "Clio to Miranda [Mrs. Aaron Hill] on her Verses on Sleep," "On Reading Seneca," and "To Mr. Savage on his Misfortunes." More work remains to be done identifying Fowke's poems in different periodicals and anthologies. I am currently preparing an edition of her poems.

5. I presented the argument for Fowke's authorship of these poems in a paper, "Martha Fowke Sansom as the 'Amorous Lady' in the *Barbados Gazette*," at the Midwest Society for Eighteenth-Century Studies meeting in Milwaukee, October 1993. Five of Fowke's poems appear under Martha Sansom (née Fowke) in Roger Lonsdale, ed., *Eighteenth-Century Women Poets* (Oxford: Oxford University Press, 1989), 84–91. Three poems from the *Barbados Gazette*, attributed to "The Amorous Lady," are printed in Lonsdale, ed., *Eighteenth-Century Women Poets*, 145–49.

6. See Maureen Duffy, *The Passionate Shepherdess: Aphra Behn 1640–89* (London: Methuen, 1989), 255. Comparison with Sappho may have been encouraged by the recent publicity Joseph Addison had given to the "bewitching Tenderness and Rapture" of the Greek poet; see Lawrence Lipking, *Abandoned Women and Poetic Tradition* (Chicago: University of Chicago Press, 1988), 80–83. Giles

Jacob in the poem "To Mrs. Fowke, with the Second Volume of My Lives of the Poets," addressed her as "thou *Sappho* of this Isle in Fame" and sketched the line of male poets, from Milton and Spenser to Pope and Granville, as poetic models for her: "Read these well thro', then Write, then Draw, Design, / And all their Talents in thy Verse will Shine" (*Human Happiness. A Poem adapted to the present Times, With several other Miscellaneous Poems* (London, 1721), 43–44. (The British Library copy [164.l.76] has a MS date of 1720.) In the July 1720 issue of *Mercurius Politicus*, "Eugenius" wrote: "But we have lived to see even a *Greek* SAPPHO, and a *Roman* TIBULLUS infinitely surpassed by an *English Lady*, I mean the Immortal *Clio*, whose late *Epistles* of *Love*, and a *disinterested Friendship*, must claim the universal Esteem of all true Judges either of Wit or Poetry" (p. 64; I owe this reference to Joanna Lipking). However, the objectivity of this is questionable; it may well be an advertising puff.

7. Ros Ballaster, "Seizing the Means of Seduction," in *Women, Writing, History: 1640–1740,* ed. Isobel Grundy and Susan Wiseman (Athens: University of Georgia Press, 1992), 101.

8. *The Athenaeum*, 16 July 1859, 78.

9. Clarence Tracy, *The Artificial Bastard: A Biography of Richard Savage* (Cambridge: Harvard University Press, 1953), 63.

10. Roger Lonsdale's introductory biography in *Eighteenth-Century Women Poets* is a useful summary of the facts of her life. The brief note under Fowke in Janet Todd's *A Dictionary of British and American Women Writers, 1600–1800* (Totowa, N.J.: Rowman and Allanheld, 1985) has been superseded by the entry in *The Feminist Companion to Literature in English,* ed. Virginia Blain, Patricia Clements, and Isobel Grundy (New Haven: Yale University Press, 1990). Note, however, that Fowke was born in Hertfordshire, not Herefordshire.

11. See Felicity Nussbaum, *The Autobiographical Subject* (Baltimore: Johns Hopkins University Press, 1989), esp. chap. 8; Nussbaum does not discuss Fowke's memoirs.

12. See Sidonie Smith, *A Poetics of Women's Autobiography* (Bloomington: Indiana University Press, 1987), esp. chap. 3, "Women's Story and the Engendering of Self-Representation," a stimulating exploration of the complex gender-related theoretical issues raised by the web of fictional strategies, literary tradition, and sexual authority.

13. Elizabeth Thomas, when old, ill, and desperate, prepared an account of her life intermixed with private letters, published posthumously in two volumes as *Pylades and Corinna* (London: Printed for E. Curll, 1731–32). In 1740 Mrs. Delany wrote an account of her life at the "earnest request" of her close friend the Duchess of Portland (*The Autobiography and Correspondence of Mary Granville, Mrs. Delany,* ed. Lady Llanover [London, 1861–62], 1:7 ff).

14. Current reference sources and the inscription on her tombstone gives 1690 as her birthdate, but the parish registers of Hertingfordbury, where she was born, give the date of her baptism as 12 May 1689 (personal communication from the Archivist, Hertfordshire County Record Office).

15. Bodleian Library, MS Rawl B130. The extended family was large, since Martha's great-grandfather Roger Fowke and his wife, Mary Bayley, had had nineteen children, and there were large branches of the family in Ireland and Virginia. Gerard Fowke comments on eccentricities and "distraction" (mental instability) in some members of the family.

16. Thomas Fowke's first wife was the widow of Sir Anthony Vincent, and his second was the daughter of the wealthy Governor Codrington. Neither marriage

produced children who survived to adulthood. The marriage to Mrs. Chandler produced two sons and two daughters, according to Burke's *Complete Peerage*. Martha does not mention the two youngest; possibly Burke may be in error, since Fowke's epitaph says she was her brother's only sister.

17. Eliza Haywood, *Memoirs of a Certain Island Adjacent to the Kingdom of Utopia*, 2d ed. (London: Printed and Sold by the Booksellers of London and Westminster, 1726), 1:43.

18. Patricia Meyer Spacks has commented on the salience of the father-daughter relationship in a number of eighteenth-century women's lives; see *Imagining a Self: Autobiography and Novel in Eighteenth-Century England* (Cambridge: Harvard University Press, 1976). Fowke is unusual in that her father was essentially involved in the ambitions and rewards she sought as a writer.

19. In Haywood's combination of fact, fiction, and advertising copy in epistolary form, *A Spy upon the Conjurer; or, A Collection of Surprising Stories, with Names, Places, and Particular Circumstances relating to Mr. Duncan Campbell* (London: Sold by Mr. Campbell; and at Burton's Coffee-House, Charing Cross, 1724), she comments about Fowke: "Never did Woman sollicite the Affections of a Man with more Ardency than she did yours [the unnamed peer to whom the letter is addressed]; and, failing in her Aim, never did any Woman take half the pains to appear virtuous, as she did to be thought the contrary" (52). In this work Haywood explicitly denies the common gossip that alleged Fowke was the mistress of this peer, although doing so in terms intended to insult her erstwhile friend. In *Memoirs of a Certain Island* (1:46), Haywood asserts that after Fowke's marriage, "her inclinations now appear bare-faced, and so monstrous impudent is she in pursuing the gratification of them, that she waits not for being address'd, nor thinks it beneath her to make the first application."

20. Laetitia Pilkington, *Memoirs with Anecdotes of Dean Swift, 1748–1754*, 3 vols. (New York, Garland, 1975), 1:13–15. See also Anne Blount's description of her misguided youth when she reveled in the praise of her father and his friends for her wit, and how her brother "cured" her of poetry (Lonsdale, ed., *Eighteenth-Century Women Poets*, 185–88).

21. In 1723 Steele wrote to Mrs. Martha Ceney that he could not pay her and that she should take the letter as "a dismission of ye Lodgings at Fullham" (*The Correspondence of Richard Steele*, ed. Rae Blanchard [Oxford: Clarendon, 1941], 181).

22. Rodney M. Baine, *Defoe and the Supernatural* (Athens: University of Georgia Press, 1968), 169.

23. Richard Savage, *The Poetical Works of Richard Savage*, ed. Clarence Tracy (Cambridge: Cambridge University Press, 1962), 73.

24. William Hylton Longstaffe, "Notes respecting the Life and Family of John Dyer the Poet," *The Patrician* 4 (1847):421; Ralph M. Williams, *Poet, Painter, Parson: The Life of John Dyer* (New York: Bookman Associates, 1956).

25. Savage, ed., *Miscellaneous Poems*, 209–10.

26. Savage, ed., *Miscellaneous Poems*, 100–101.

27. Katherine Philips, *Letters from Orinda to Poliarchus* (London: Printed by W. B. for Bernard Lintot, 1705). For the Blounts' circle, see Valerie Rumbold, *Women's Place in Pope's World* (Cambridge: Cambridge University Press, 1989), 48–82. Pope's satiric depiction of this platonic concept may reflect common gossip or his personal sexual frustration:

> Philomede, lect'ring all mankind
> On the soft Passion, and the Taste refin'd,
> Th'Address, the Delicacy—stoops at once,
> And makes her hearty meal upon a Dunce.

Epistle to a Lady, lines 83–86, in Alexander Pope, *Epistles to Several Persons,* ed. F. W. Bateson (London: Methuen, 1951), 55; Rumbold, *Women's Place in Pope's World,* 57–58.

28. Antonio Verrio (1639–1707), described by John Evelyn as "that excellent painter," worked extensively both at Windsor Castle, and at Burford House, Nell Gwyn's house in Windsor, where he painted erotic mythological scenes. His own house in Windsor was presumably similarly decorated. See Ellis Waterhouse, *Painting in Britain, 1530–1790* (Baltimore: Penguin, 1953), 87–89; Robert R. Tighe and James Edward Davis, *Annals of Windsor* (London, 1858); and *Victoria County History: Berkshire,* 3:19.

29. James Grantham Turner, "The Libertine Sublime: Love and Death in Restoration England," *Studies in Eighteenth-Century Culture,* 19, ed. Leslie Ellen Brown and Patricia Craddock (Lansing: Colleagues Press, for American Society for Eighteenth-Century Studies, 1989), 99–115.

30. The influence of the *Tatler* and the *Spectator,* particularly on women, has been illuminatingly discussed by Kathryn A. Shevelow, *Women in Print Culture: The Construction of Femininity in the Early English Periodical* (London: Routledge, 1989). For general discussions of some of the changes in attitudes at this time, see G. J. Barker-Benfield, *The Culture of Sensibility: Sex and Society in Eighteenth-Century England* (Chicago: University of Chicago Press, 1992).

31. Lawrence Stone, *Broken Lives: Separation and Divorce in England, 1660–1875* (Oxford: Oxford University Press, 1993), 78.

32. Cited by Susan Staves, in "Recent Studies in the Restoration and Eighteenth Century," *Studies in English Literature* 33 (1993): 672.

33. The prospectus for *Letters from a Lady of Quality to a Chevalier* appeared in 1720; the volume itself has a date of 1721. A separately paginated "Discourse" contains an attack on Fowke as the woman who initiated relationships with men and sent them verses. Haywood then prints some apparently authentic verses: possibly Haywood gained access to a genuine letter of Fowke's. See appendix B.

34. See George Frisbie Whicher, *The Life and Romances of Mrs. Eliza Haywood* (New York: Columbia University Press, 1915); Christine Blouch, "Eliza Haywood and the Romance of Obscurity," *Studies in English Literature* 31 (Summer 1991): 535–51; and Gabrielle Firmager, "Eliza Haywood: Some Further Light on her Background," *Notes and Queries* 236 (June 1991): 181–83.

35. Haywood, *A Spy upon the Conjurer,* 51–53. The contents page draws attention to this as "A Strange Instance of Vanity and Jealousy in the Behaviour of Mrs. F——."

36. Philip H. Highfill, Jr., Kalman A. Burnim, and Edward A. Langhans, *A Biographical Dictionary of Actors, Actresses, Musicians, Dancers, Managers, and Other Stage Personnel in London, 1660–1800* (Carbondale and Edwardsville: Southern Illinois University Press, 1982).

37. See Blouch, "Eliza Haywood and the Romance of Obscurity," 535–51.

38. Savage, *Poetical Works,* 73.

39. The Earl of Egmont notes in 1730 that he stopped by Sansom's lodgings in the Temple and saw "his wife and child" (Diary of Viscount Percival, afterwards

1st Earl of Egmont, *Historical Manuscripts Commission: Manuscripts of the Earl of Egmont* [London: His Majesty's Stationery Office, 1920–23], 1:97).

40. *Dictionary of National Biography*. The definitive account of Hill's life remains Dorothy Brewster, *Aaron Hill: Poet, Dramatist, Projector* (New York, 1913). Important letters and poems illuminating Hill's relationship with Fowke are reprinted in this edition in appendix A. Hill's letters to Savage containing references to Fowke are in *The European Magazine* 6 (1784): 189–94; 277–82.

41. Cited in the "Life of Aaron Hill," prefixed to *Dramatic Works of the late Aaron Hill Esq.* (London: Printed for the Benefit of the Family, 1760), 1:x.

42. Hill printed "Cleora"'s tribute to Mrs. Manley on her death in 1724, one of the few critical tributes that took Manley seriously as a writer, not just a titillating scandalmonger or erotic writer (*The Plain Dealer*, no. 53, 2d ed. (London, 1734), 1:444–45. The same issue of the periodical promised to give accounts of three living women writers, a promise never performed; it seems probable that Fowke would have been one of the three.

43. Hill, *Dramatic Works*, 2:393; internal evidence suggests that this is addressed to Fowke.

44. "Hill and his circle were consciously creating a climate of kindness and benevolence which had as its object nothing less than the reformation of manners based on the universal cultivation of social love"; see Leon Guilhamet, *The Sincere Ideal: Studies on Sincerity in Eighteenth-Century English Literature* (Montreal and London: McGill-Queen's University Press, 1974), 78–80.

45. For Hill's letters and poems to Fowke, see appendix A. His poem on his wife's death has been reprinted in Roger Lonsdale, ed., *The New Oxford Book of Eighteenth-Century Verse* (Oxford: Oxford University Press, 1987), 303–5. Hill's wife, Henrietta, wrote poetry, including generous tributes to other women, including Fowke. A few of her poems are printed in Hill's *Works*, but they seem to have been heavily revised by Hill.

46. Margaret Ezell draws attention to a similarly sophisticated self-presentation, utilizing both romance conventions and narrative strategies, in the late-seventeenth-century memoirs of Lady Elizabeth Delaval; see her "Elizabeth Delaval's Spiritual Heroine: Thoughts on Redefining Manuscript Texts by Early Women Writers," *English Manuscript Studies, 1100–1700* 3 (1992): 216–37.

47. In his classic sociological study, Goffman draws attention to the techniques of impression management as part of social interactions: "when one's activity occurs in the presence of other persons, some aspects of the activity are expressively accentuated and other aspects, which might discredit the fostered impression, are suppressed"; see *The Presentation of Self in Everyday Life* (Garden City, N. Y.: Doubleday Anchor, 1959), 111.

48. Aaron Hill's association of Clio with writing from the heart can be seen, for example, in his lines, "*On a Blank Leaf of* Colin's Mistakes *in* Clio's *Window*":

> Taught, by *her* Power, to feel the Passion strong.
> Thou hadst disdain'd the devious Turns of Art,
> Look'd—and *improv'd*—and drawn the moving Song,
> Not from thy mimick memory, but thy *Heart*.
>
> Savage, ed., *Miscellaneous Poems*, 211–12.

49. Karen Davis, "Martha Fowke: 'A Lady Once Too Well Known'," *English Language Notes* 23, no. 3 (1986): 32–36, seems to have been the first to suggest this and it has entered standard reference sources; see the entry on Fowke in

The Feminist Companion to Literature. It may be the result of confusion with the autobiography of Deborah Sampson, who served as a soldier in the mid-eighteenth century, which was noted in the mid-nineteenth century as existing in an extensive unpublished form.

50. Longstaffe, "John Dyer," 422.

51. It is possible that these lines may have been edited by Mallet, since Thomson wrote to him, "Notwithstanding of all your objections, I belive [sic], you could, with a little Trouble, make Clio's Verses very pretty——lovely" (*James Thomson [1700–1748]: Letters and Documents,* ed. Alan D. McKillop [Lawrence: University of Kansas Press, 1958], 36. However, since Mallet did not revise his own dedicatory verses, it is perhaps less likely that he reworked Fowke's.

52. *British Journal,* 24 Sept. 1726: "Clio must be allowed to be a most complete poetess, if she really wrote those poems that bear her name; but it has of late been so abus'd and scandalized, that I am informed she has lately changed it for that of Myra." Cited in Whicher, *Life and Romances,* 128.

53. "On the Celebrated Clio's designing to publish her Poems," *Read's Weekly Journal,* 16 June 1731, cited in *James Thomson [1700–1748]: Letters and Documents,* 35.

54. In 1708 Arnold Sansome, Esq., was the Comptroller of the particular Receivers in the Custom House (Edward Hatton, *A New View of London* [London, 1708], 2:654). Sansom was admitted to the Society of the Inner Temple in 1712, presumably as an established attorney, but he was in continual trouble with the authorities about the payment of his dues, and his chambers in the Paper Buildings were finally disposed of in 1726 to another tenant (personal communication from Mr. I. G. Murray, Archivist of the Inner Temple). Dudley Ryder, a young law student at the Inner Temple in 1715, mentions Mr. Sampson, an attorney, who acts as his informal tutor; he may be Arnold (*The Diary of Dudley Ryder, 1715–16,* transcribed and ed. William Matthews [London: Methuen, 1939], 31, 35, 230, 362). It is not clear how Arnold relates to John Sansome, Steele's school friend and later legal adversary (see Calhoun Winton, *Sir Richard Steele, M.P.* [Baltimore and London: Johns Hopkins University Press, 1970], 128–31, 135–36); they may have been brothers, since they both had a father who was a Commissioner of the Customs around the turn of the century.

55. The pervasiveness of such imagery can be seen in the section of songs called "The Female Lover," a separately paginated section of *The Cupid,* 2d ed. (London: Printed for J. Osborn, 1739), an anthology of verse from the preceding four decades.

56. Diary of Viscount Percival, Earl of Egmont, *Historical Manuscripts Commission: Egmont,* 1:423–24.

57. From a letter to the editor, 16 Jan. 1781, in the *Gentleman's Magazine* 51 (1781): 22.

58. Brewster, *Aaron Hill,* 191.

59. Hill, *Works,* 1:133.

60. Hill, *Works,* 1:265.

61. *Monthly Review* 6 (1752): 148–49.

62. The Oxford English Dictionary notes that "autobiography" was not used until the nineteenth century, and Dryden uses "biography" as a learned term for a branch of history. Even in mid-century, Samuel Johnson was writing the Lives of the Poets, not their biographies.

63. Most discussion of the genre of autobiography focuses on male writers from the later eighteenth century on; see Laura Marcus, *Auto/biographical Discourses:*

Theory, Criticism, Practice (Manchester: Manchester University Press, 1994), esp. chap. 5, for a discussion of the theoretical basis of criticism of the genre.

64. See Elspeth Graham et al., eds. *Her Own Life: Autobiographical Writings by Seventeenth-Century Englishwomen* (London and New York: Routledge, 1989).

65. J. Paul Hunter, *Before Novels: The Cultural Contexts of Eighteenth-Century English Fiction* (New York: Norton, 1990), discusses the complex matrix of news, history, fact, and fiction which formed the early novel.

66. See the preface to *Mrs. Manley's History of her Own Life and Times. Publish'd from her Original Manuscript*, 4th ed. (London: Printed for E. Curll, 1725).

67. Cited in Ballaster, "Seizing the Means of Seduction," 97.

68. Sandra M. Gilbert and Susan Gubar, *The Madwoman in the Attic* (New Haven: Yale University Press, 1979), 50.

Textual Note

THE copy text used for this edition of *Clio* is that of the Lilly Library, Indiana University, Bloomington, Indiana. Call number PR3291 A1 642.

Collation: 12mo. A^4 B-I^{12} K^8; description: (i) title; (ii) blank; iii–viii dedicatory material; 1–163 secret memoirs &c; 164 blank; 165–207 songs and poems; 208 blank.

Long "s" has been normalized. Original spelling has been preserved as possibly authorial but the following errors have been corrected:

Original text		*This edition*	
25.	Pardon, me, my	71	Pardon me, my
46.	By	81	My
86.	Fulham	99	Fulham.
98.	on the Back of	104	on the Rack of
120.	somethtng	113	something
136.	[not of Hearts]	120	(not of Hearts)
142.	to Town Freedom. I languish'd for,	123	to Town. Freedom I languish'd for,
145.	heseemed	124	he seemed
169.	Mind	135	Mind.

CLIO:

OR, A

SECRET HISTORY

OF THE

LIFE and AMOURS

Of the Late celebrated

Mrs. S———N———M.

Written by HERSELF, *in a Letter to* HILLARIUS.

LONDON:

Printed for M. COOPER, in *Pater-noster-Row.* 1752.

CLIO's PICTURE.

Oh! gentle *Hamond,* whilst a Brother shines,
Immortal in thy Friendship, and thy Lines,
Place me a Neighbour to the dear-lov'd Name,
Nature has pair'd us, let me share his Fame.
I ask not Lawrels, they are here resign'd,
My Chaplet must be of a softer Kind,
Oh! let the Bay my longing Temples bind.
If all the Graces in his Person shine,
Oh! think the Muses have befriended mine;
And while their Lustre o'er my Olive' spread,
I envy not the Shine of White and Red.
Here let the Muse perform the Painter's Art,
And strike the Picture of my Face and Heart.
Poetry's call'd the Image of the Mind,
On mine the Soul and Body both are join'd,
Large is my Forehead made, not wond'rous fair,
But Room enough for all the Muses there.
Full are my Eyes, and of a harmless blue,
As if no Wound they meant, no Dart they knew,
My Eye-brows, arching o'er, a Shade bestow,
Veiling the Dullness of the Eye below.
Nature, so niggard to the upper Part,
Fell to my Lips, and gave a Dash of Art.
Oft have I heard the faithful Lover swear,
That Poetry and Love were shining there.
Even and white my Teeth, but rarely shown;
In Life I've little Cause for smiling known.
The Loss of Friends fell on my tender Years,
Dash'd ev'ry Hope, and turn'd my Smiles to Tears.
A gloomy Sweetness on my Features hung,
Sorrows my Pen, and trembles on my Tongue;
Slow is its Speech, and with no Musick fraught,
Wronging the Richness of my Soul's best Thought.
But whither is my mournful Pencil stray'd?
My Hair, dark brown, wants not *Ducela*'s Aid,
Flows in the Wind, nor of the Comb afraid;
Beneath my Waist in nat'ral Rings descends,
Or pliant to the artful Finger bends,
When it betides that Dress and I are Friends.
Easy my Neck, but of no dazzling white,

Veil'd by the Lawn from the enquiring Sight.
My Shoulders fall, as Nature's self informs.
Small are my Fingers, nor too plump my Arms;
To the nice Eye no Transport they afford,
But to the Ear pressing the tender Cord.
Then my Cares murmuring with a lower Breath,
Drop from my Eyes, and weep themselves to Death.
My Waist but gently by the Whale-bone bound,
Is not a *German,* but an *English* Round.
My Feet with no ungraceful Motion tread,
Tho' *Isaac*'s Steps are from their Mem'ry fled.
To decent Height my Stature is inclin'd,
Worthy the Muses and a gen'rous Mind.
To thy kind Eyes *Clio* submits her Form,
Whose Verse can give it ev'ry absent Charm;
Thou, in whom Art, and Love, and Nature shines,
Immortalize my Picture with thy Lines.

The *Dedication* of my Heart and Life.

TO
The Monarch of all my soft Desires;
The End of all my Wishes;
The Inspirer of my Heart;
The Adoration of my Soul;
The Elevater of my Thoughts;
The Immortalizer of my Songs;
The Charmer of my Bosom;
The Life of my Soul;
The Heaven of my Repose;

This is most fondly, most passionately, most respectfully addressed, by

His devoted, adoring
CLIO.

To the Inspirer of my Soul, but Sweet Disturber of it.

Oh! divine *Hillarius,* till I was inspired by your lovely Eyes, I did not imagine my Life worth my Concern. I meant to die undistinguished, and to sleep amidst the Lumber of the World. But your heavenly Beauties have warmed me with nobler Sentiments; for your sweet Sake I would be immortal: I would excell in every thing as I do in Passion for my lovely Charmer. But for Love's Sake, most Adorable, preserve me at least in your Heart; there let me live: nor am I unworthy of such a Residence, who adore you so perfectly, so respectfully, so ardently, and will do to my last Breath. I know not how soon I may in Absence or Death lose the Joy of gazing on you, and my Hand be rendered incapable of this sweet Employment. Receive therefore this Assurance from my Soul, that I will live and die filled with Adoration for you. That since the first Moment I beheld you my Heart has panted for nothing else; my Eyes and Arms have been insensible of all other Pleasure, and, in Absence from you, acquainted with no Joy. I have mourn'd incessantly, while Business or Friends have engaged you too often. Oh! *Hillarius,* how have those Accidents wounded my Soul! if you were ever to blame, sure it was in afflicting me so deeply. Oh! if you have a Heart, why did it not beat with *Clio*'s Anguish? why was it silent when mine was torn to death with Love and Sorrow? Oh! insensible *Hillarius,* will it be to your Glory that you have pierc'd to Death the most faithful of all Women? How will you answer it to your God, that has made you so lovely, that you have used that Beauty to make me wretched? Oh! how sweetly might it have blessed me! how might it have softened all the Misfortunes of Life, by shining on me often, and blessing me in Absence with tender Letters! Are you not afraid, oh! too assured Charmer, a Day may come, when the neglected *Clio* may return this Coldness, and transplant herself to some kinder Bosom?

To the for-ever-lovely Hillarius.

Guide of my Life, Inspirer of my Muse,
Sweet Patron of my Lays, thy Spirit infuse;
I court no other's Care, no meaner Name,
But his who charms my Soul, to guard my Fame.
If *Julius* liv'd I would address to thee,
King of my Soul, and only Lord of me!

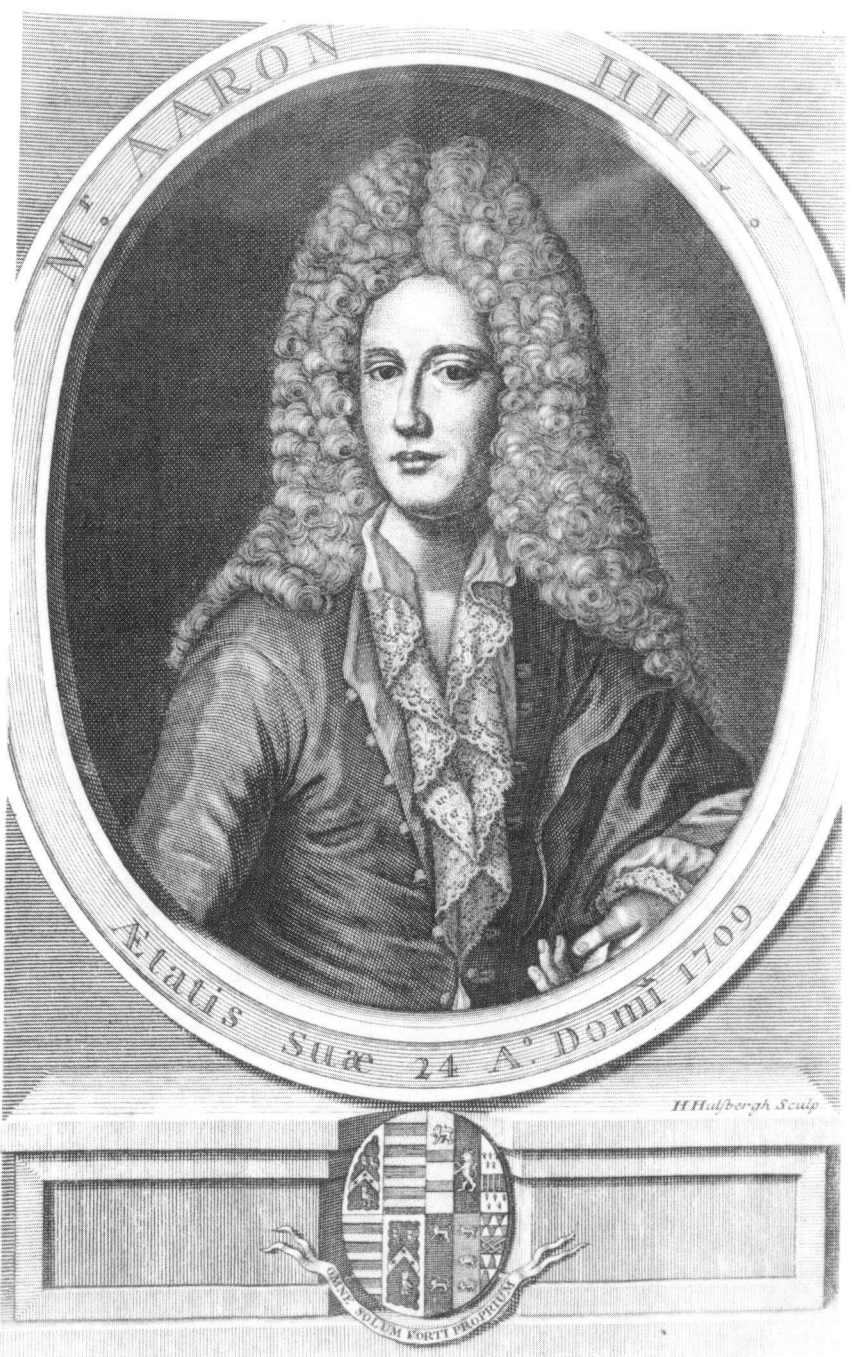

Aaron Hill. Frontispiece to *A Full and Just Account of the Ottoman Empire*, London, 1710. (Photo courtesy of The Newberry Library.)

> Let not the World imagine I design
> To charm its Malice, or to make it mine;
> So false, so vain its Praise, I would not gain
> The common Trifle with the smallest Pain.
> No gaudy Title shall my Life defend,
> Nor shall it but to great *Hillarius* bend.
> Oh! bright Protector, to thy Arms receive
> My Life and me, then we, indeed, shall live.

SECRET MEMOIRS, &c.

I had the Happiness of being born of Parents that I am as proud to own, as if they had left me fortunate and rich as they could wish. The Civil Wars deprived my Grand-Father of a very large Estate in *Staffordshire,* where our Name and Family lived and flourished ever since the Conquest. It is originally a *French* Name, and has been worn by Kings abroad and Princes here, and is still in a Way of appearing well to future Ages, in my dearest Brother, and the other Branches of it.

The Revolution was not kinder to my poor Father than the Civil Wars to his; after his Royal master was forced to leave his Kingdoms, he laid down a very handsome Command in the Army, not being able to submit to the Tyranny of Oaths. This was an unhappy Thing for his Family, and obliged him to retire into *Staffordshire,* where my Mother had a good Jointure, and they were received with the utmost Respect. But it created Wonder, that the most polite and witty of all Men, could pass his Hours in the Country, where the Pleasures are so different from those in Town, and where the courser Senses are only entertained. Eating and Drinking are their highest Pleasures, the chief Design of Retirement is lost, which was to indulge the Soul in Learning. This way of Living makes it gross and unrefined, dead to Wit and fine Conversation. My poor Father languished in this stupid Scene some Years, far from his native Element, which was refined Love and Pleasure. Pardon, my lovely Friend, this little Digression my Pen is fallen into. And now permit me, ere I say any thing of my own Life, to give you the Pictures of those I owe it to, whose Memories are dear to me. I have already said something of my Father, but methinks not enough for one I so dutifully and passionately loved, and one I would render charming to you. Oh let me bring you acquainted. How do I anew deplore his Death, which has robbed him of your sweet Commerce, unless you will now bless him with

[1]

SECRET MEMOIRS, &c.

I Had the Happiness of being born of Parents that I am as proud to own, as if they had left me fortunate and rich as they could wish. The Civil Wars deprived my Grand-Father of a very large Estate in *Staffordshire*, where our Name and Family lived and flourished ever since the Conquest. It is originally a *French* Name, and has been worn by Kings abroad and Princes here, and is still in a Way of appearing well to future Ages, in my dearest Brother, and the other Branches of it.

Page 1 of Fowke's Life, from *Clio*. (Courtesy of the Lilly Library, Indiana University, Bloomington, Indiana.)

your Regard. How would his Soul have been charmed with you who are so charming? I feel his Loss again, and shed all my Tears as if he dy'd but yesterday. He knew the World he then liv'd in, but he did not know you the only Ornament of it: Nor did I live myself till I had the Blessing of beholding you. But to finish this Pourtrait which your Beauties take me every Moment from; He was tall, graceful, and well made; his Complexion was the darkest brown, but something so sweetly commanding shone through that Gloom; I have often thought it like some lovely Evening, which charms beyond the Day. Till he was thirty he had the finest shining dark Hair in the World, long and flowing in large Curls: He had large dark Eyes full of Love and Fire: His Lips and Teeth were beyond Description, and had something inchanting in them: His Hands were equally fine: Thus was his Form adorned by Nature, and his Soul worthy of it. He was good-natured to Excess, and the most amorous of all Mortals. Heaven had designed him for a Lover rather than a Husband. The Chains of Marriage press'd him to Death. He was well-bred and modest, and so happily assur'd he knew not the Pain of Blushing; so lively was his Wit, he never study'd a Moment in either Writing or Speaking, yet did both to Perfection. His Address had something so powerfully charming, that even the Duke of *Marlborough* used to say, he wondered he did not ask him all things, who could refuse him nothing; and this great Man was not famed I think for granting. My Father had been bred in his first Years in the Court of *France,* and distinguished there; at Nineteen he returned to *England,* and was favoured by all the Gay and Witty, even by the King himself, who was *both* in Perfection. My Grandfather was Store Keeper to the *Tower,* and his children well received at Court; 'twas there the Widow of Sir *Anthony Vincent,* a Beauty and rich, fell in Love with my Father; she was thirty, and he not twenty; the Shade of Years between them created much Uneasiness; Jealousy hastened her Death; she took with her a very large Jointure, which forced the young Widower to Marriage again. The Daughter of Col. *Codrington,* Governor of the *Leeward Islands,* was then thought one of the greatest Fortunes in *England,* she was an only Daughter, and her Father had above Ten Thousand Pounds a Year. My Father found means to board in the very School where she was, and soon married her. He was passionately fond of this Lady, for she had every Perfection. The old Governor forgave them, and received them to his Favour. He sent for them to him, where she died, and left only one Son, which the Grandfather designed to share his Estate with his own Son the witty Colonel *Codrington;* but Death at eighteen Years robbed him of this Darling. My Father, after his Lady's Death, hastened to *England,* where he married my Mother, a handsome and rich Widow: But Love had little to do in this Affair, though she was a very lovely Woman, and a most excellent Manager, but knew not how to charm my Father's Heart. She was devout, but could not pray herself into his Affections; but she found all things in the Heaven she address'd, and though not fondly, they lived civilly together; and what cemented them a little more was my Birth. The little Fondness I have for myself, and the tender Remembrance of the Persons I have spoke of, has perhaps detained me too long; pardon me, my heavenly Friend. And now I will speak of her you honour with your Regard, the only Pride and Blessing of her Life.

I was born the 1st of *May* some Years after the Revolution; your divine Muse has blessed that Day in the sweetest Manner; for which I shall for ever bless you; and never was any Daughter received with so much Joy. From the first Hour I was dear to my Father's Heart; and I have heard him affirm he has stolen from his most agreeable Friends to attend my Cradle; from the Moment of my Birth to his Death he placed his chief Happiness in me; my Mother and he only agreed in this Point; the Fondness he wanted for her he overpay'd me, and she had the Goodness to receive it there with Pleasure.

A Year after I was born they were blessed with my dear Brother; but I have heard them since say, they received that Happiness but coldly. When he was very young he was insensible of this Distinction. As he throve in Beauty, he was as much my Favourite as I was my Father's; as if my young Soul had prophesied of his future Perfections, or meant to atone for the indifference of his Parents, I suffered every Time he was corrected, so much, that my Father in pity to me used to spare him. We were both born in *Hertfordshire,* at a Seat of my Uncle *Cullen*'s, in the sweetest Place upon Earth, the very Air seemed to breathe nothing but Love; there sure I drew in those tender Sentiments first, which are now glowing in my Heart. Let me not appear too romantick, if I paint to you the Beauties of that Place; if I lead you to sigh by those Streams, and to slumber in those Groves, where the God of Love might sweetly wander. The House is large, built after the modern Manner; the Rooms are spacious and well designed; the Hall, which is most beautiful, is laid with Marble, and is raised to the very Top of the House; the Gallery round it is finely adorned, with an Echo where the God of Musick would delight to warble. It was hung with the finest Instruments, and several large Christal Branches for Lights. The rest of the Rooms were equally handsome, and the Furniture very fine; from all the Windows there is a most delightful Visto, where the Eye is sweetly entertained with a thousand Varieties, Wood and Water, flow'ry Meadows, and a very fine Park, well filled with Deer. I never saw Shades more beautifully formed than here, where Art and Nature agree so well together. Oh that I had been bless'd with your sweet Company there, that my Eyes had gazed on you with their first Light, and never parted to this Moment! The Gardens and Park descend from the House in a very agreeable Manner, and many of the Walks are entirely covered from the Sun. Here I began my Life, here I could end it.

The Hours of Childhood passed pleasantly over, with the continual Endearments of my Father and Mother. What encreased their Fondness was my ill Health, which seemed to require their utmost Tenderness. They found it very hard to raise these Atoms. My Soul seemed often willing to sally from my Bosom, as if it foretold its future Agonies, and would elude them. From *Hertfordshire* we went into *Staffordshire,* after a little Stay in *London;* my Brother had been sent there before us, to my Grandmother. I cannot tell you, my divine Master, the Joy I had to find him again; I had pined for his Absence. It was in this Country my Mother became a Catholick, to the Surprize of all her Friends in Town; but I cease to wonder at it, when I remember the fine Sense of her Converters. Religion appeared in its true Beauty, in their Chapels and Conversations; tho' so young, I found myself charmed with it. My Mother indulged my Inclinations, and my Father permitted her to breed me a Catholick. I must confess I was pleased with their Devotion, though not naturally devout; I tasted a Pleasure in their Admonitions, where Gentleness was always mixed with Devotion. I was caressed by the wisest and most religious of our Friends; and all those who meant to endear themselves to my Father and Mother found the Way by praising me. It yielded my young Mind a Sweetness, but a fatal one; it wakened a Vanity in me, which I have hardly yet been able to suppress, and which has led me into many Mistakes: The Homage I received then gave me a Passion for it, which will never entirely dye. I would warn those, who have the Care of Youth, against this Misfortune. Every Day I grew dearer to my Father and Mother. I devoted myself very young to Reading, but was so unhappy to choose such Books as rather diverted, than informed, my Mind. My Mother had a Closet finely furnished with the best Authors, but *Cassandra* and *Cleopatra* were my Favourites. I read there with Pleasure the Empire of Women, and doubted not of finding an *Orondates*. I could think of nothing below a King or Prince. I began from that Moment to despise the Country Gentlemen; our Neighbours appeared Savages, and I often wondered, my Father and Mother could endure them. This gave my Heart too exalted Notions, and has since occasioned a thousand Disappointments. The Leisure, that Reading afforded, I applied to Musick and Dancing. I had the best Masters for both, and began to excel in those Trifles by my Father's Care, who had a fine Taste in these Things. I had then an Inclination to *Latin,* and began it with my Brother, but my weak Health would not permit so many Exercises. It seemed to languish under the Oppression. My Father endeavoured to change my Studies; he sent for a *French* Woman from *London,* but I never was very fond of that Language, and had an Aversion to the *Hugonots,* which prevented my pursuing it; yet I at last wrote it and spoke it tolerably well. About this Time I apply'd myself to Writing, with greater Fondness, than any thing. I was too young for a Master, therefore I stole Copies, and by myself formed such a kind of Hand, as this. I learned in haste and secret; 'tis no wonder I am so little perfect in it. From *Cowley* and *Ovid* I collected the most tender Parts, and addressed them to my Father. He was charmed at my little Theft; he shewed them to all his Friends, and his dear Child was his continual Discourse. How, my most lovely Friend, was I pleased with his Praises! I redoubled my Care, and not a Day passed without writing him a Letter. The Prudence of my Mother grew concerned at my pursuing Trifles so much; she possibly foresaw this Humour might encrease with my Years. She locked up her Books, my Pens were burned, and I bound down a Prisoner to my Needle. This was the first Misfortune I knew. Never did romantick Lady deplore her self more than Miss *Patty.* I looked upon this as the highest Affront. I did all my Work wrong, and nothing succeeded, I undertook. I secretly mourned the Loss of my dear Pen and Ink, as if I had lamented a Lover, but I would not complain to my Father, lest he should resent it to my Mother, too severely.

My Mother addressed herself to her Father Confessor on this Occasion; he was a Man of true Piety, and of fine Sense, of a most Angelick Composition. He used to call me his little Saint, and I had for him the most religious Duty. One Day, after I had ended my Confession, he gently reproved me: My dearest Child, says he, I both rejoice and mourn for you; you have Sense beyond your Years, and your Soul is sweetly adorned; Heaven designed it for itself. Oh let me early reclaim it from profane and loose Poets: Let me introduce you to the heavenly Company of Saints and Angels, who languish to converse with you, who are jealous of *Ovid* and

Cowley; I must have you shine amongst them, and make my Favourite the Favourite of Heaven. He spoke this with such a divine Air, mixed with Sweetness, that my Soul burned with Devotion, a holy Shame covered my Face; on my Knees I received and thanked his heavenly Care, and from that Hour looked upon him as my Guardian Angel; my Heart sighed after Heaven with the same Ardour it now does for you: Nor do I find any Difference in its Passions; but that I now adore an Object I have seen. For many Years I was under this Gentleman's holy Council, and happy in it. He was a temporal as well as spiritual Friend. I deplore that I have lost him by Death or Absence; he was an Honour to his Profession; he was of the Order of *Jesu,* and most truly devout. I can never remember him without Tears; would to God I could still converse with him, to fortify my Soul against your Absence, a Misfortune most wounding to me.

We left *Staffordshire,* and returned with our whole Family to *London;* we lodged in *Pallmall,* where an odd Adventure befel us; I was then about nine or ten Years old; my Books were restored to me, and I was more in Favour than ever; I was called the Wit of the Family, and now made Secretary to my Father and Mother. I answered for them all their Letters of Compliment. I was very proud and happy in this Employment. My Father made me his Confidant, and I often dictated his Love Letters for him, and that in such a tender Manner, he had too much Success with them. I began to scribble Verses of my own, or I thought them mine. My Memory treasured up all Things. I had long Poems by Heart. I wrote Verses for my Brother against his Breakings-up, which were too much approved. I grew so vain of all this, that I would converse with none but People of the finest Sense. I was raised above the usual Follies of my Age. We lodged in a *French* House to improve me in that Language; the Master of it was young, handsome, vain, and a *Hugonot;* he seemed necessary to my Pleasures, and still conducted me abroad to all the Places that afforded any Entertainment, the Parks and Plays, with my Brother. I looked on him as something extreamly below me; I know not why, unless from the Duty he pay'd me, and my natural Vanity. My Father had a great Confidence in him, or he would not have trusted his Treasure with him. I know not whether it was Love or Whim, but the poor Man grew very melancholy; he sighed whole Nights, neglected his Affairs, and seemed lost to himself; as to me, he no longer entertained me with Stories, but walked with the Silence of a Shadow. My Brother was his Bedfellow, and used to complain he could not sleep for his *French* Friend. We knew not what to make of this Change.

I had no Notion any common Soul could be in Love; my Mother imagin'd it Religion, and lent him the most composing Books of that kind; but the Illness was not in the Head so much as Heart, he still grew worse, nor had he Courage to seek any Remedy. One Night, about twelve o'Clock, we heard a very odd Noise, Groans mingled with Stampings, and loud talking, with my Name often repeated in a very distracted Manner. My poor Brother run down to my Father, and assured him, Mr. B—— was gone distracted, and he believed, for his Sister. Soon after, about half a Dozen *Hugonots* ascended the Stairs in a very violent Manner, and said my *Mother* had bewitched the Man above with Popery, and *I* with Love. It was in vain to argue with these ignorant inraged Creatures. My Father thought it best to retreat to a Neighbour's, till this Storm decreased. We all went out of the House in a very disorder'd Manner, and soon after beheld the Books, my Mother had given him to read, and some little Presents, she had made him, all burnt together, which they imagined would end the Charm. It was very well we escap'd with our Lives, for it seems they had threaten'd before to murder us. From what I have seen of the Madness of these People, I cannot but think the immortal *Lewis* had more than Reason to drive them from his Country.

This was the first of Love, that concerned myself, I ever heard of, and the oddest. It began in Flames, without any Fiction, and gave me a Terror for such Passions. My Father fixed in a very handsome House in *Albemarle-street,* near St. *James*'s, in a very agreeable Neighbourhood: A Relation of our's, a very sickly Man, desired to finish his Days with us; he was very rich, and always affirmed, he would leave me his Fortune, having a Fondness for me from my Cradle. I looked upon him with a Gratitude and Care, I thought he deserved; he was very young, but so deaf that the rest of the Family seemed to neglect him; I often stayed out of meer Pity with him, and endeavoured to make him forget ill Health. I used to play to him on the Harpsichord, which tho' he heard but imperfectly, seemed extreamly to oblige him; on his Part he grew polite and well-bred, tho' naturally morose and peevish. I was a kind of Oracle to him, and nothing pleased him that any other did or said. My Innocence and Good-nature had so far engaged him, that he resolved to marry me; he proposed it to my Mother, who seemed to approve it, as Interest induced her; but my Father, who studied my Happiness in a more refined Manner, was entirely against it. He could not think of sacrificing my Youth to such Misery; nor was I less against it, for I had Pity, but no Love.

What hastened this Disagreement was a foolish Accident; I was

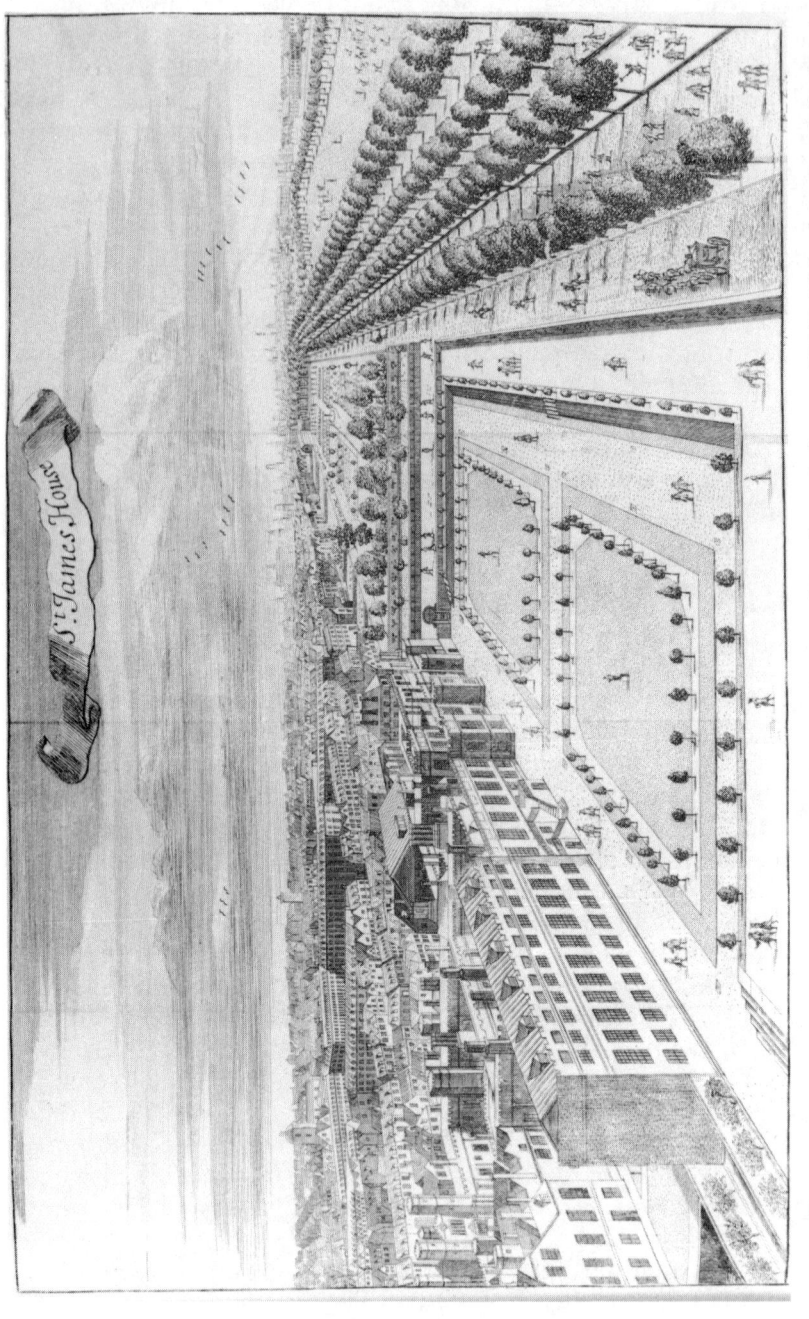

View of St. James's Park and Palace, from John Stow's *Survey of London*, ed. Strype (1720). This view shows the royal palace of St. James and the fashionable area to the north of it. St. James's Park to the right where Fowke often walked or sat was visible from Hill's garden to the south. (Courtesy of the Lilly Library, Indiana University, Bloomington, Indiana.)

very often permitted to go to Plays, but was still attended by some grave Person that I could neither laugh nor cry, as I pleased. One Day I was left at home to entertain my sickly Lover, who entreated me to go to the Play with him: it was *Oroonoko,* my Favourite; I knew not how to resist this Temptation, but feared being known, or possibly meeting my Father there; but against this we provided a Mask. My Heart was too innocent and young to dream of further Harm, in this, than my Father's Anger. But it happened to be a very dear Play to me; for at our Return I found my Father and Mother both enraged against me; I was most severely reproved; I confessed very innocently, where I had been, and asked Pardon for the first Fault: I was forgiven, but my poor Lover never was. My Father, who never loved him, now looked on him with Aversion, and desired him to leave his House, which he did, and Life soon after, for having lost in me the only Pleasure of it, he languished to Death. He often sent to intreat I would see him in his Illness, but my Father would not suffer it, which was much too nice. He died, and left Twenty Thousand Pounds to entire Strangers. I lamented for this poor Gentleman, though he had little but Love to recommend him: As for the Money, it gave me no Concern: I had every thing I wished for in the affectionate Care of my Parents.

Thus, my heavenly Friend, ere I was fourteen, I lost my second Lover, no less unfortunate than my first; I began to think Love an unlucky Thing, and resolved to preserve my Indifference, which I did some Years. One Day, as was usual, I was kneeling behind my Mother at Mass, in *Arlington-street.* My Heart was truly devout, and my Eyes lifted up to Heaven. I had laid down my Prayer Book for some Moments, and was much surprized when I took it up to read what was wrote with a Pencil.

[*Oh heavenly Creature, look back on a poor Mortal, who dyes for you.*]

I was much surprized and troubled at this Discovery. I blushed extreamly, which my Mother wondered at, who often regarded me, to keep me close to Devotion, which I still continu'd without once turning my Head. I still prayed, but in a different Manner. I entreated Heaven to defend my Heart, to keep it still to itself. When Prayers were ended, I rose with some Confusion, fearing to see the Author of the Lines I had read. But I could not help observing him from his bowing very low, and offering his Hand to lead my Mother to her Chair. I must confess my Eyes had never, till then, seen so fine a Form. He was very tall, gracefully made, and near twenty; his Face was very sweet, and all his Features perfectly beautiful; but what I observed most, as he lead my Mother, the finest fair Hair in the World, which descended very low, to his Waist; he seemed genteel and modest. After he had put my Mother in her Chair in the most respectful Manner, he offered his Hand to me. He endeavour'd to say something, but trembled so, he could not; thus we parted. At Dinner, my Mother enquired of my Father if he knew such a Gentleman; she described his Person and Civility: Whilst she was speaking, a young Lady, who was my Bedfellow, a Nobleman's Daughter of *Ireland,* told my Mother, she was assured the Person she spoke of was her near Relation, just arrived from *France,* where he had charmed all the Ladies. He is, says she, Sir C—— B——l——n's Son of *Ireland;* I may call him his Heir, for his eldest Brother has resolved against Marriage. I heard this Discourse with Indifference, for I had found Admiration, but no Love. Oh how different are they? your divine Beauties have taught me to distinguish, or rather to join them together. In the Afternoon, the first thing I saw was my new Lover, who came to visit his Cousin; we were together when he came: I had more time then to survey him, which I did with Caution, for I saw and pity'd his Disorder; which I have found since is the Symptom of a sincere Passion. He spoke but little, yet what he said was tender and respectful. He begged Pardon for the Liberty he took in the Morning of Writing. He laid the Fault on Love; nothing could be more polite or charming than this Lover, yet was my Heart insensible to him. I felt neither Pride nor Pleasure in the Conquest. I retired, as soon as Civility allowed, to my darling Books; I own his Beauties and his Love deserved a better Fate. He often visited his Relation, who still pleaded warmly for him, and often, by some Art or other, brought us together. My Mother was not displeased, this Gentleman being a Catholick. My Father had his Pleasures abroad; so we passed the Moments very agreeably. I was pleased, though not charmed: He used to bring with him a Relation to entertain my Bedfellow: He was a very agreeable Man, and had something of a pleasing Sadness, which more engaged me of the two. I imagined I liked him most, but it was truer much, that I was in Love with neither. My Lover used to complain of my Coldness in a Manner, that would have warmed any other; but my Hour of Love was not yet arrived. He had a very sweet Voice, and used to be ever singing some tender Song of his own making. One Day, as we were sitting in an Arbour in a neighbouring Garden, or rather he was kneeling at my Feet, he sweetly sighed in Musick,

CLIO

1.

O lovely Maid, whom I adore,
  I sadly prophesy,
When this poor Victim is no more,
  Who dyes, who dyes for thee,
Thy Eyes will kinder Looks impart
To some ungrateful careless Heart.

Oh if the Dead can suffer Pain
  What Torment will it be!
'Twill force me into Life again,
  Again to dye for thee;
But first to pierce the faithless Breast,
Who wounds my Ashes, and thy sacred Rest.

My Soul found something very moving in these Words, and returned them *extempore,* if I can remember, in this Manner:

Oh generous Youth, what can I give
  To Tenderness, like thine!
Ah! on some gentler Bosom live,
  Till Love has waken'd mine.
I see thy Merit and approve,
Be kind, and call my Friendship Love.

Let it suffice thy tender Heart
  And pass for a Return,
That it confesses thy Desert,
  And may hereafter burn.
Thy Sighs and Tears may happy prove,
And charm my Pity into Love.

Wou'd to God it may, my Angel, he cry'd, wou'd to God it may. As he lifted up his Face (which was all charming) I saw it covered with Tears. My Soul was touched with real Pity, and I have often wondered, Love did not enter it that tender Moment; and much more am I amazed now, when I recollect Mr. *B*—— was not unlike my heavenly Charmer, neither in Shape nor Air. He was something taller; but I must own, 'till I beheld you, I had never seen any thing so lovely. Pardon me, my adorable Friend, if I break every Moment from my Life to speak of you, who are dearer to me. Oh, you have more than enough revenged my Indifference.

But to return to my unhappy Lover. We parted that Evening:

Some Weeks after, he was press'd by his Relations to leave *England*, where he was only meant to make a little Tour. He told me of this with the utmost Sadness, and anew implored my Pity, that I wou'd suffer him to offer himself to my Father. I could not think of this, I resolv'd to see the World ere I fetter'd myself. I intreated him therefore to leave me to Time, and promis'd I wou'd receive no other whilst he was single. With a breaking Heart he prepared to be gone; when we parted he was dress'd in deep Mourning, which added to the Beauties of his Face; a sort of Languishment was there which pleaded for him, and I must own I never saw him so handsome; the Concern he was in was more moving than Eloquence. After a thousand Sighs instead of Words, he look'd me a most tender Adieu. I felt some little Sorrow, but soon forgot it, my Books amus'd me; he wrote often from *Ireland*, but I found it easier to refuse his Letters than himself; I continually sent him such Answers, intreating him to obey his Friends, that at last he married a good Fortune, and an agreeable Lady, but not to his Taste; for not long after his Health declin'd, and he dy'd in the Bloom of Youth and Beauty, the Desire of all Hearts but mine. His Memory is much dearer to me than his Person was, and I often weep over it to this Moment; 'tis possible his sweet Shadow will accept my Tears after Death, and I offer them sincerely, if you permit them, my sacred Friend. Oh! that it was possible you lov'd me enough to be jealous of this Tribute, how happy should I be!

Thus, heav'nly Guardian of my Soul, I lost my third Lover. My Stars were very whimsical. A greater Misfortune succeeded this; my poor Mother dy'd, and left me amidst a thousand Temptations; shelter'd by her Piety and Care, I was safe; with Shame I confess, I felt this Loss in every thing ere I truly sorrow'd for it; my Heart was fondest of my Father, and saw no Danger while he was left to bless me; but this Blow even removed me from his Wing.

In losing the best Wife in the World he lost her Jointure, on which was his chief Dependance. My Brother was in the Army, though a School-Boy. The Number of Masters I had grew expensive, as indeed House-keeping did; therefore he gave it over, and was once more persuaded to go into the Army, where he had yet very good Interest. His chief Care was to place me well, in whom his only Happiness was center'd. An old Lady, a Friend of my Mother's, desired the Care of me; she had three Daughters older than I, who, my Father hop'd, were wiser too. I lived there some Months, but found a mighty Reverse in my Fortune; the old Lady was artful as a Serpent, she had been a Beauty, and remained a Coquet, at least, for her Daughters. Half the young Fools in Town rendezvouz'd there, we danc'd, play'd at Cards, and the young Ladies went to Church, but 'twas for Lovers.

My Religion bore me another way, which I yet preserved, though not desired by my Mother in her Illness, she left my Soul to its own Way. The good Father, I some time ago mention'd, still bless'd me with his Advice, which preserv'd me amidst the Follies of this House; nor was this the only Mark of his Care, he press'd my Father to settle some Fortune on me, which my Mother had not Time to do; he was eternally of Service to me, and came to *London* on Purpose; if his Eyes should by any Chance see this little Book, I intreat him to receive my everlasting Acknowledgements; but I fear Heaven has call'd his sweet Soul thither; may it still watch over me!

I continued with these Ladies, till I found both my Character and Money in some Danger; the House was ever haunted by a sort of Men I had, till then, been a Stranger to; the old Lady meant to catch Fools for her Daughters. I was abounding in all sorts of fine Cloaths, which were laid by till my Mourning was out; but my fair Friends, without my Leave, adorned themselves every Day in them. I was ashamed to take Notice of this, and bore it good a while, till I had no farther Reason to complain, for all my fine Laces were worn out. It was Time then, I thought, to remove, which I did, by my Father's Orders, to a Relation's in *Devonshire-street*. The few Things I had of Value remaining, the Ladies were so good to take out of my Cabinet, which made it light of Carriage. Forgive me that I mention these Trifles, never any one lost them with less Concern. In this Place the Scene was intirely alter'd, I liv'd in very good Order, but not happily, the Gentlewoman of the House, though a Cousin-German, was no Friend.

I had very little Liberty, and began to mourn the want of it; I had no agreeable Friend to converse with, and few Books; in fine, I was a kind of half Prisoner. I durst not again complain to my Father, but wrote a Letter to the young Lady, who liv'd with us at St. *James's;* there I lamented myself, and painted my good Cousins in proper Colours; this I did only to amuse myself. In the Letter I happened to call my Father old Gentleman, they imagining this Word wou'd ruin me with him, the Letter was seiz'd and open'd, and delivered to him. His Tenderness often brought him to see me, and one Day, to my vast Confusion, he shew'd me this Letter. Never did I know the Passion of Shame before, I trembled and turn'd pale, and was sinking down.

My Father, who was divinely tender, pity'd my Concern, and gently reprov'd me for calling him old, a Thing his Gaiety hated; I begg'd Pardon a thousand times, he as often forgave me: What a Pain it is to offend those that love us? I cou'd less forgive myself that foolish Word, than my Father could. The rest of the Letter he approv'd, and from that Moment removed me from my good Relation's, who I have never convers'd with since; they knew my Father was at that Time settling all he cou'd upon me, and they meant to prevent it. This was the first Malice I met with in the World, and most unnatural from my own Family.

My Father convey'd me to a Niece of his own, a very lovely good-natur'd Person, who had liv'd with us some time when my Mother dy'd. I was very happy in her Friendship, and nothing could be more delightful than the Place we liv'd in. Our Garden look'd over *Spring-Garden,* where we could, unseen, see all the Company, and after the Company of a Night was retir'd, there we us'd to walk: A thousand Birds attended us with their Musick; my whole Time was pass'd in Reading. Here I had Time to indulge that favourite Passion again, more than ever. My Cousin's Closet afforded very entertaining Books, which were left her by our Grand-mother, who was a Wonder of her Kind.

I liv'd here as my Soul could wish, without the least Grief, but in the Distance of my darling Brother, who was then in *Ireland.*

We were sitting one Evening by the Water's-Side, to which our Garden descended, when a little Boat pass'd by us with a full large Sail, attended by another Boat without any. Two Gentlemen saluted us as they went by, and toasted our Health: The String of the Sail was ty'd to the Boat, and a sudden Gulf of Wind overturn'd it. The poor Gentlemen were swimming in the Water, but I believe so unus'd to that Exercise, that if our Cries had not call'd the Neighbours to their Aid, they would have been lost with the Surprize; and incommoded by their Cloaths, they were taken out of the *Thames;* and, our House being nearest, we offer'd them to repose themselves there; the Watermen, who were very well dipp'd too, bore them along.

They were put into Bed, and refresh'd with warm Wine; when a little recover'd, they desir'd to see the Ladies that had been so compassionate to them. They paid us their Thanks in a very handsome Manner; and soon after I found the Elder of the Two had been Physician to my Mother: My Cosin perfectly remembered him again. He seem'd to apply his Thanks and Discourse to her, as the other did to me. From that Time our Acquaintance began. The Physician's Friend was about two and twenty: He had something in his Face and Mein agreeably tender, but nothing fine or graceful.

The Danger I had seen him in, recommended him more than his Person: And I found a kind of Compassion for him more than I had been sensible of before; 'tis possible he had Art enough to discern this. His Friend had told him who I was, that my Family and Fortune would be the raising of his; that he would use his Interest with my Cousin, whose Care I was under. They often renewed their Visits, and at last we saw them every Evening: Solitude, and seeing them often, inspired us with something like Love. My poor Cousin at last grew fondly in love with her Doctor, who was indeed a more engaging Man than the other. Her Lover, and she, still join'd in praising mine. He was a young Merchant, and his Family, and Education, but mean. I saw something servile in him, which my proud Heart could ill reconcile itself to; but Art and Time season'd this Dislike. He was artful in studying proper Diversions for my Youth. He was ever making Balls, of which I was the Queen, the Hours and I danced on with little Consideration. I lik'd the new Pleasures he every Day found for me, much more than the Man; he rather grew useful to me than charming: He was ever inventing little Journeys to amuse me. He shew'd us *Windsor,* and *Hampton-Court,* and all the fine Buildings about Town. All this pleas'd me extreamly, as it was new to me. At last, my Lover thought himself so well in my Favour, that he propos'd Marriage: I started at the Name; 'twas a State I ever abhor'd from the uneasy Life my Father and Mother led. I told him my Aversion, which appear'd to grieve him extreamly. He had a good deal of Cunning, but not much of Honour.

Soon after my Father was alarm'd with the News of this Lover. He was proud, and could not bear the Thoughts of receiving him into his Family. He talk'd to me about him; I very innocently and sincerely told him every thing. With Tears he intreated me to see him no more, to have better Hopes for myself. He told me he design'd me for a Nephew of his own, who he expected every Day from Sea: A Man of Sense and Honour, suited to my Soul, who was rising in the World. I listen'd to my Father as I would to Heaven, I assur'd him I would obey him while I liv'd, and that I would break off this Affair. When my Lover came next, I receiv'd him very coldly, and told him I must obey my Father. He seem'd to weep, and after imploring, in vain, a Reverse of his Fate, we parted, and I thought for ever.

The next Day the Relation my Father had spoke of, returned to *England,* and soon after desired Leave to be in the same House with *us,* where my Grandmother had brought him up, with the young Lady I liv'd with. I had not seen my Cousin many Years;

his Sense and Manners were improv'd very much; He was far from handsome, yet he appear'd very agreeable to me. He became a most passionate and tender Lover; his Sentiments were more refin'd than any I had yet heard. We convers'd eternally together, nor were ever parted a Moment. He retir'd from his Friends and Business to give himself up intirely to Love. Living together gives a Tenderness, I know not how to define: It supplies a thousand Charms: The Lover may improve the soft Moments to his Advantage. He watches the tender Motions of the Heart, and succeeds more in a Month, than the distant Lover in an Age. The little Time we were together I found it so: My Heart soften'd at his Tears, and return'd his Vows. He was perpetually studying to engage me: I saw nothing of the World but himself, and he took Care to conceal me from it. He made my Solitude so pleasing to me, that indeed I had no Wishes beyond it. What made him dearer to me, was the Fear of losing him soon, and to a thousand Dangers: These Fears create Love. I was happy that there was no Probability of marrying him soon, that would have been more sensible than parting with him for ever; so averse was I still to Marriage.

My Merchant was dead to my Memory; my Cousin had defac'd him there: He had represented him in such Colours, that I despis'd, or rather forgot him. My Cousin was now oblig'd to go to Sea again; I was tenderly concern'd to part with him: It was the first real Grief I had tasted. My poor Lover was carried on board half dead with Sorrow; it was certain he left his very Soul behind him, and to this Moment passionately loves me. Could he have staid longer with me, he had establish'd himself in my Heart, but Youth and other Objects wore off those Impressions.

As soon as he was gone, my Merchant returned; but I would neither receive his Letters nor Visits. But after my Cousin left me, my Father was alarm'd, by some busy Friends, that I might relapse into my former Inclinations; they advis'd him to hurry me into a Boarding-School, to be severely guarded. This was offering a Violence to his own Heart, which lov'd my Happiness.

He plac'd me under the Care of an old Governess, who had formerly been one to King *William*'s Queen. He desired I might be treated with Indulgence: He did not design I should be tormented with the foolish Learning of the School, which he knew I was above. Behold me, my ever charming Conqueror, in close Captivity! far from my dearest Friends, from my sweet Books, and beloved Retirement; I who had been Mistress of myself, ador'd by three Lovers, and a Kind of Wit, to be thus debas'd! I must say it was the wrongest Thing my Father ever did, and was near leading me to my Ruin. It is the worst Education upon Earth, no fine Mind can endure it. I speak with warmth against this, who have felt the Misery of it. I was intirely out of my Element: I now look back with Tears on my late lost Liberty. I wrote my Complaints on all the Windows!

Dear Liberty! O take me to thy Arms!
I pine to Death again to taste thy Charms!

But even in this Place I possess'd one Happiness, which was the Conversation of Miss *H——d,* a Lady of much Wit and Merit, something elder than I. We there began a Friendship, that, I hope, will last with my Life. We us'd to agree in playing our old Matron a thousand Tricks, till she grew weary of us.

It was now my Trafficker appear'd again: As I have said, he had low Cunning, he knew how to intrap us, as the Traders call it, tho' not to charm. He rightly judg'd Confinement might sink my Spirits to him. He wrote the most humble, fawning Letters: He had brib'd all the Servants to deliver them, and us'd to pass whole Days, walking in *Hyde-Park,* with folded Arms (our Windows look'd in there) where I every Day saw my Lover. He appeared then very differently in my Eyes; every thing he did had some Beauty; I forgot his mean Fear: in fine, I grew to like him, having nothing else to like; where I only saw Trees, old Women, and little Girls, he appear'd very lovely; Marriage itself was not then so abhor'd, and I resolv'd to release myself at any Rate. He begg'd Leave to write to my Father, and to wait on him, which I now permitted. He fell at my Father's Feet, and implor'd his Permission to see his Daughter, on whom his Life and Happiness depended. My Father's Heart was mov'd with Pity, and the Humility of the Man; he permitted him to see me once a Month, on Condition he would not press me to marry, without his Consent. In this Time he behav'd so well, he won to his Party even my Governess, who now pleaded for him, much more than my Heart, which was often weary of him, and languish'd to find something of greater Merit. He had not Sense enough to discern this, and thought himself secure of me. How dull are the Souls of common Men! My Governess, who wish'd me gone extreamly, seem'd to hasten this Affair. My Father therefore, at last, consented, but very heavily, I was remov'd into the *Strand* to buy Cloaths for this fine Wedding. How was I pleas'd to find myself at Liberty? 'Twas that I only wanted. But my Merchant is now trying to out-wit himself: He imagin'd, if he seem'd to retire, my Father would add to my Fortune, rather than lose him. Never was Wretch more mistaken. He told his Design to me; I was not displeas'd with it; hoping it would break off this dull Affair. I therefore acquainted my Father, that the Merchant seem'd willing to defer his Marriage a little while, till his Fortune was more worthy of me, and hop'd this would oblige him, it having been once his own Desire.

I knew very well how this would work on my Father's Soul: He mus'd some Moments, and then said, Yes, my dear Child, I will defer this Marriage—But it shall be for ever. And I now command you on my Blessing, never more to see that mean-spirited Villain: I see this is a Trick, and I hope it will make you think justly of yourself, and him: Thank Heaven, which has so early deliver'd you from Meanness and Misery.

I promis'd my Father never more to receive him, to return his Letters, and to despise him: which I did. Never was miserable Creature more disappointed! never was there a happier Resolve for me than this! From that Moment all things went wrong with him; his Credit sunk, and after some Years, vainly endeavouring to regain me, he married a very good Woman, and a Fortune, which both left him. He fail'd three Times, and became more unhappy than I wish'd. It is not six Months ago, since I was forc'd myself to relieve him, being reduc'd to a Garret, and to want all Necessaries of Life, but what he receiv'd from my Hand.

Thus, my most Adorable, I escap'd this Danger. My Father was cur'd of all his Fears, went into the Country to his Regiment, and left me Mistress of myself in Town. I pass'd the Hours very gaily: I liv'd with a young Lady, agreeable to my own Humour. Every Moment was diverted with something new: I had Lovers, but such as did not disturb me, nor indeed please me much. Amongst these, I had a Cousin-German, a Man of Fortune, who had liv'd some Years in the Country; he now came to Town, and was charm'd with his new Cousin, but he was far from my Taste: The Man of Pleasure, and the 'Squire, were awkardly blended together, and he was marry'd to a peevish Beauty, who despis'd him; all this disgusted me: his Presents, his Letters, and Person was refus'd. In fine, he had not the Art of Charming, which he wonder'd at.

Permit me to leave myself a Moment, to give you a little History of my Cousin's Lady, which will present you with a true Picture of the Pair: This is not likely to be seen by any but your heavenly Eyes, or I should spare the Follies of my Relations.

His Lady was a Man of Quality's Daughter, and was, besides being a Beauty, a very good Fortune. She was address'd by all the best Estates in the Country, but none pleas'd her so well as my unmeritorious Cousin. His Face was fair, his Cheeks rosy, and fashion'd more to carry off any thing, than a fair Lady; but this was nothing.

The God of Whimsy, not of Love, resolv'd their Union; she leap'd from a Window into my Cousin's Arms, who convey'd his fair Prize to *London,* where she was the Admiration of the Town, a little while, but it grew weary of her, as did her Husband, who began to languish for new Beauties. He left his Lady to sigh alone, but Chance took pity on her. In the same House, an old *Irish* Gentleman lodg'd, who had been a Man of Pleasure, and was still gallant: He took Compassion on this fair Victim, and us'd to amuse her Hours. The Husband was well contented, and pass'd away his Time as Wine and Youth directed.

But one Evening returning early home, he was much surprized to find his Wife abroad, nor could he hear where she was gone. He inquir'd for his Friend to comfort him, but found they were both flown together. After passing some Months in *Ireland,* he invited the Wanderer to return, which she at last consented to do; but has ever since hated him with the utmost Disdain. I have gone, my heavenly Friend, a little out of my Path, to give you an Idea of this Lover. I had another at that Time, far more agreeable, who had Youth and Wit. He abounded in Ridicule, and sometimes was dull enough to sacrifice his Passion to it, 'till at last we laugh'd Love out of Doors; but I must confess, he had something amusing enough in him, but was not intirely to my Taste. How sacred a Thing is Love! It will not indure Jesting.

About this Time of my Life, my Youth and Pleasures were interupted by a violent Illness, which I received by sitting too long under the sweetest Trees in the Park. But, oh, I forgive that Injury, and adore the Place, for it is now blest with your looking on it from your sweet Windows. I no longer reproach them, but rather wish I had continued there till this Moment.

I languish'd long with a Fever, that near destroy'd my Life. It was then, my ever charming Friend, I lamented the Loss of a Mother, and the Distance of a Father. My Distemper increased, and no Hopes of Recovery were left, but the Country: I went therefore to *Fulham,* where I was us'd with such Tenderness and Care, that my Health reviv'd every Day; and at last I was perfectly well. The Place agreed with my Soul as well as Body; I was charm'd with the agreeable Walks, and delightful Solitude. The sweet *Thames,* which, you know, passes by the Foot of the Garden, entertain'd my Eyes; and the agreeable Meadows, which were scatter'd on the other Side: How refreshing are the Arbours, fill'd with the

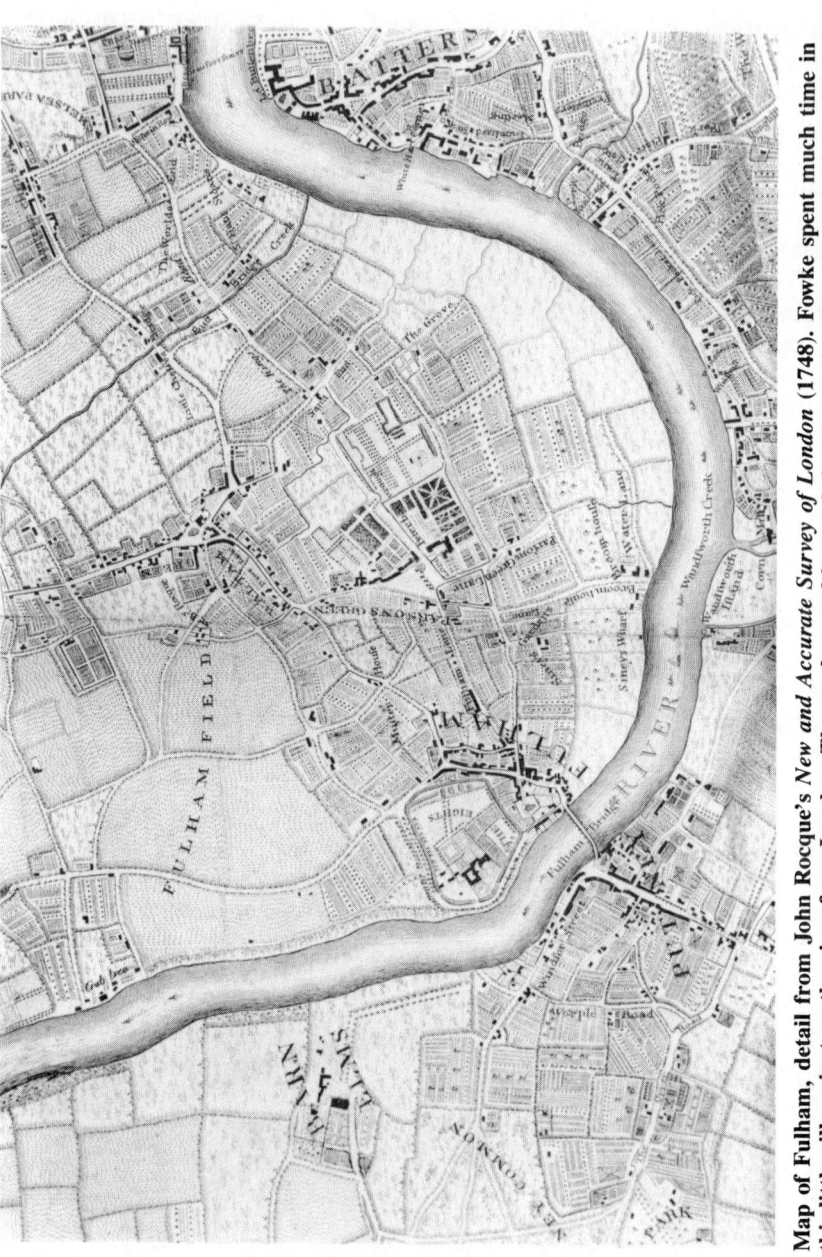

Map of Fulham, detail from John Rocque's *New and Accurate Survey of London* (1748). Fowke spent much time in this little village just up the river from London. The gardens and houses belonging to the Cenny family (spelled Siney on this map) with whom she lodged are visible in the center. (Courtesy of the Lilly Library, Indiana University, Bloomington, Indiana.)

softest Melody of the Spring! How cool are its Grottos, defended from the Day, as if form'd for Love and Friendship! I us'd to wander there with my Book or my Muse, and sweetly lost to the World, here I sigh'd,

> *Oh Heav'n, whate'er you else design,*
> *Let this sweet Solitude be mine:*
> *The Trees that shade, the Streams that shine.*
> *On this mossy Pillow resting,*
> *Nothing here my Soul molesting.*
> *Let not tyrant Love invade me,*
> *From his killing Arrows shade me.*
> *I have heard how others languish,*
> *And have wept to grace their Anguish;*
> *But never let this Bosom prove,*
> *From its own Pangs, the Force of Love.*
> *Every Guardian Angel save me,*
> *With the Freedom Nature gave me.*

The Angels heard my Prayers for a great while, and I liv'd in Paradise without a Serpent. I was happy in my Books and Friends, when the most terrible Misfortune of my whole Life befell me, the Loss of my dear Father. Oh let me collect Strength for this Part of my Life, I bleed when I think it over, and feel all those Agonies he suffer'd; I need not, were I able, to repeat the dreadful Manner of his Death; it wou'd wound your generous Soul too much, and you've already heard it.

Never was any Sorrow more real than mine: Part of my Life, the dearest of it, was lost at this Time. My Blood was shed by the same Hand. Nor Friends, nor Reason, could perswade me to pity myself. I resign'd my Soul to Grief, and indulg'd the fatal Sadness. My very Muse deceiv'd me, she could not sing for weeping.

> *Like a poor Flow'r, I pale and dying lay,*
> *Torn from the Stalk, which weeps its Life away.*
> *A thousand Dangers prest on every Part,*
> *Grief rent my Youth, and prey'd upon my Heart.*
> *The Night and Day was all to Tears resign'd,*
> *Death shook my Form, and shadow'd o'er my Mind.*

My Loss was inexpressible, and I find it more every Day, and this Instant more than ever; when the Ashes of the Dead are wounded by the Malice of the Living. My Griefs bleed anew, to find the Grave is not a Retreat from Envy, there I hop'd to rest with my poor Father; but the Scorpion *Haywood* will bear her Sting even thither.

I hear she even violates the Dead, who never had the Misfortune to see her, and has committed no Crime against her but in giving me Life; she taxes him with Follies he never heard of, my Soul knows him innocent of every Charge.

Sure this wretched Creature's Mind is as harsh and unlucky as her Features, that neither Death, nor Innocence, can intreat her; how much worse is this female Fiend than the Villain that stabbed my Father's Bosom, who darts the Poison of her Pen in his very Dust; may it perish there, nor rise again to hurt the World!

Pardon me, my Angel, while I am speaking of this Devil; till now she had not Power to afflict me. Oh, take me to your heav'nly Protection, and defend me from this Tygress, who delights in my Misfortunes, and pursues me in all that is dear and sacred to me, my Friends, my Reputation, my Parents, and even my adored *Hillarius,* who is dearer to me than all these, or Life itself; there she wou'd strike me; but I trust in Heaven, and your divine Sweetness, you will preserve me from her; what can I expect, oh my Adorable, from the Tongue that will not spare even you, the sweetest and most lovely of all Mankind.

But to return to my former Sorrow: I past whole Months devoted to Grief, my Brother was still in *Ireland,* and I without any Friend or Relation to comfort me or assist my Affairs; but the Murderer was executed, and I did all Things that the most tender Duty required. My Soul was sunk in Melancholy, and my Health languished almost to the Grave. I conversed with nothing but what fed my Sorrow, Musick and my Books, that I appeared the Shadow of Death.

I was one Evening, which would have seemed sweet to the Happy, walking in the most gloomy Part of our Garden, when a Lady and Gentleman passed by me. My Eyes were bent to the Earth, and I in the deepest Mourning. I observed they turned back again with Surprize, and followed me so fast I could not well avoid them. When they overtook me I found the Lady had been a Neighbour, and once a favourite Friend; she presented her Husband to me, who till then I had not regarded. He was a kind of Man the World calls handsome, well made, and not unlovely to other Eyes, but mine were blind with Sorrow; they both appeared extreamly pleased at meeting me so unexpectedly; they pitied my Concern, and seemed to share it with me. In walking with them I found they had been my Neighbours some Months, and were fixed in a very handsome House that looked into our Garden, where

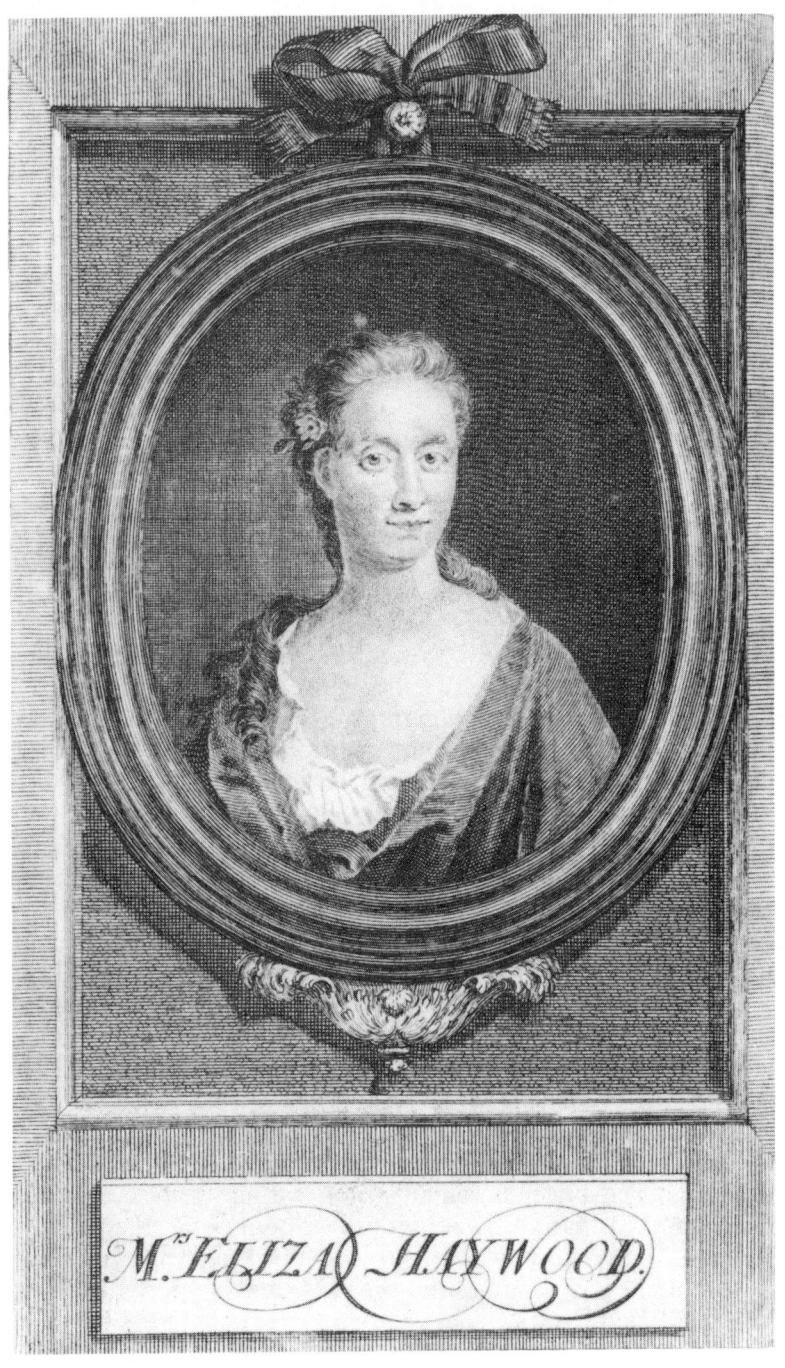

Eliza Haywood. Frontispiece to Vol. 1 of *Secret Histories, Novels, and Poems.* London, 1732. (Photo courtesy of The Newberry Library.)

they invited me that Night, and pressed me to go, which I could not civilly refuse. From that Hour, for many Months, we were seldom asunder. Their Coach, their House, and every thing were at my Service, till Love was pleas'd to part us, by entering into the Gentleman's Head, where there was Room for twenty Cupids. I lamented this Change, and foresaw it would break our Friendship. I grew more reserved, and made but short and cold Visits, and only wanted to break off entirely; but as I retired the Couple grew fonder of me; they both complained of my Neglect, and forced me to be often there. When I was absent they lived in a perfect Storm. Mr. *B*—— grew to hate his Wife, and she him; he reproached her with not looking and speaking like me; in Return she assured him I hated him, and disdained him, which was really true, and that he owed my Company entirely to her. In this she did me Justice, for of all Creatures he was most disagreeable to me. Not Love itself could make him seem lovely. He knew little of the divine Part of the Passion, and had no true Regard for Women. Young as I was I discovered this, and resolved every Way to avoid him. His Praises were disagreeable. I was careful in never passing a Moment with him without his Wife. I endeavoured to reconcile their Quarrels, which were much higher in my Absence. His Lady often intreated me with Tears to be with them for her Sake, whom indeed I only considered. We often went to take the Air, but the poor Coach Glasses were still wounded between them.

One Day, after Dinner, we were sitting in their Arbour, when Mr. *B*—— left us to sit by himself in another Part of the Garden, which I rejoiced at, but in a few Moments he intreated me to walk that Way just to speak to me; I was very unwilling to go, but his Lady compelled me; when I approached his Arbour, he conjured me with a very grave, but assured Face, to hear and to forgive him the last time he should ever trouble me. He took the Advantage of the Confusion he raised in me, and with uncommon Assurance spoke to this Purpose:

I find, Madam, to my Despair, the Coldness you entertain my Passion with, and all its Proofs; you see me miserable without Pity, and dragging at once the Chains of Love and Marriage. I cannot believe that Youth and Sweetness is without some Flame, nor can I imagine myself an unworthy Object; but I suppose you sacrifice me to imaginary Honour, to the cold Maxims of your Grandmother, or to the Friendship you have for my Wife; she merits nothing from either of us; for your Sake I try to suppress my Hatred, but you give nothing in Return.

I stood with Horror to hear this Creature, but was flying from him, when falling at my Feet he held me so fast I could not move; I will never leave this Place, says he, till you promise to smile upon me; and here I swear to merit your Regard. I will leave all things for you, my Wife, my Children, and Country. I will fly where we are not known, marry, and settle all my Fortune upon you. You are young and friendless; if Love will not incline you, let Interest.

Never was Soul so shocked, nor so full of Resentment! I trembled with Anger, so that I could not speak, but bursting from his Arms, I gave him a severe Blow on the Face; There, Villain, says I, take my last Favour, and boast of it. His Wife overheard some Part of the Discourse, which obliged me in Justice to myself to tell the rest, and to assure her I never more would enter her House where I was so affronted. She endeavoured to appease me, and implored me to continue my Visits. He retired into his Closet, where he locked himself up all Night, equally enraged with his Wife and me.

I never more returned to this House of Terror, and avoided all Places where I could hear of them, or meet them. On his Part Love turned to Hatred, and he made it his Business to injure me as much as was in his mean Power. Soon after, I thank Heaven, he left the Place and me with a thousand Curses. It is yet a Pleasure to my Memory that I acted so justly in that Affair. I have told you most religiously the Truth, as if I were addressing to my Creator.

Thus, my Guardian Angel, I escaped this Rock; I think blameless and innocent; but I was not long ere I was driven on another far worse, which wounded me more severely.

About a little Mile from us a near Relation of mine lived, who was a very famous Oculist, and had some of his Patients in the same House with him; amongst the rest a very agreeable Lady of a good Fortune, whom I had formerly known in *London,* and was happy in meeting there. I was often with her whole Days together. There was other Company in the House, then unknown to me; amongst others two blind Gentlemen lately returned from *Turky,* where they lost their Eyes: I never saw more melancholy Objects: They were both about thirty, Men of Sense, and not disagreeable. My Soul was sincerely touched with Pity for them both, but most for one of them, whose Person and Manner appeared more engaging, and who shewed me an uncommon Regard. He was tall, genteel, and well-shaped, and had the Remains of some Beauty, which even his Blindness had spared. The Compassion I had for this unhappy Gentleman carried me often to my Cousin's; at last I almost lived there. I used to read to Sir *William M⎯⎯y⎯⎯d,* and walk with him. The Melancholy that still hung upon me made me delight in dismal Objects, and lament them. I was never so well pleased as when I could be of any Service to Sir *William;* and indeed I grew happier than I had been since I lost my Father. I pitied the Misery of others so much, that I in some manner forgot my own; and Heaven shewed me the Tenderness I bestowed on the Unfortunate. The Summer began to decline, and I could not go so often to my Cousin's as usual; nor could the Blind walk to me unless Love had led him, for the Ways grew very bad, and the Days short. Sir *William* could not bear this Distance. He was resolved to shorten it, by living in the same House, and leaving his dearest Friends for me. I knew this would create some Remarks, but could not prevail with Sir *William* to stay where he was, nor indeed could I press him extreamly, for his Company grew very agreeable to me; nor was I pleased without it. In fine, he came to Mr. *Cenny*'s. We continually walked or sat together. I was seldom a Moment from him, or if I was, it gave him the greatest Pain, and me no Pleasure. I dined always with him, and rendered him all the little Services at Table that Pity directed. He would not eat but from my Hand, nor drink, unless I first touched the Glass. In walking, his Blindness permitted him to lean on my Arm. At Night we sat up late together. I used to read him to Sleep. Nothing could please him but my Discourse, Reading or Playing. I have seen him transported with Mirth at my Prattle. I invented a thousand Stories to entertain him, and left all my Friends to devote myself to him. I was too young and artless to imagine this more than Pity; nor did I dream his Love, but Gratitude for my Care. The World was more concerned for us than we were for ourselves. It was angry that we retired from it; for we had left every body for one another. It began to talk severely: The Wise called me imprudent: The Cunning fancied that which was noble Pity, meer Interest, which my Soul was above: The Ill-natured still treated it worse, while Heaven knows nothing was more innocent than my Heart. I was too happy to heed these Prattlers, but was pleased to have a new Occasion of shewing my Regard to Sir *William*. His Relations grew alarmed, and fancied my Design on his Title and Fortune. But all this only augmented our Regard; and Anger gave a higher relish to it. Sir *William* was eternally praising me, and presenting me to his Friends, and desired they would use their Interest with me to marry him, for the Admiration he had for me made him tremble to propose it. This extreamly perplexed them. They consulted, wondered, and railed. We laid a thousand little Schemes to teaze 'em; which all succeeded, to our infinite Pleasure. Never were People better pleased with themselves, or less concerned for the

World. But all this while we rather talked like tender Friends, than Lovers, for I own I meant no more. But at last Sir *William,* in the most passionate and respectful Manner, assured me he adored me; that his Life and Fortune were at my Service; and entreated I would bless the Remainder of his Days, which else would be miserable. This Discourse inspired me with no Design, but of liking him more, yet without a Thought of giving myself up for ever. I thought it nobler to be compassionate than rich, and that Marriage would take from the Beauty of my Pity. I returned him my Thanks for the Honour he imagined I deserved, and assured him, whilst he thought in that manner, I would continue my most tender Respect. I had then Abundance of what they called Lovers, but would receive none. My Heart was taken up more than I thought or durst examine; still I dreamed this was only Pity; till Sir *William* was obliged to go a few Miles to a Relation's. Our parting was too soft for Friendship. He was long ere he could leave me, and I as unwilling to part with him. In this little Absence I found myself extreamly uneasy. I sighed every Moment, I knew not why, and counted the Hours till he returned, which was in a few Days, but so pale and altered, it appear'd his Shadow. Receive me, he cry'd, oh my lovely Friend, nor part with me again, but to the Grave! I have suffered more than Death in this short Absence. I cannot live without you— Oh you must be always mine! He held me in his Arms, which I could find tremble with Joy. We every Day grew dearer to each other. I was then indeed as blind as he. I gave him every Perfection, and began to love in earnest. How did I want a Friend to guard me from this Precipice, where Love was leading me, to warn me of this Serpent, who was sucking out the Sweetness of my Soul, and laying every Art to destroy it!

Honour, that Guardian Angel, can alone
Give Life to Love, and fix him on his Throne:
Or if from Beauty Passion ever springs,
How short its Reign, how ready are its Wings!
Or if from Wit the trifling Flame is born,
Soon it expires, and grows our Reason's Scorn.
'Tis artless Tenderness, and Honour join'd,
Can only triumph o'er a noble Mind.
With these Hillarius *leads my Soul along,*
How soft the gentle Chain, and yet, O God, how strong!

Oh let me break once more from your divine Beauties to Sir *William!* but the Descent is so great, I can hardly bear it, and must recover Breath to proceed.

One Day I was obliged to go to Town, which I very seldom did; but at my Return, early in the Evening, I found Sir *William* retired to Bed, and, his Servant assured me, very ill. I hasted to his Bedside, infinitely afflicted. He started up at my Voice, and embracing my Neck, he could not speak for weeping. My Heart was most tenderly moved at his Tears; a thousand times I intreated him to tell me the Occasion of them. At last, with a deep Sigh, he told me he must leave me; that his Relations had been with him that Day, with a Physician from *London,* who both affirmed that Air was fatal to him; that wrong Methods had been used with his Eyes; and they must have him near them in Town: But lost in Grief, he cryed, I will lose all Hopes of Sight or my Life, rather than part with you a Day. My Soul is bound up in this Bosom. Here will I sigh my last Moments, unless I could contrive some way to be bless'd with Light and this together, of what Comfort would it be to see a World I should despise without you. Oh think for me, my sweet Angel! think for me soon! soften my Despair! say I shall not lose you! No, says I, dear Sir *William,* you cannot lose me; comfort yourself; Love will inspire us with some Method. His Tears still flowed, and mine mingled with them. At last I left him to repose, or rather to think of preventing this Separation. He sent early to intreat me to his Chamber. His Looks seemed more composed, and Hope shone on his Face. I have not slept one Moment, says he, to-night, and shall sleep no more, unless you bless my Proposal. I will, with your Leave, take Lodgings in Town, where there shall be Room for you; or rather I will implore you to please yourself with an Apartment to be in it some Time, and only secure me one near you. What can the World say of this? How can you or they help my desiring to be with you? Who will wonder at it? or not wish the same? We already live in one House. It will not be new to continue so, or at least all the Fault will be laid on me: And it is in our Powers to silence them by joining for ever.

I liked the first Scheme much better than the last. I never entertained a Thought of marrying Sir *William*. I told him I wished this could be managed with Prudence; and, to avoid Reproach, we resolved to consult some Friends of ours in it, whom the World calls wise. But I unhappily found those who rather studied my Pleasure than my Interest. They gave me such Reasons for this as I could wish, and such as transported Sir *William*. I therefore moved to *Red-Lyon-Square,* and in a few Days Sir *William* came thither. We lived for some Time agreeably enough, but the Scene quickly changed. When I imagined we should be most happy, he grew peevish, jealous, and melancholy. I had very little Company, but that little disturbed him. Nor could I ever leave him without finding him sick, or out of Humour, at my Return. He used to examine how I was dressed; every Patch or Ribbon grew a Sin. Whenever any Friends were with me, he bribed his Servants to enquire their Names, and to listen. See my weeping Lover, adored *Hillarius,* grown a Tyrant. The Pity and Tenderness I had for him made me endure this some Time; though I often reproached myself with this Submission, and saw too plainly that Love had led me wrong; and I must ever confess this one of my greatest Mistakes. It was hard to retreat, but I only waited a happy Hour to break my Chain, which my Lover did not imagine. It cost me some waking Nights, and many Tears, before I could resolve.

One Morning I went earlier than usual to his Room, in order to leave it for ever. He begun in a very grave Manner to preach to me Retirement and Prudence, and told me his sincere Passion was the Occasion of this Discourse. I coldly thanked him, and assured him I would both please the World and my self, by leaving him with all possible Haste; that I had already taken Lodgings in *Bedford-Street,* which I had done to convince him of my Prudence, that I did not desire an entire Separation, and should often wait on him, when I could be of Service to him. Never was any wretched Mortal more surprized. He colour'd, trembled, and frown'd, and confess'd the Devil in every Action. I own I secretly triumphed at his Anguish; for his Tyranny and Ill-manners had murder'd Love; his Spight and Passion choaked his Words, and I left him in Silence. I heard afterwards he behaved like a Madman; and alarmed the whole House. He found me out, and implored my Return, but in vain. He came himself, and intreated, but to little Purpose, only sometimes I passed a few Hours with him, but never more with any Happiness. He appeared to repent, and to accuse himself, but was too late. About this Time my long absent Brother returned from *Ireland,* and my cousin from Sea. And, to compleat my Happiness and Cure, they lodged in the same House. I did not find it hard to transplant my Tenderness from that ungrateful Soil.

Behold me once more pleased and happy; but my dark Angel still hover'd over me.

Sir *William* would often visit me in meer Malice. He sometimes found my Brother with me, for whom he now laid his Nets. He put on all possible Tenderness and Respect before him, and to him. He presented, he intreated, 'till my Brother grew charmed with him, and wonder'd at my Indifference. I had not let him into our Quarrel, but only gently warn'd him of his Humour. But his Art was too strong for me; and my Brother believed him an Oracle.

He was at first eternally praising me to him, and that way secured him. And when he had him fast, he opened all his Griefs to him, complained of my Treatment, and implored my Brother's Interest to reconcile me; which he vainly attempted. He laid before me the Charms of Title and Fortune with a Man that adored me: But I was deaf, tho' for my Ease I appeared to listen.

In the mean while Sir *William,* who did not succeed as he wish'd, renew'd his Complaints; and at last I grew more uneasy with my Brother and him than I had been before. I had not the Liberty of seeing any Friend with Ease, for these Guardians were ever at my Elbow. I had no Comfort but in lamenting myself to my Cousin, who grieved with me. When good Fortune once more returned to my Embraces, my Brother was recalled into *Ireland,* but, ere he went, after embracing Sir *William,* whom he now called Brother, he recommended me to his Care, desired him to advise me, and to inform him of my Conduct. Sir *William* was highly pleased, and now thought me more in his Power than ever, and again returned to his old Tyranny. From which I resolved to break once more. My Cousin was again obliged to go to Sea. And now I had nothing to please me in Town. I resolved therefore a Tour to *Bath,* with a Lady who was then going. I broke this Design to Sir *William,* who was distracted at it, vowed to inform my Brother, who had trusted me to his Care; but I took the Liberty to leave my Guardian for ever. Never was poor Prisoner more rejoiced who had broke his Chain; on the other part, never was Jailer more enraged. He leaped into a Boat, and went to *Fulham,* bursting with Rage and Malice. There he said every thing it could inspire; but they knew his Malice too well, and only laughed at it, which was a new Wound to his illnatured Soul.

I removed to the Lady's I was to go with to *Bath,* whose Company and House were perfectly pleasant. Our Evenings were passed in the most agreeable Company. We had Wit and Musick, and continual Entertainment. I now began to live, and recover my Repose. My Spirits rose, and I was myself. But even in these gay Moments I sighed for a soft Captivity, and Life was insipid.

From hence, with a Heart entirely free, I began my Journey to *Bath,* a Place I had never seen. There I found a kind of new World, but pleasing enough to me for that Reason. I had some Relations there, who were the shining People of the Place. These made it their Pleasure to introduce me to all Diversions, and to the most polite. I found myself agreeable to them, and caressed by the Fair and Witty. Our Lodgings were ever filled with these; on the Walks we were more crowded than the rest; the Ladies lost their Lovers, and began to complain and envy; but the Hours flew on. Here I became acquainted with Mr. *Wicherley,* who had Wit without Politeness, and a Levity improper for his Age. He was very little to my Taste. I was much more to his, and would Love have consented, I might have been Wife to this Poet; but my Heart was averse.

There was a Gentleman, young, and not unhandsome, who used to be eternally with us. He always danced with me, and conducted me to all publick Places. He sent me such Books as could best entertain me, with the Presents that were usual in that Place. The People called him my Lover; but I had very little Tenderness for him. His Company was rather habitual than delightful. He was bless'd with an overflowing Fortune, which kept him in a happy Temper. He was ever gay and obliging, rather than tender. When an Accident happen'd that obliged me to drop this Lover. We were invited by a Gentleman, who lived in the same House, to a *Bath* Breakfast, which is generally given at parting. All my Friends were there, and every one had somebody to address himself to. This Gentleman, as usual, entertained me, but after a different Manner. We were leaning out of a Window when he hastily slipped a very fine Ring off his Finger, and placed it on mine. It is but just, says he, the finest Hand in the World should be so adorned. I grew very angry at this Liberty; and with a just Resentment gave the Ring back, which in refusing, dropt out of Window. This alarmed all the Company. They were run down in a Moment; and I, the most concerned, pursuing with all haste, when, to my unutterable Surprize, I saw him lock the Door, and myself in his Arms. Never was I seized with such Shame, Horror, and Anger. They all assisted me, but in spight of my Resistance he threw me on the Bed, and I him on the Floor, where he fell, cursing his Disappointment, Love, and his Stars. I rose trembling, with Fear and Passion, whilst this Monster rolled upon the Floor. Rise, says I, Villain, and see me no more. I then flew to the Door; he followed on his Knees, and implored my Pardon and Silence in this Affair. I ran down Stairs with my Hair and Dress disorder'd, where I found the Company had recovered the Ring, and had even forgot, in their Search, my Absence. My Lover sneaked out of Doors; and from that Moment my Soul had an Aversion for him. He used all the few Arts he was Master of to reconcile me by our Friends; but I returned his Letters, and all his Presents, and never after would suffer him to see me. This was the chief Adventure of that Place, of which I grew a little weary.

But after parting with this robust Lover, I found a softer, more to my Taste. Colonel *K——r* was then at *Bath,* and extreamly admired; he danced to Perfection, and was polite and well bred. These were attended with a respectful tender Passion, and though happy in his Person, Family and Fortune, he did me the Honour to wish me his; but I was not yet fond of Marriage, nor wise enough to consider I was then offered the most agreeable Man, and a Rank worthy of my Care. How foolish, how blind is Youth! I cannot enough accuse myself this Mistake. I had a Crowd of other Lovers, not worthy my remembering, or your divine Thought; but I left them all, and retired to Town by the Way of *Oxford.*

How was my Soul entertained with that sweet Place! where Learning inspires the very Air. I saw all the noble Buildings. I was enamoured with the Walks, and wished there to end my Life. Here my Passion for Reading awakened again, and I resolved my future Life should pursue it. The Civilities and Charms of that Place made me leave it with Tears, and sigh thus as I parted from it.

> *Fair flow'ry Vale, oh dear Retreat,*
> *And Treasury of all that's sweet,*
> *Why is my hapless Youth refus'd*
> *To taste thy Charms, with Toys amus'd?*
> *Here let me sigh in thy sweet Shade,*
> *Or be by thy cool River laid.*
> *Drive me not from thy deathless Store,*
> *Nor leave my Mind undone and poor.*
> *Adorn it with a lasting Name;*
> *For oh it swells and pants for Fame.*
> *Not all the Trifles of my Kind*
> *Can stop my ever-soaring Mind,*
> *For Immortality design'd.*
> *It will, it must, it shall be great,*
> *And rise above the Medium of my Fate.*

The Beauties of *Oxford* staid upon my Soul, and sweetly played on my Memory, even after I came to Town; and I was favoured with Letters from the most obliging and ingenious there: Amongst the rest, Mr. *Hally,* a most worthy and agreeable Friend, who sought and deserved my Friendship.

After I came from *Bath,* I lodged some Time in *King-Street* by St. *James*'s Square, where I had the Happiness of a very gay Neighbour, Sir *Harry B——y.* He was a Lover, but very unrefin'd, which secur'd me from him. We only, or chiefly at least, conversed like *Pyramus* and *Thisbe* through a Wall, for I lay next Room to him. Never was amorous Knight more angry with his Stars than he with this poor Partition, which was defended with a Chain, which sat more uneasily upon him than that of Marriage. He used to sigh, to serenade, and to toast me, but in vain. Love would not enter amidst Wine, and Noise, and Levity. It sought a more sacred Palace. Alas! there requires little Virtue to refuse the Half of Mankind. 'Tis a Justice to ourselves, 'tis a Love for ourselves, makes us justly unkind to them: But I know not why this should be called Virtue, which is but natural, as to fly Fire and Water, and all the Enemies of Life. No, my adored *Hillarius,* this ought not to wear that divine Title. Oh need I say what Virtue is! 'tis to adore *Hillarius,* and him divinely as I do, without Reserve or Interest; to sacrifice the mean Incense of the Crowd to the heavenly Passion to live for him alone, to languish for him amidst the Praise and Adoration of the World: This is Virtue, to love the Virtuous, and truly Noble. I look down with Contempt on the mean Mortals who confine Virtue to the narrow Compass of the Body: Sure it is seated in the Soul, or rather your divine Breast is its Treasury. I will not, with other dull Authors, ask Pardon for this Digression: No, my Angel, all Things else are Digression. You are the darling Subject of my Soul; and when it leaves you to speak of any thing else, I offer it a Violence not be express'd.—Oh must I go back again to talk of my self!

Thus the charm'd Traveller his Sight regales
A while, with shining Streams, and flow'ry Vales;
Treasures the Prospect with devouring Sight
To charm the Way, and entertain the Night.

But I return to tell my sweet Charmer.—The Cousin he has heard me speak of sometimes in this little Account, was again returned from Sea, more my Lover than ever. With his Tenderness he brought me to love Retirement again. Love made him jealous, and for his Ease I resigned the Park, the Play, and every idle Amusement. I seldom saw my *Bath* Friends, and lost the Relish of 'em. Such a Force has even the Shadow of Love over the Mind; for I have since learned I was not truly in love; The Pleasure of being beloved, made me dream I loved.

In that faint Tenderness I could survey
A Dawning of the fierce approaching Day;
And from the Sighs Imagination drew,
The Constitution of my Soul I knew.
It waited only till your Beauties came,
Then every Wish was kindled into Flame.

I was indeed happy enough in the soft Conversation of my Cousin. We used to sit and walk, and almost live together, till our gentle Kindred grew jealous, and endeavoured to divide us; but that only could be compleated by the Winds and Waves. Ere he went away, he conjured me to leave my joyous Neighbour. His poor Heart trembled for me, amidst Bars and Chains; but he was more secured by my Promise. He took a very tender Leave; and I really believe he had a real Passion for me; and, as I said, I had as much for him as he knew how to inspire.

Behold me now, my lovely Master, dreaming of Rocks and Sands at Sea, and mourning for my absent Lover; but I soon found there were Shelves and Quicksands on shore more to be really fear'd.

I was seated in the most agreeable Part of the Town, St. *James* Street, on the Terrass, where I saw all the World; but, I conjure you to believe me, without being charmed with it. I often retired to sigh in a back Dressing-Room, where I had a Harpsichord. I have played away whole Afternoons, without going down Stairs. The Gentlewoman of the House was a little Coquet, and a kind of half uninform'd Beauty: She was ever drest out, and trying to catch the Eyes of the Spectators. She had as little Sense as a Statue, and so far like one, she turned as she was set by Flattery. There was always a civil Distance between us: I resigned all her Fools to her; and was extreamly in her Favour. They were People of some Fashion, and lived in a very handsome Manner. It was here the gay Cousin I left at *Bath* introduced his Grace of *B——fort* first to me. I had, before I saw him, addressed a little Poem, on the Death of Mr. *Edmund Smith,* to him, and he came to thank me. From a Patron, he grew a Lover, and as passionate a one as he could be. But I had no Notion of his Love or Title; he was too general, and sought the Body more than the Soul. We could not agree in our Sentiments. I found him a coarse dull Lover. He desired me to instruct him in *Platonick* Love; but he was a strange Scholar, and I grew weary of him. This I have Reason to believe, he never ascended to love any thing so respectfully as he did me. We have had many laughing Hours together, but no tender ones: He had extream Good-nature, but knew only the Forms of People; he was a Stranger as to the Minds; nor could he tell the Manner of Charming. If the Lady refused five Hundred Pounds a Year, his Love was confounded, and all at a Loss. This arose from his mean Education: His Grandmother's Maids were all the Goddesses he knew for some Years; and they were so far mortal as to receive all his Quarteridge. He had a very small Allowance, and that laid out in this mean Manner; which led him to think wrong of Women.

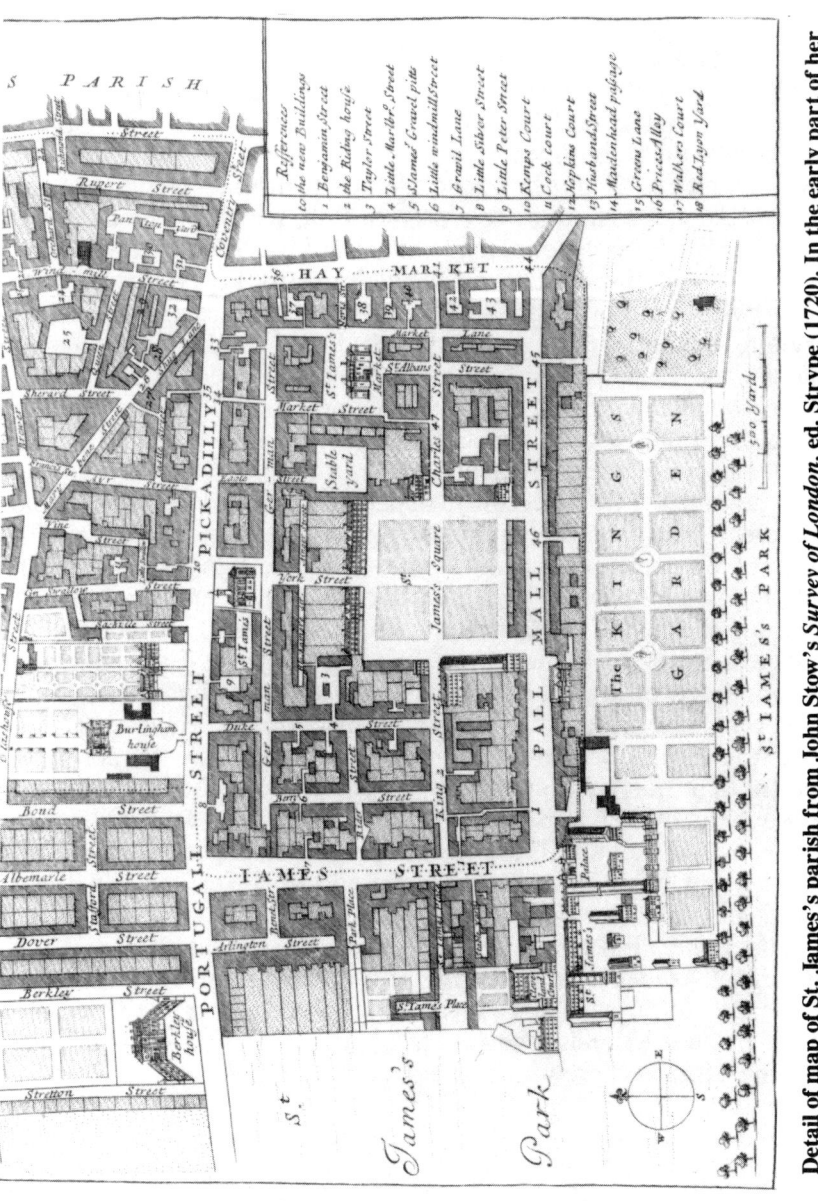

Detail of map of St. James's parish from John Stow's *Survey of London*, ed. Strype (1720). In the early part of her life Fowke often resided in this fashionable area of London. (Courtesy of the Lilly Library, Indiana University, Bloomington, Indiana.).

We used to wonder at one another; he at my Dullness to Interest, and I at his way of addressing. This kept us at a very happy Distance; though the World was so good to talk warmly of us, and to make his Grace much happier with me, than I could; for I most religiously profess, we were innocently gay together, and no more.

About this Time an Adventure befell me that gave me more Pain, though in itself as innocent.

Some Friends of mine, whose Names I intreat you'll spare me for their Sakes, invited me to a private Ball, which the Gentleman, whom I thought my Friend, made himself: I was fond of this foolish Diversion, and thought to excell in this Mistake. Vanity led me thither with another Lady I was very fond of. I found all Things very fine, beyond what I dream'd of, and the Company very agreeable. I was presented to 'em as a Person of great Agility. As I looked round the Room, my Heart seemed to choose one Gentleman beyond the rest; he was tall and genteel, or I thought him so; and his Face seemed to assure me he thought as kindly of me. After he had very respectfully, himself, presented me with Wine and Sweet-meats, before any of the rest, he intreated to dance with me. I secretly rejoiced at his Choice, and gave him my Hand with some Pain and Pleasure. We entertained one another without much Regard to the rest of the Company; I saw, or hoped I saw, a peculiar Civility to me, for I found I know not what for him. Everything he said appeared engaging, and I began to fear the Night would end too soon. How little, oh divine *Hillarius,* do we know what approaching Hours design us! Nothing could be more tenderly respectful than this Gentleman. The Lady who conducted me hither was sent for by her Husband sooner than the rest were willing to go, for the Musick and Entertainment were both very elegant. My Friend departed in haste, but whispered me, a Servant and Light should remain at her Back Window; and she left her Partner to see me safe home. I was too much pleased to suspect this, and too innocent. I danced on as securely as if my Guardian Angel had led me along; but at last the Company prepared to be gone; I looked round, but my Friend, who was to conduct me, was slipped away with the Hours. I grew a little concern'd at this; but the Person who had danced with me offer'd his Service very gravely. It was late, and I alone, and a Stranger to the rest of the Company. I saw it was the Custom of the Place to see the Ladies home; I therefore gave my Hand to my Partner, who led me into a Hackney Coach, that waited, and which he told me my Friend had left on Purpose. I knew not why, but my Heart began to tremble as if some Danger was near it. I sighed to myself, and now wished to be safe at home, though my Lover behaved as I could wish. The Coach drove to the Back-Door, as directed; but how was I surpriz'd! we called, we beat at the Door enough to raise the Dead, but no Light appear'd, nor Servant; we stay'd above an Hour to no Purpose. It was extream dark, late, cold, and rainy. I knew it impossible to get Entrance into my Lodgings, for there I left word I should lye in the ——— The Gentleman seem'd concern'd as much as I, and acted his Part very well. He spread his Cloak over me, and we walked and stood at the cruel adamantine Door till I was starv'd to Death. At last Mr. *S.* implor'd me to mount the coach, to defend us from the Weather.—The Wind blew, the Spouts pour'd, the Coachman grumbled, the Horses groan'd, and I sigh'd. Never were more deplorable Objects. I purpos'd sitting in the Coach till the Windows open'd; but the Coachman, an Actor in this tragic Farce, would not permit it on any Terms. My Soul was truly perplex'd, and sick with Vexation, when my Lover surpriz'd me with a Confession. He fell on his knees in the Coach, and implored my Pardon for what he was going to own. 'Tis I, said he, Madam, am chiefly guilty of all this Trouble, which your Innocence mistakes for Chance. It is Love and I have contrived all this. I heard him with Grief and Wonder; nor thought it yet possible there could be such Art. See, says he, divine Creature, your Power over me. I confess myself a Villain: I sacrifice my Friends and your's to your Displeasure; but since they have join'd to afflict you, I will hate them and myself. The Ball, the Design, the Coach were mine, and all in order to make you so. But I already repent, punish me as you please. But oh have Pity on your lovely self, dearer to me than my Soul. Leave me to my Disappointment, to stab myself. But where will you wander to be insulted this bitter Night. Oh be tender of yourself, and trust me once more, after this Penitence! I have long adored you, and Love laid this Scheme for me—but it costs you too dearly. Receive my sincere Penitence, and let my future Respect convince you, I love you above myself. My Lodgings are near; all Things are safe and silent there; not a Mortal can see you; my Life shall defend you; nor any but this Heart now beating for you, know of this Blessing; and I most religiously swear to be commanded by you this Night and ever. Without giving me leave to think or speak, he ordered the Coach to drive to *Pall-Mall*. The Sadness of my Soul made it appear a Herse to me. I could not talk for Grief. We arrived at the Door, where we saw a Light, which instantly retired, and the Door was opened. Mr. *S.* took me in his Arms, and carried me in. We went up Stairs, where all things were very gay and fine, Lights and a Table spread with every thing polite. By the Order of all this, and by every thing I saw, Mr. *S.*'s Confession was true, that I was betrayed by my Friends, and designed his Victim; but my Soul took other Resolutions worthy of itself. Never was more melancholy Company than I, nor ever were so many soft Things thrown away on a Heart. After we had sat almost silent, at least on my Part, for some time, he began to implore me, for my own Sake, to take some Rest. I told him I would try to repose a little in the great Chair, if he would please to leave me. I saw this was not the Rest he meant, and, kneeling down by me, he tenderly intreated me to go to his Bed, which should be sacred to me, and presented me the Key of his Chamber to lock myself in, while he only begg'd Leave to guard me in the outward Room. I received the Key, and grew a little easy, to think I should be once more alone, and safe. I wished him a good Night, and withdrew into the Bed-chamber, which I locked, and went into Bed, thinking myself very secure. My poor Spirits were almost sunk to Death, and oppressed with Fatigue and Grief. In fine, I fell asleep, which lasted not long. I started, and found myself inclosed in the Arms of Mr. *S.* How was I amazed and terrified! I burst into Tears of Anger and Sorrow. I implored his Pity, and he mine; he wept, he intreated, but in vain. We lay after this Manner; nor could I break from his Hold. Never were sadder Hours past on both Sides. Never were such different Complaints. I knew not how to get from this Precipice, but by a little Art, the first I had ever used. I promised him, if he would safely release me, I would consider the Merit of that, and be some time grateful. I conjured him to trust to my Pity and Generosity; which at last he did. I rose, and huddled on my Things, still trembling with Fear.—After kissing my Hand, and weeping over it, he let me out of his Chamber, to which I found he had another Key. He softly opened the Street-Door, and I hurried out, and walked faintly along to my Lodgings, where they were just up. I pretended I had been up dancing all Night.—Pale, and cold, and sick, I threw myself into Bed, and slept a few Hours; when I rose, I heard a Gentleman had waited below some time for my waking, who said he had danced with me over Night, and came to inquire my Health. He was brought up into the Dining-Room; but how shall I tell my Charmer the Confusion I received him with, or the sad Reflections that crowded on me. Not Innocence itself could defend me from Shame, when I reflected how lately I had broke from his Arms; nor was he less concerned, for I indeed believe he had a Passion for me; and 'tis possible even his Disappointment increased it. He spoke little, but that after so tender a Manner, that my Fears begun to retire, and Smiles take Place. I endeavour'd to comfort him, and seem'd to value his Generosity at a high Rate. Again I promis'd him to think of it, and ever to esteem him. When the Danger was over, I confess he appeared more agreeable to me; and still, as I talked to him, my Liking returned. His Conversation was very sweet and pleasing. For some Months he visited me continually, and I found something of a Tenderness for him, but no violent Passion, which he used to deplore, and think himself very unhappy. In this Time he offered me very fine Diamonds, and Presents of all Kinds, but I received none; nor did I find my Youth fond or dazled with these Trifles. He was ever sighing before me. At last I believe he grew weary of losing his Hopes and Hours, and resolved to try his last Art. He therefore offered, in as respectful a Manner as such Discourse could bear, his Fortune, or any Part I would choose, for a Settlement, and assured me I should have every thing in such a Way that it should set me above Reproach; nor should my Character suffer as he could contrive it; and were he happy enough to have any Children of mine, they should be his only Heirs; that he would enter into the firmest Obligations not to marry, unless I would my self accept of him for a Husband. He confess'd the other more agreeable to him, and only as Love liv'd longer when unconfin'd; and that he would be mine eternally, and only mine. Whilst he was talking in this Manner, my Soul felt a just Disdain to hear its Body bargaining for;—but I conceal'd my Anger, and told him I would think for him. We parted that Evening, and for ever. I left my Lodgings, and retired again to *Fulham*. I wrote him word I was gone into *Staffordshire* to a Relation's, and would never see him more. I know not how he received this Retreat, for I have only since, and that within this Year or two, seen him in Publick—He always turns pale; and I always avoid him.

Pardon, my Heaven, this long Account. I have been more particular in order to give you a true Draught of my Soul, which I think is not without some little Virtue, even what the World calls so; 'tis possible indeed there was Pride and Niceness in this Refusal; but rather it was Want of a violent Passion, such as I now burn with for you. I cannot value myself too much upon it, for I fear it might be partly the Want of a proper Address in him. Be it what it will, we parted, he to some kinder Mistress, and I to my beloved Shades, where Love was not much my Care. I offered up but few of my Sighs at his Altar, but treasured them all for you.

Accept, my Angel, all the Tenderness of my Heart, till now never truly charmed.

Survey me again at *Fulham,* where I had Amusements enough, and more Lovers than I sought after, but most of these of the lightest Kind, such as could not make me happy. Sometimes Fops fell in my Way: These are strange insects, such as I despise.

One of these, who had a good pretty Person, joined to a Pertness of Wit, addressed me; all his leisure Hours were employed in writing Billets. I happened at that time to be his reigning Goddess; he powder'd for me, and really thought he sigh'd for me, whilst he had only a Passion for his dear self. I have often observed him seated over against a large Glass, where he has ogled his own sweet Person as he spoke to me. He was what the Dull call a happy Man amongst the Ladies, a Wit, and a Beau. I never saw a more perfect Coquet than this Creature. He used to drop very tender Letters on purpose to show me his Success in other Places. No Comedy ever represented a more accomplish'd Figure. He was a Poet too, or rather a Thief that way, which I used continually to discover and laugh at. Often have I said to myself,

> *Empty Trifler, couldst thou see*
> *Ought to give thee Hopes of me,*
> *I should then myself despise,*
> *And chide my dull ill-judging Eyes.*
> *But their Looks are too sincere*
> *To perswade thee thou are dear.*
> *See my Heart is all unmov'd;*
> *See thy Vows are disapprov'd.*
> *Retire, poor Trifler, nor consume*
> *Thy borrow'd Wit, and Beauty's Bloom.*

In fine, I grew so weary of this Lover, that I dropt him much to his Surprize, and my Ease. About this time I had another just the Reverse of this, a most whining doleful Mortal, who used to terrify me with Complaints. His Person was very disengaging; nor could I bring my Heart to endure him, upon which he threaten'd to destroy himself very often; but at last he was so good to resolve to live and to forget me, to my great Comfort; but I hear he complains of me to this Hour.

I had at this Time very little Passion, but for divine *Shakespear*, who used to pass whole Nights with me. I devoted myself to his Beauties, which I found improve upon me. Oh how transporting he is! Sure there is a heavenly Likeness between your Souls.

> *In every lovely Line of his I find*
> *A sweet Resemblance of my Charmer's Mind,*
> *That Godlike Glow which with inchanting Art,*
> *Pours all its Flames into the Reader's Heart.*

> *Bless me with that sweet Power, and I'll forego*
> *All but thy Love, the only Joy below.*
> *Oh much too charming, thou mayst well resign*
> *Half that sweet Art, when my Lips press to thine.*
> *There breathe thy Soul, its Harmony infuse,*
> *And give immortal Beauty to my Muse.*

I was so inchanted with this old, yet for ever new Lover, that I used to carry him all Day in my Arms, and at Night he was my Entertainment. He inspir'd my Dreams, and first made me sigh after Immortality. I seldom left the dear Garden, where I was extreamly happy. If I parted from it, it was only to a favourite Neighbour, who was one of the most agreeable Women I ever found; her Humour was gay, her Taste polite, her Wit entertaining, and her Friendship most desirable. She help'd to render my Solitude very charming. Never did I taste the Beauty of Friendship so much as in this engaging Person. She understood the World, herself, and me, most perfectly, every Thought of my Soul. She had a very sweet Voice, and remembered all the most modish Songs in King *Charles*'s Time, with the Beauties of that Age, their Virtues and their Failings. In comparing them with ours, I could only find they were more gayly faulty than at present. Love, or what they call'd so, was the Fashion of those Days.

Whilst I am bless'd, my adored Lover, with your divine Regard, I sigh not after their Wits or Beauties; rather I rejoice they are dead, who would have been such powerful Rivals to me.

> *If* Cleveland *had survey'd thy Charms,*
> *She wou'd have left her Monarch's Arms,*
> *And chilly* Churchill's *Forms declin'd*
> *For the bright Sun-shine of thy Mind.*
> *Or had the lovelier* Mazarine
> *My brighter King of Beauty seen,*
> *Variety she had not known—*
> *But sigh'd for thee the Soul of Love alone.*
> *She wou'd have lost her loose Desires,*
> *And burn'd for thee with more religious Fires.*

Pardon my interrupting Fondness, sweet Charmer of my Heart; 'tis ever with Pain I leave you to speak of my self; 'tis a kind of Death you force me to suffer.

As I have said, my Thoughts were wholly charm'd with Reading and Friendship, when an Adventure broke in a little on their Harmony.

We had at *Fulham* a young Lady of a very handsome Fortune, joined to a Person very pretty and engaging: she did not want Sense, nor any Charm, in my Eyes. A young Gentleman of a good Estate had seen her in the Country where he lived, and pursu'd her to Town, extreamly in Love. He address'd her with very good Success. Amongst the rest of her Acquaintance, I was invited to see this Lover, and give my little Judgment of him. He was low, but gay and witty; well-shaped, and indeed perfectly pleasing, without being intirely fine. I spoke of him in such a Manner to his Mistress, that from liking, she grew, I fear, to love him; when, by the Caprice of our Stars, he liked me, I know not why; for I religiously affirm, I had then no kind of Tenderness for him, no Design to engage him.—But from the Moment he saw me he grew cold to his first Pursuit, and too often declared his Heart was intirely devoted to me, without considering he lost both a Fortune and a Beauty. I protest I had no Joy in this Change, rather I beheld it with Pain. I had neither Inclinations nor Ingratitude enough to use this to my Advantage. I most generously try'd to reconcile these Lovers. I knew Envy would be busy at our Expence. He would be eternally with me. His Father pressed him to marry, but in vain; nor was he more successful with me. I own he was very agreeable to me, but I resolved to conquer that. Wounded with his Disappointment, he retired very melancholy into the Country, without taking Leave of the Lady he once lov'd.

O how capricious is ill-grounded Passions! How few Moments do they live! In some few Months, to forget me, he marry'd a Fortune, but a very terrible one, as deformed as the other was lovely. He laid this Misfortune at my Door. He is since dead, and was never happy.

After his Retirement into the Country, I had the ill Fortune of stealing another Lover of a different Kind. This was a Son of *Eden*, a Gardener, but the most polite I ever saw; he had not only read his Mother Earth, but the admir'd *Shakespear*, and with some Success. He spoke of his Beauties not ungracefully. His Person was tall and handsome; his Dress very modish, and I assure you I have seen worse Figures in the Side-Box. He was very rich, and offer'd a Jointure wou'd have excus'd my Descent, had Inclinations pleas'd, but they were proud and nice.

He had agreed with Mr. *Cenny* for one of his Daughters, and the Match was more than half made, when I unhappily, and undesignedly, interposed. In fine, I refused this *Adam,* who retired to his Paradise without a Wife, and left me to my beloved Garden—I thank Heaven, without a Husband. Oh why did I ever part with lovely Liberty, but to you! why did I not treasure it up to offer at your divine Feet! How sweet is the Bondage I now am bless'd with! Oh I will bear these dear Chains to my Grave.

Thy heavenly Laws are sweeter to the Mind,
Than all the Pleasures of the Unconfin'd.

Never was Mortal happier, or more disengag'd than I in these Hours. I was adored by my Friends, and favoured by the Muses, fortunate in my Acquaintance, which were but few. Envy and Malice were not intirely silent; but they could not alarm my Innocence. The Duke of B——t often visited me, but without Success. I protest to your divine Friendship, and to the God who has bless'd me with it, I cannot impute this to any thing but the little Regard I had to the Trifles of Fortune which he offered me in vain. I had no tender Thoughts for him. See me, adorable *Hillarius,* courted to shine in the World; but Love was not yet waked in my Bosom, nor could any thing charm him from his Slumber, but your inchanting Softness, and everlasting Beauties.

My Cousin, whom I've not lately spoke of, now returned once more from Sea. I had still some Tenderness for him, but no ardent Passion; continual parting had almost murder'd Love, defacing those tender Impressions I once dreamed would last for ever; but I own he wanted many fine Qualities to inspire and preserve Love. He had a brutal Jealousy, which offended the Delicacy of my Soul. He would often, for slight Appearances, break out into violent and mean Resolves; which at last disgusted me; for Tenderness and fine Manners is the Food of Love. Permit me to give you an Instance or two of this Humour.

In the same Ship with him was a young giddy Rake, one of those who are ever dully boasting of Favours they never received.

My Cousin, whose Soul was fond of me, one Night was drinking my Health to this Fool, and so imprudent to name me; the other smiled, and assured him, he was not the only happy Man in my Favour. He hinted himself, and described me, as my Cousin, blind with Jealousy, thought, perfectly.

Never was Man more miserable than this mistaken Mortal; he hasted trembling to Shore, and rose Post all Night, and was at *Fulham* by Break of Day. He flew to my Bed-side, pale as Death, the very Picture of mistaken Rage. He could hardly speak—Here, Madam, says he, receive your Letters, no longer dear to me; and here is your Picture, half defaced with my Tears. I have armed myself with Resolution to take leave for ever, well convinc'd I have been betray'd.

I was amaz'd and griev'd, lost in thinking what could be the Meaning of all this. When he grew a little calmer I inquired the Reason, which he told me with great Assurance. I was for some time too angry to undeceive him, but at last I convinced him his Friend was base, and he deceived; that it must be some other who had assumed my Name, and at his Friend's coming to Town desired this might be explained. He seemed to believe, and shew'd all possible Signs of Repentance. He found what I had assur'd him true.

This Boaster carry'd him to see this Person, who had done me the Favour to wear my Name. See, my Angel, how liable Love is to Mistakes! how often he falls into them! Oh my Heart knows too much of these soft, yet fatal Errors. I was then a Stranger to them, and perhaps had not Pity enough for them,

> *Till on the fatal Shelve my Passion drove;*
> *Oh God, what killing Fears attend on Love,*
> *What Agonies of Thought, no Pen can paint;*
> *Oh thine are Pangs, too sharp for all Complaint.*
> *When the poor trembling Heart to Grief resign'd,*
> *In Silence mourns, and can no Language find:*
> *Far worse than Death these bitter Moments prove,*
> *Extended on the Rack of doubtful Love.*
> *Then all the Wounds his Arrows first have made,*
> *Bleed o'er again;—again are open laid,*
> *While pale Despair, and ever-trembling Fear,*
> *Pours Death into the Soul, and stabs the Ear.*
> *The cold and dewy Limbs confess the Pain,*
> *And the Mind bleeds thro' every breathing Vein.*
> *This is a Shipwreck my poor Ease has known,*
> *And I can draw its Torments from my own.*

There was no curing this unhappy Relation of mine of this Disease; he was eternally relapsing, which broke in upon the Harmony of our Loves.

I had most tenderly recommended my Cousin and his Interest to the Duke of B——f——t, in whose Power it was then to serve him; he had promised to use his Endeavours for him, and desired to see him and to serve him. Too well I knew the Pride and Jealousy of this Person, to imagine he would wait on the Duke, whom he regarded as a Rival.

But I contrived, for his Service partly, a Relation of ours should invite us to Supper, who was intimate with the Duke, and first introduced him to me. I perswaded my Cousin to guard me thither, he was unwilling to go, but more to let me go without him.

In fine, we went, and found every Thing fine and entertaining. But how was my poor Lover disordered, when the Duke of *B——fort* took me out to dance. I wish'd to have avoided giving him this Pain, but it could not be. I chose him a fine young Lady to dance with, and told him softly that I felt his Uneasiness, and would contrive to drop the Duke, if he would be easy; but that was impossible, I saw his Heart bursting with Grief, he neither minded his Partner, the Dances, nor the Company, his Soul was so out of Tune; the Duke very civilly address'd himself to him, but in vain.

All the Company remark'd his strange Behaviour, which I endeavoured to excuse. I pretended Illness for his Sake, and danc'd no more with the Duke that Night, which occasioned our breaking up sooner than was intended.

Some other of our Dancers were to go our Way, which was a new Torment to my poor Cousin; he long'd to complain, and thought he had a long Charge against me. He could not speak in the Coach, but was obliged to wait on the Ladies Home; but as we went Home I put my Hand to his Face which I found all in Tears; he press'd it between Grief, Anger, and Love. Pity kept me waking that Night, as Sorrow did my Cousin.

The first Person I saw, was this melancholy wretched Lover kneeling by my Bedside. He told me, he had pass'd the Night in Tears, that Love had made him the most distracted of all Men; he implored me to forgive him, and to leave *London,* that he might recover himself. I never indeed saw a more deplorable Object, his Face was too sad a Witness of his Griefs. I forbore to wound him more, and hasted with him to *Fulham,* where a few Days composed his Soul; and mine, full of Pity, again forgave him.

Oh my Angel! what a Difference there is in Jealousy! how respectful and tender is yours! while you complain you grow more charming, and the Soul receives you with redoubled Ardour.

His was a coarse Uneasiness, and Love was asham'd and troubled at this Disturber of his Repose, the dull Waster of his tender Hours, who threw his Sweets regardless by him, and only lived upon the Bitter.

> *Oh to thy heavy Kind impart*
> *Thy soft Complaints, thy heav'nly Art.*
> *Thy gentle Murmurs, thy sweet Tone,*
> *Thy speaking Sighs, when Love makes known*
> *His Agonies with an expressive Groan.*

> *When the fond Eyes with kind Reproaches flow,*
> *And all the soul is delug'd o'er with Woe;*
> *When the cold trembling Hand, with every Press,*
> *Speaks the poor breaking Heart, and begs Redress.*

He was unblest with this kind of Eloquence. At last his Fellow Waves redemanded my elemental Lover. I resign'd him rather with the decent Grief of a Relation, than of a tender Mistress.

I was once more left to my dear Liberty, and sometimes pass'd some Hours at *Kensington,* with a Friend of mine, who had Life and Spirit enough. We amus'd the Moments gaily, but innocently; some of them we pass'd in Town at the *Park* or Play.

She carry'd me to a Friend of her's, who was a Painter, and perswaded my Vanity into sitting for my Picture, a Folly I had never before committed; for since my Hours of Childhood, I never dreamt I was handsome—or more than tolerable. I imagin'd my Eyes were only meant to read with, and the rest of my Features for their proper Offices. Flattery had made but few Impressions on me yet—nor was I aware of its Dangers.

The Painter and his Wife, who indeed were both well-bred agreeable People, and understood the World very well, receiv'd me rather like an Angel than a Mortal; they distinguished me from all their Friends, and courted me in such a manner, that I cou'd not help being pleasingly surpriz'd; little did I dream it was Interest, and not me, they address'd. I resolved sincerely to serve them; I recommended them to all I knew, and would let no Day pass without some Instance of my Friendship; my Heart lay open to their Survey. Never was a more sincere and passionate Friend than I was to these People. Amidst their Caresses I often stole down to *Fulham,* to be sweetly lost in that Garden; but every Time I went I saw Mr. C—— and his Wife in Tears, as if unable to support my Absence. How was I obliged and deceived! often in Pity to their Intreaties, I stay'd in Town longer than I wish'd.

In their House were some Ladies entertaining enough.—One was an old Beauty, who had yet fine Remains, and Wit and Art enough to supply the Loss of Bloom; she had a Daughter with her, a fine and very lovely Woman, who then mourned a faithless Lover. I found Pride and Anger had a greater Share than Tenderness.— She had been once the favourite Mistress of C——k the Chamberlain; the *Atalantis* gives a full Account of this Pair, their extravagant Passion, and sudden Disagreement. She sigh'd indeed incessantly, but I more than fear, it was for a gilded Chariot, and all the fine Things she had lost in her Lover; yet, methought, I pity'd her restless Nights and melancholy Days, and gave her all the little Comfort I cou'd; now she no longer wants it, and has found in a new Lover all she mourn'd in the old.

Her Mother, who had out-lived the tender Part of Love, was very entertaining; she wou'd sometimes, wittily enough, ridicule its Torments. Amongst this Company I pass'd many agreeable Evenings; and about this Time it happened, I was obliged to make some Stay in Town, in order to compleat an Affair of my Brother's: I was to lay down some Money for him, which I had offered.

This was an unlucky Stay for me. One Morning I saw Mrs. C——y by my Bedside in Tears, which of all Things move me most. For God's Sake, says I, my Friend, what is the Matter, and why do you afflict me? if there is any thing in my Power, freely command me; I live but to serve my Friends. She very handsomely thank'd me, and told me, that Morning some Demands were made on her Husband, for Debts of hers in her former Husband's Time contracted; that she feared he must be ruined for them; unless some Friend would lay down the Money.

I am glad, say I, Madam, this is all; pray accept these Lottery-Tickets, which I have happily by me for your Service; they will sell for two hundred Pounds; and I shall rejoice if this, or all I can command, will make you easy. I gave her the Tickets out of my Pocket, which she received with Transport, after a thousand Flatteries. The Joy I had in serving these People is not to be expressed so easily, as felt by your most generous Mind; they were less nobly pleased, and I envy them not their mean Joy.

I never thought of taking any Security, nor of demanding a Payment till I wanted the Money again, which is to this Moment unpaid. Nothing but Joy and Civility was seen in this Family, till Love flew over it with his Wing, and shadow'd this Scene.

The Painter was a Man of Wit and Address, and had Art enough to engage a Substance as well as express a Shadow. As I was one Day sitting for my Picture, how was I surprized to see the Artist at my Feet imploring my Pity. I was dumb with Wonder at this Change, and could only bid him rise; but he continued to kneel, and talked of Love with the Air of Distraction.

I rose from my Seat, and left him pursuing me on his Knees, when his Wife entered the Room; she seemed surprized, but I have too much Reason to fear this Plot was laid between them, from their future Baseness.

He rose in some Disorder, and I left the Room, to let them adjust this Affair. I would not leave the House rudely, but after Dinner pretended I was obliged to go into the Country on Business, and would sometime soon return. The Gentleman impiored my Pardon, and the Wife herself seemed to intreat for him, and laid this Misfortune on my Charms as they called them. In fine, I left this Family, and never after would live in their House, though I continued to serve them. In some Months they took about five hundred Pounds of my Friends, but yet could they never forgive my Coolness.

See, my Adorable! what Dangers waited on my Innocence. From that Time they were hardly my Friends, vex'd with their Disappointment; but as I had done wondering at the Falsehood of these People, another Misfortune threatened me.

A Relation of mine, a Man of Fortune and Distinction in *Ireland*, came to *England;* his first Visit was to me. He was old, but perfectly well-bred, good natur'd, and polite, and what the World called a fine Gentleman. The near Relation he had to my Family, where he us'd to be always, when in Town, made me look on him like a kind of Parent, and he treated me always like his Child. My dear Brother had received a thousand Favours from him in *Ireland,* where he was one of the Lords Justices. He had been a good successful Courtier in the Reigns of King *Charles* and King *James,* and had married a Daughter of Chancellor *Hide*'s, which rais'd him more Ways than one. His Lady had her Gallantries, which ended in parting.

I give you, my darling Love, a little Sketch of this Lover, for so he soon became.

He was so kind to concern himself in my paying the Money for my Brother, and seeing it laid out to his Advantage. I thought myself happy in such a Friend; I was often at his House, his Coach and Servants were ever ready to attend me; he was so well received in all Places, that his Relations made no ill Figure. One Day I was returning my Thanks with all the Gratitude I cou'd, when I observed he changed Colour, and after a deep Sigh, said, Wou'd to Heaven, my most lovely and dear Child, you had Reason to thank me!—Wou'd I were only a Friend, but I am—oh! forgive me, I am a Lover, a designing artful one, pursuing your Youth, and endeavouring to steal the sweet Innocence I should defend; but oh! you must pity, or I must die. Not all the Experience of my Life, not all the Falsehoods of Women, not my Wife, not my Age, can secure me against you. I am undone unless I can be yours. I reproach myself, but to what Purpose? While I look on you, all the Flames of my Youth burst out anew, and I perish. Your Softness, your Good-nature, your Modesty, your Person, must, if possible, be mine. Amidst these Words he embraced me so ardently, that my Youth could hardly break from his Arms. I was astonish'd and griev'd at this Discovery, having ever imputed this Relation's Tenderness for me to Good-nature and Friendship. After some Moments Silence, What, says I, dear Sir, have I done, to deserve the Grief you now give me? If I am so unhappy to please you, punish—punish me by seeing me no more; fly from this unlucky Person, and forget her. But Love was deaf as well as blind. Whilst I was speaking, he was laying a thousand tender Schemes. Oh suffer me, says he, my dear Angel, to carry you into *Ireland,* where it will be in my Power to make you as fortunate as you can make me blest. You may live with my Sister, or if with me, who can accuse us? My Age, my Behaviour, and our near Relation, will defend us from Censure. You are alone in the World, and may possibly be one Day tempted to bless one who adores you less. I was so much perplex'd that I left him, and retir'd into another Room, where I shed a thousand Tears for this Conquest, and resolved to hide myself from this Lover.

I retired to *Fulham* without taking Leave, whilst Mr. *R.* was looking over the whole Town for me. He sought amongst all my Friends for me. At last, almost distracted, he came down to *Fulham,* where he found his Fugitive. I could not perswade him to return to *London,* though he had continual Interest at Court to pursue. Nor would I suffer him to be in the same House with me. He took a Lodging as near as possible, in a little Cottage. How resolute, how humble is Love! It would have been a kind of Farce for his Brother Justice to have seen him sighing in bare Walls, who had been indulged in all the Pleasures and Grandeurs of a Court, and happy in its chief Beauties. He has often protested to me, he was better pleased to wander in our artless Garden with me, than with all the past Scenes of his Life. But I often forsook him here, for his Love grew tiresome to me; and he was soon recalled into *Ireland.* Never did I see a Heart more afflicted than his at leaving me. The hurry of Business, and the Pains of hopeless Love, finish'd his Days in *Ireland,* from whence he often writ to me a thousand tender Invitations, but I still refus'd them. He had a polite gentle way of Writing, which I have rarely met with, but had in his Youth been too much abandon'd to Women of little Sense and Virtue, his Mind had else been more adorn'd. He was a faithful Friend, a passionate Lover, and the best Relation I ever saw. I own I lamented his Death, and wrote something on it like this:

> *Oh where are now thy amorous Fires,*
> *And all thy Train of soft Desires?*
> *Thy tender Schemes forgotten rest,*

> *Thy silent Heart sleeps in thy Breast.*
> *It springs no more to hear my Voice,*
> *Nor can it sorrow, or rejoice.*
> *Thy Arms no more will fold my Waist,*
> *Nor tremble to be close embrac'd.*
> *Happy art thou, Death overpast,*
> *Which rolls upon my Youth so fast.*
> *Ev'n whilst I write my Sands decline,*
> *They fall, and soon will mix with thine.*
> *A few short Years and I shall be*
> *Cold as thy Tomb, and all unmov'd as thee.*

After the Exile of this Gentleman, I rested some time from Lovers. I was fond of this Repose, too sweet and soft to last.

My beloved Brother, who from *Ireland* was settled in *Spain,* sent me his Picture by a particular Friend of his, of whom he wrote me the best Character in the World. They had been Fellow-Prisoners together, which had created an uncommon Dearness between them.

The Gentleman brought me the Picture, and I received him as one loved by my darling Brother; but I was at that time so intirely given up to Reading, that I little observed his Person, on which I had no Manner of Design; but his Soul, it seems, was fill'd with softer Sentiments, and felt for me such Tenderness that it could neither express nor hide.

When he first did me the Favour of a Visit, he found me in the Garden beneath the great Tree, which my Charmer has honoured with his Regard. My Dress was plain and rural as possible; for then I had no Thought of pleasing, nor a Wish to be much beloved; yet has he protested to me that this Carelessness undid him more than all Art could have done, which I was far from dreaming of then. We took a Survey of our Garden, which he very civilly prais'd. I did not remark any Disorders in him till some time after this. I wou'd fain present him, my Angel, to your View; but Time has borne the Image of him from my Mind, that it's possible I should not do it Justice.

He was tall, but not of the divine Height so lovely in you; his Limbs were robust, and wanted the Delicacy of your's, but manly and proper for *Mars,* to whom they had been devoted. He was genteel, as his Strength would suffer him to be. His Features were strong and lively, and spread over with a good Humour that had some Charms. He was generous, and esteemed very well bred. His Soul was suited to his Person; he had Sense, but not too refined. His Hours had been divided between Love and War; the latter had not allowed him Leisure to approach the other as he ought; rather he had seiz'd his Pleasures than intreated them, or rather they had never reach'd his Soul. He was a Stranger to the divine Tenderness of a Lover, and at first but a rude Scholar in that heavenly Science. He visited me very often, I knew not why, nor did I think much about it. Sometimes I mourn'd to resign my ador'd *Shakespear*, for his Company.

I imputed his repeated Visits to the Friendship he had for my Brother, but at last they were so long, and so frequent, I knew not what to think; nor could I help observing his Face grown pale, his Voice faint, and all his Manner changed. He often complained of having been ill since he saw me, which was now every Day. I never saw any man so alter'd. He was naturally, as I have said, bold and assur'd, but was now grown silent, tender, and a kind of Coward.

One Day, as we were sitting together, I perceiv'd his colour change, and his whole Frame disorder'd, more than usual. I rose to call some Assistance, but ere they could come, his Spirits were lost, and he seem'd dying; but we recover'd him again. While his Senses were thus confus'd, we heard him groan, and saw the Tears flow from his Eyes as they were clos'd. I own I was touched at this Sight, though I knew not my self the Cause. As soon as he was a little recover'd, and the Servants retir'd, with the Tears still flowing, he intreated my Pardon. I am miserable, says he, but I thought of dying, rather than of troubling you; but my Soul has not obey'd me; it lingers in this unhappy Body, 'till it has deserv'd or begg'd your Pity. Oh I die for you! regard me as the most passionate and most sincere of all Men. I have endeavour'd to suppress this Passion, but see it has subdued me! Smile on me, and I will live! Pardon my odd Address; I have not been used to intreat, and perhaps appear less tender and respectful than I mean to show myself;—but my Senses are not yet return'd. Here he sigh'd for some Moments, and seem'd intirely devoted to Grief. I fear'd a Relapse, and with all the Gentleness my Surprize permitted, intreated him to walk back to the House. He rose, and leaning on my Arm, I convey'd him home. But the whole Evening was pass'd in Sighs and Tears on his Part, and cold Civility on mine. He left me that Night, and returned early the next Morning, nor ever left me for some Months after. Sometimes he lay in the next House, and sometimes in the Town, but seldom went to *London*, where he was said to be dead or married.

He was a Man of a very large Fortune, and one of the best and noblest Families in *Ireland*. He had a very happy Interest in the present Government, and in a fair Way of being what he pleas'd.

But what was this to me? my Soul languish'd after something more lovely.

My Friends surrounded me, with Intreaties to marry him; he bribed their Interest, and made such Offers of Settlements as would have tempted the Mercenary. He implored in publick, and did all the Extravagances a Lover cou'd. I heard him with Pity, but no Love; but he had Hopes in Time to soften my Soul, since he saw it disengaged; and indeed I believe I had married him to please the World, had not his Affairs press'd him to *Ireland.* He left me with the utmost Anguish, and a Promise to return soon.

In our Acquaintance, he had introduced a Friend to me, whom he held extremely dear; and whom he made his Confidant in his Passion for me. He was a Man of Wit and Pleasure, devoted to the lightest Part of Love, and had convers'd with those that knew not to please above a Day; he had a Passion to charm, and when he had succeeded, he soon forgot the Obliger.

This Gentleman I had laugh'd with, and meant no more, for I saw his Soul was not capable of a tender or lasting Passion. He had foolishly and meanly confess'd the Names of some who had made him happy, which I used to receive with Scorn, and repaid still with dull Advice of Constancy, a Thing he knew little of; Truth was not his Element; but the honest Heart of my Lover was laid open to his View, who was as unreserved as this was artful. It has often created my Wonder there could be any great Friendship between such different Souls.

Mr. *B*——*s* at his leaving *England,* most tenderly recommended me to the Care of his Friend, and beg'd to be every Day informed of my Health, which was then much disordered; the other gave a thousand Promises of guarding the Treasure of his Soul; but he was no sooner in possession of his Charge, than he endeavoured to betray it; first, by a thousand little Arts that wore the Face of Friendship; and after, by an assured Declaration of Love; nor did it suffice to speak his own Passion without rididiculing his Friend, trying to expose every little Fault, even the Dulness of trusting him. Did not Mr. *B*——, says this Creature, know how I adored you? yes, he saw my Eyes speak it, and every Action: nay, I have told him of it most sincerely, and desired his Excuse if I preferred my Happiness to his. See, he leaves me to your Pity, nay, he love me so, he would intreat for me, and means to serve me by his Absence.

I cannot express, my only Blessing, how my Soul was affronted, and disdained this Trifler. If I ever felt any Tenderness for Mr. *B*——, it was to find him thus betray'd. I left him with a Look of

Disdain, nor ever more wou'd receive him as a Friend. Imagine his Pride so disappointed, and contriving to revenge itself. An Occasion offered soon after—too soon.

Oh! forgive me, my heavenly Charmer, if I pause here a little, to gather Force to continue my Life in this approaching Scene; the most unlucky Turn of it, for which I eternally must lament. I was now bless'd with Youth, Freedom, and Friends, but without knowing the true Value of these Blessings.

There was an unfortunate Friend of Mr. *Cenny*'s who had failed in Town, and was come to *Fulham* to make up his Affairs. He had many who assisted and visited him in his Retirement; but the chief and most civil was Mr. S——; who was then, indeed, what the World calls a pretty Gentleman, and what I thought so. His Face was lively and handsome, and his Manner very civil. He was not in perfect Health, having languished long with an Ague; but he had something in him that I more than liked, which was improved by his liking me. There was a Beauty methoughts in his Care of the Unfortunate, and some in his Love for me, which he shew'd from the first Moment I saw him. My Thoughts had been long disengag'd; nor was it a Wonder they should now take a softer Turn. He was ever near me, and employ'd all the Arts of a Lover to engage me; and what of Entertainment his own Mind was not adorned with, he found for me in some Amusement. He presented me with Books and Musick, and whatsoever he saw my Soul fond of, till it grew so of him; yet even then, when Gratitude mingled with Affection, and both were inspired by Retirement, there wanted much of that noble burning Passion I now find for my adored Charmer.—Mine was tender Inclination, rather than Adoration, as my Soul shew'd in its Letters, where it is ever truly painted. Oh God, how different are they from what my Heart has pour'd out to you its divine Master! They abounded with Thanks, or a gentle Civility, but no Transports or Torments; those only are sacred to you. But could even the Warmth I then had been sustained with its first Beauty, it was enough to have sweeten'd Life. But oh, how few have your godlike Art of improving Love, or being eternally dear! Who but you can grow upon the Soul! Who but you can seize it with sweet Violence, that it can receive no other Object! Mr. S—— rather made a Part of its Happiness than was its all. If a Change had happen'd, if Coldness or Death, I could have lived beyond it; that it is not so now, may the righteous God be witness, who has stamp'd my Soul with such awful Sincerity, such never-fading Truth!

> *When at thy sacred Feet I vow my deathless Flame,*
> *I swear (not by love's transitory name,)*
> *By him that breath'd this Soul, and warm'd this Frame:*
> *May he dissolve it whilst my Tongue implores,*
> *And my charm'd Heart religiously adores,*
> *If it in Life or Death has any View,*
> *But to be lov'd (sweet Soul of Love) by you.*

Never did my Passion arrive to this Extreme: before rather it delighted than pain'd me; for I must confess, with everlasting Gratitude, Mr. S—— deserv'd a very tender Regard. His Love was mix'd with Friendship, and I believe he never sincerely sigh'd but for me.

His Education had been good, but not noble, which was his chief Misfortune; the polite Part of the World had not fallen in the Compass of his View. His Days had been sacrificed to the morose God of Business, and his Nights to the wanton God of unrefin'd Pleasure, which had not given his Mind that Delicacy of Taste as I wish: 'tis this I lament even now, and is the sad Occasion of many unhappy Hours. Alas! the generous Soul is not to be hir'd, but to be eternally woo'd and charm'd; I have a thousand Obligations to Mr. S—— but I would receive them as marks of his tender Affection, not as Badges of Slavery, to bind me down to mean Servitude, such as he expects. But to return to our happy Hours, the Holidays of Love. I was then happy, and deservedly so; I was devoted to his Tenderness, and willing to yield to it my Heart and Time. He was ever with me, nor had I Leisure or Inclination to receive any other.

I have already told my divine Lover Mr. B——s was in *Ireland,* and not beloved when in *England,* and now less than ever; I forgot, or rather never had truly remembered him. His disappointed Friend was glad to aggravate my Coldness to him: Revenge had made him a faithful Spy. He informed Mr. B——s, for whom he was neglected, but with so much Malice, that it almost distracted this poor Gentleman; he hasted over, and left his Friends and Affairs in the utmost Confusion; so indiscreet is Jealousy!

He waited not to refresh himself after his Voyage, nor almost for the Winds to bring him, but the Night he came to Town hurried to *Fulham.* Love and Grief had not added to his Beauty, and my Heart was filled with a sweeter Image; my Coldness was increased, and I fear I received him too indifferently; he was pale and all unlovely, and his Words in very improper Order, or rather none at all. I am come, Madam, says he, to charge you with my Distraction, and my Death; but first I will be revenged of him who has robbed me of you. I know his Name, and where to find him. He need, poor Gentleman, but have looked into my Heart. To imagine Mr. S—— was in any Danger, and for my Sake only, increased my Regard. I coldly told Mr. B——s, I should not account to him, nor his Friend, for my Conduct; that I would give myself where I pleased.

He behaved much like a Madman, and left me, as I feared, to find out Mr. S——. It was then I found that I regarded him more than I imagined; I flew to Town, and intreated his Care of himself for my Sake. Never did any Heart appear more charmed and grateful than his; and promised an everlasting Acknowledgment of the Sacrifice I made him.

See me, my guardian Angel, dealing away my Interest, and the most faithful Lover, to giddy Inclination, whose phantastick Fires had seized on my Heart. It was now I wanted your divine Assistance and Counsel in this important Moment of my Life. I had no prudent Friend to advise me, and Love was a fatal Counsellor; he presented these two Gentlemen in such false Lights, that my little Discretion was easily misled. Mr. B——s was certainly the most sincere of all Men, and truly generous; he was unskilled in the little Flatteries of Love, for his Soul was all Truth and Honour. I lament I lavished away this faithful Lover; I had not then Compassion enough for what I made him suffer; my Coldness and Neglect almost cost him his Life. He often visited me, but his Passion and Grief were too strong to let him appear agreeable. It is strange, the more I saw him the more I forgot him. Love and Jealousy made him do, and say, a thousand odd Things: He disguised himself like a Porter to run on Love's Errand, and waited at the *Temple* to watch my going in with a Design of murdering me, or Mr. S——. Love had made him a Kind of *Othello*. He used sometimes to write me very tender Letters, full of Complaints, but mixed with such Distractions that I trembled to read them. One Day he intreated me to see him, to preserve his Life, for he had sworn neither to eat nor drink till he saw me. He had died away at Court, and had but just recovered Sense to write to me.

I went and found him, indeed, dying, as I feared; his Face was pale as Death, and his Eyes sunk, his Hands trembling, and his Soul almost going. This melancholy Sight struck me with the utmost Compassion; I wept for his sad Condition, and implored him to live for a Heart more worthy of him. In obedience to me he received some Nourishment, and from that Day grew a little better. What did not this poor Gentleman suffer for me? Oh! I have tasted his Torments since, and have languished with his Pains. I prevailed on him at last to return to his native Air, where his Health slowly recovered. He left me with a half-broken Heart; he struggled long with this unhappy Passion; he returned to *England,* again to sollicit it, but in vain; my Inclinations were more strongly engaged, for the fear of losing me made Mr. S—— doubly assiduous; no Day past without giving me new Proofs of his Devotion; he devoted himself intirely to my Pleasures, and grew more a Lover than you wou'd imagine.

He had a little retired House near *Windsor,* where I used to pass many very happy Moments. Nothing could be more romantickly sweet than this Place; it seemed formed for Love, far from Noise or Business. The Gentleman it had belonged to was a fine Painter, he had spread the Ceilings and Wainscot with *Cupids;* every Room had some soft Device.

> *Here lovely* Venus *her* Adonis *griev'd,*
> *Here her fair Bosom with Distraction heav'd,*
> *While mourning* Cupids *bending o'er their Darts,*
> *Gave dying Looks to the fair Queen of Hearts.*
> *The artful Pencil kindles soft Desire,*
> *And warms the Wishes with a dangerous Fire,*
> *Th' attending Lover sees the Passion rise,*
> *Watches the heaving Breast and streaming Eyes;*
> *Pours in his sighs, when the dissolving Heart*
> *Gives way; and no Reserve to take its Part.*

Whilst we lived in this sweet Solitude, a Friend of Mr. S—— came to give him a Visit. There had been a very long and firm Friendship between them. This Gentleman was not young, but a Man of plain good Sense, and happy enough in his Person and Fortune. He had been formerly what they call a Man amongst the Ladies, which had left a little Vanity behind, yet not enough to make him disagreeable. Mr. S—— received him with much Joy, and presented him to me; my Thoughts were at this Time so much engaged, I hardly regarded this Stranger, at least very coldly; but he had the Misfortune to look on me with other Eyes.

From that Day, which was fatal to his Quiet, he became a faithful Lover, and an unhappy one; for his Honour prevented his imploring my Pity, but by Sighs and Looks. Love is not always blind, Mr. S—— discovered his Friend's Disorder, and grew concerned at it. One Day he took him into the Garden, and there told him his fears; the other very generously confessed his Passion, and in such a Manner, that Mr. S—— almost pitied him; and assured him he would resign any thing but me to his Quiet. This was an ill-timed

Compliment, for nothing would make Mr. A——s happy, but the only Thing he cou'd not part with. He coldly thanked Mr. S——, and affirmed to him, he would conceal his Misery from me, whatever he suffered, and sacrifice his Love to Friendship and Honour. Indeed he was faithful to his Word, tho' I believe no Lover ever endured more to keep it. I always avoided being alone with him, fearing to hear what I too plainly saw; therefore I hastened Mr. S—— to leave that delightful Place, and return to *Fulham*. But I shall never forget the extreme Grief Mr. A——s discovered at parting. I have heard him since protest, his Soul was then torn from him, and that no Time can heal the Wound.

He has indeed been a very faithful Friend to me ever since, and done me a thousand kind Offices, tho' Hope was lost. He has undergone the anguish of intreating for another, whilst he was dying himself; he has often brought me Letters from Mr. S——, which he would trust no other with; he has delivered them with Sighs, and I have often seen the Tears burst from his Eyes; which he has charged on Friendship, and said proceeded from the Pity he had for Mr. S——. He has often conducted me with a breaking Heart to these Chambers, and been as miserable as Jealousy and Despair could make him. But Time, I hope, the soft Healer of all Distresses, has been a Friend to him, for I delight not in giving Misery.

Whilst the Hours flew on smoothly as I could wish them, an Adventure presented itself which served but for an Amusement. In my Leisure Days, which were but few at that Time, I used to ride out, or sometimes go up the River.—I was waiting one Day for a Boat at the Water-side, when one put into our Stairs, which had only one Gentleman in it, to whom I found it belonged, and who very civilly offered it me. Mrs. *Moor* and I jumped into the Boat, and were very gay all the Way to *Richmond*. I never indeed was merrier in my Life; I had none of my present Cares, but was devoted to the God of Laughter; nor was the Gentleman more serious; he made Love, but in a trifling Manner.

He was a perfect *Cupid* in Beauty, fair as a *Venus,* and well-shap'd; his Face could engage the Eye for a Minute, but no more. At Landing he very civilly waited on us to *Kew,* where I was to stay some Hours; I took leave, as I hoped, for ever; for I was grown a little weary of him already, nor was he a Kind of Man formed to charm my Soul.

When I came to *Richmond,* in the Evening I found him there; he left all his Company to attend on me all Night; we danc'd together, and laugh'd again; tho' he seem'd to put on a more serious Air on his Part. The next Day I went back to *Fulham,* and had not

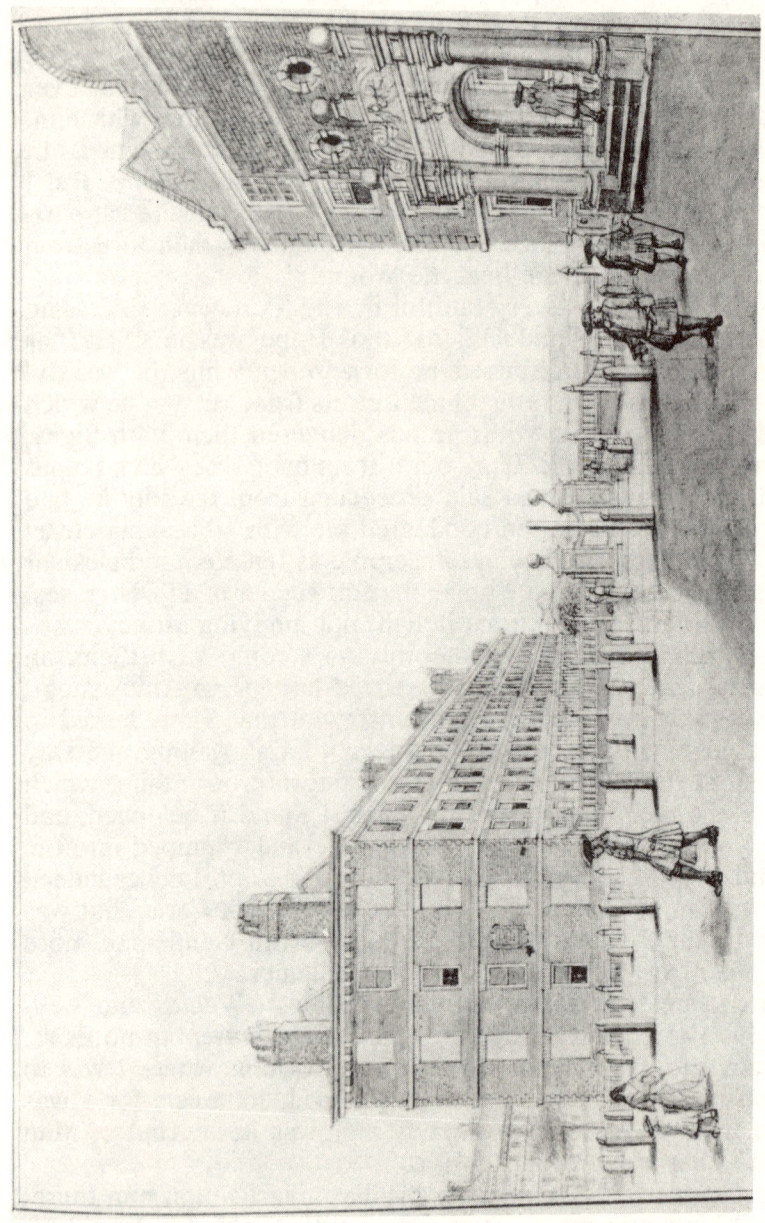

Early eighteenth-century watercolor sketch of the Paper Buildings in the Inner Temple. This handsome building, overlooking the Thames and attractive gardens, contained the legal chambers where Fowke lived when she wrote *Clio*. The woman and child walking toward the building show the domestic side of life in this center of legal activity.

been there many Hours, when my new Lover appeared to me. I cannot say the Sight was pleasing to me; I was sick of his Beauties, and languished by that Time to be alone.

The very thinking of Mr. S—— was more agreeable to me than this new Substance. He staid some Hours, and from that Day, for many Months, eternally solicited, but in vain; my Heart had no Inclination for him; he wrote tenderly and well, but nothing pleased me truly that he did or said; his Temper was as sweet as his Person, but he could not charm me; Ill Success was so new to this Gentleman he could not bear it. His Health began to languish, the Roses and the Lillies faded away, and at last he grew pale as the dying *Adonis*.

I wanted Love for this lovely Object, but not Compassion; I went to him in Town, as he intreated, and found all his Relations weeping round him; he was in the most violent Fever I ever saw, but still handsome. I could not see him dying, and for me, without suffering some of his Illness. The Care I show'd in seeing him sometimes recovered him again, much to my Wish. When he was well enough to bear it, I advised him against his inconsiderate Passion, and generously repeated what I had often told him, how deeply I was engaged to Mr. S——. I entreated him to think of me but as a Friend, or rather to forget me, who had tho' innocently, wounded his Repose. This was a very severe Lesson to a young and passionate Lover. But Time will conquer all Things; I forbore seeing him, and withdrew myself gently from his Correspondence, and at last I believe he ceas'd to be unhappy. He married a Woman of Quality, Beauty and Fortune, who was charm'd with him, tho' I was not. 'Tis not long since I saw him at *Hampstead,* where he, sighing, told me, no Change of Fortune could restore his Quiet, tho' he had try'd even Beauty, Time, and Marriage; he implored me to give him an Evening to paint his Misery, but I would never see him unless by Chance.

After I had dropt this Lover, I grew much easier; Mr. S—— still visited me, and I still preferred him to the rest of the World.

At this Time I had a Friend, who was very agreeable and dear to me, at *Parsons-Green,* Mother to the present Dutchess of *Bolton:* I need not then say she was a Woman of Gallantry, or rather had been so; but there appeared some Beauty to me, in choosing the most lovely Man in the World, the unfortunate Duke of *Monmouth;* he wanted your divine Soul, oh! heavenly *Hillarius,* to render him completely charming. This Lady was a Woman of Wit, she had been Maid of Honour and a Beauty, her Mind was still handsome; she used to entertain me with all the past Gallantries of the Age she had shone in; she had read very much, and was a very accomplish'd Woman. She favoured me with her tenderest Friendship. She had a Son in the Army, a very pretty agreeable Man in his Person and Manners, but had not his Mother's Soul; he wanted that Sense and Flame, which made her Conversation so sweet; yet was he thought, by the Ladies, a most amiable Man, and sought by them extremely.

I often saw this Gentleman at his Mother's, where I passed whole Days with him, but without thinking of him as a Lover; at last I found he thought of me more tenderly than I wished. He was eternally there, nor could I avoid his seeing me Home on Nights, it being often late, when I left his Mother. In these Walks he used to discover his Passion, and not ungracefully, though unsuccessfully; for still Mr. S—— possest my Inclinations. He often formed Excuses and Messages to see me at home, till at last Mr. S—— grew uneasy, and I ceased going to *Parsons-Green,* or being at Home when Mr. *Crofts* came.

I found it no easy Matter to free myself from this Lover; he was a Soldier, and not soon repulsed. Had not my Heart been so far engaged, I know not where it could have reposed better, for his Temper was faithful and sweet, and I have seen few in the World more engaging, till I beheld your heavenly Beauties, and your all-superior Graces.

I endeavoured to avoid all Trouble of this Kind, having neither Pleasure nor Design in them, but found it impossible. Love was minded to amuse himself at the Expence of my Ease; in those Hours I found him an arrant Boy, always playing one foolish Trick or other.

In our mighty Town, there was newly arrived a Country 'Squire, or rather he was a Mixture between a Fox-hunter and an abandoned Rake. He used to pass the Night in Noise, and the Day in Murder, destroying all the poor Animals round the Place. He was very handsome, and I may say his Form was rather fine; I have often wondered it would receive or indure such a Soul; he had been successful with all his Tenant's Daughters, and believed no Mortal could resist his Beauties; he meant to carry all Women before him, as he did the poor Birds and Beasts. He had a very large Estate, and where his Person failed, that was to conquer.

I saw this Conqueror (not of Hearts) first at Church, where he fixed his Eyes on me, as a proper Prey, many Sundays; at last he grew weary of this distant Wooing, and resolved to be introduced right or wrong. He forced a Neighbour of ours to bring him into the Garden, where he hoped to see me, as it really happened he did. I never was more displeased at the Sight of any Mortal, for I had a most terrible Idea of him. But 'tis in the divine Power of tender Inclination to refine all Things. He addressed me in a much better Manner than I could have imagined, and my Fears grew less. As we walked, I found him a good conversable Brute, and had Love trained him early, he would have made no ill Scholar. He was well-shaped, and genteel in Spight of Education; polite Conversation would have made him very charming; but I had neither Leisure, nor indeed Merit enough, intirely to refine him. After this he was as constant a Tenant of our Shade as the Trees themselves, nor was he disagreeable to me. I used to preach to him, and he avowed a Reformation. He no longer conversed with his loose or mercenary Mistresses, but offered them all up to religious Love.

The Town was alarmed at his Change, and little else was talked of but the converted Mr. *H——n*. He said his Prayers decently; and amongst Women forbore to talk of his Dogs, and Horses, and strong Beer, which he used to boast were all the stoutest in the Country.

Love made a meer Saint of him; he read the softest Poets, who before only rose to *Durfey*. At last he grew the Darling of our Corporation. He was grown so polite he studied a thousand little Presents, such as the Season afforded, and offered them with a very good Grace; he grew modest and silent, from Roaring and Ranting. I was pleased enough with my Pupil, and have past many agreeable Hours with him. I even made him a kind of Poet; in Absence, he wrote Verse, which did not want Spirit or Softness, but Numbers. I have laugh'd at his Letters beyond Measure. I have not seen him lately, so fear he is relapsed again. His Business called him into the Country, where we will leave him.

I was now *Sola* in our Garden, and a happy Wanderer there, unless I made short Visits in our Town.

At the large House that looks over our Garden, was a Clergyman of fine Sense, who loved Books and Musick; he was a *Swede,* but spoke some *English,* and admirable *French.* I was happy in the Conversation of this Gentleman, who made Solitude very charming to me. In him Religion, Learning, Love and good Manners, sweetly met together; he tenderly loved me, but in the Way the Refiner does the Diamond, to polish and refine it; he brightened my Soul, and adorned it with Discourses of his heavenly Master, and the Charms of Goodness. Our Evenings were past in this improving Manner, till he went back to *Sweden.* I first lost by Absence, and next by Death, this ever-to-be-valued friend; I could still weep over his Memory. After his Loss, I became more grave and retired; my Soul mourned this heavenly Companion, and languished for Society, while Fortune was contriving something to torment me, lest my Solitude should grow too sweet.

There came to visit me a Friend of our Family's, and mine, who had been very tender to my childish Hours, and now came to renew her Friendship; with her was an elderly Lady, who had the lovely Remains of past Beauty, and was still agreeable; her Conversation seem'd entertaining and friendly. With these two Ladies was a young Gentleman of about nineteen, genteel and gay; he had a sweet Voice, and sung to us very sweetly. I little dreamed Love meant this Youth to disturb my Moments. His Mother from that Day contracted an appearing Esteem for me. Which soon grew to a Fondness. She endeavoured to find Lodgings in the Town near me, but could provide none nearer than *Putney*. I was every Day with her, and sometimes staid many Days at her Lodgings; they were new and obliging to me, and I began to think myself happier than ever. The young Gentleman behaved with peculiar Respect, and I saw something in him I thought I lik'd; I know not what it was; we were ever together, and his Mother seemed pleased we should be so. I had the Regard of a Parent for him, and he looked on me with a Kind of Duty. 'Tis Love broke these Measures, and taught to wish and sigh for unreasonable Happiness; my Complaisance and Pity gave him strange Hopes, which he knew not how to govern. He was uneasy still to be nearer, yet had not fine Sense enough to know the Soul must be first approach'd, and with the utmost Tenderness and Delicacy. He had never seen anything but his Lady Mother, or his School-Mistress. Sighs and Tears were *Hebrew* to him, nor could he understand how greatly Love rewards his Adorers. He was young, obstinate, irregular and vain, but yet 'twas certain he was mine. He abandoned his Books, his Friends, his Amusements, for me; and in Return, I gave him my Company, my Pity and Instruction. Never had Love a ruder, yet more faithful Scholar.

He was eternally pressing his Mother to leave the Place where they were, and found a thousand Faults with it; tho' it had, indeed, no other but its Distance from me. The Water divided us, yet could not suppress the Flames of this young Bosom.

He perplex'd his Mother to take Lodgings next Door to me, which, at last, her Love for him inclined her to; nor did she then foresee the Mischiefs this would create. My young Lover still grew more enamoured, and fond to Distraction, but it became a cruel Passion to him that felt it, and me that created it; every Parting grew insupportable to him, he could not leave me one Moment, tho' Friends or Business called, and would break out into such Disorders, that good Manners would blush for him. In vain I advised him to Softness, to Respect, which alone could make him dear to me. We eternally quarrelled. I retired from the World, but some Part of it pursued me, which made him distracted; my Life became uneasy to me, and I found Compassion had chained me down to an Oar, from which I could not easily break. It was my Tenderness, not my Soul, was now engaged. Every Day shewed me some fatal Consequence of the false Step I had made. I wish'd to retreat, and often broke loose to Town. Freedom I languish'd for, or for a lovely Object, that would sweetly take it from me.

My Soul was melancholy under this Oppressor, who knew not its Softness, nor its Value; it sought to amuse itself. Mr. S—— was taken up with dull Business. He was ever dear to me, but his Passion did not take care to keep its first Beauty, dully believing he had engaged and secured my Heart. Alas, this is not easily done, it requires a thousand tender Cares, and eternal Endearments, of which only my Angel is Master. On the other Hand, Mr. G—— was lost in Rage, and rude Jealousy, and I began to be weary of him, or resolved to soften my Chain.

I was often in Town with a Lady who had lodg'd at *Fulham*, an agreeable but dangerous Acquaintance. Never did any Lover endeavour to charm more than this Friend. She flattered, she intreated me still to be with her. Her Wit was amuseing, and released me from the duller World; she was still gay, and had been handsome; but was a Coquet to Men, and severe on all Women. She lashed her dearest Friends in absence, even me, whom she courted as a Goddess.

Her House was seldom empty, her Person drew the Eyes of the Unthinking, and her Flattery the Ears of the Dull; but the most lovely and refined of her Visitors was Mr. *C*——*y,* a young Gentleman, whose Soul and Body were engaging. She took care we should meet and like one another, on purpose afterwards to torment us. She took care to blow the Passion she saw kindling in our Souls with a thousand Praises of each other; she talked of every Grace, which I saw too well, but most his Adoration for me. She watched the tender Movements of my Wishes, and threw in her Arts: she left us together, and rejoiced at our present Happiness, in order to make us miserable for the future.

I yet knew little of the World, or this fair Adder, who wounded me in her Friendship, and was charming me to Ruin; every Day shew'd me some Charm in this lovely Lover; I grew uneasy at his

Absence, and sigh'd when forced to return to *Fulham,* where he could not be often. On his Part, his Passion increased, it was too natural to seek Relief from the Object beloved. He sigh'd, he complained; but to one no less unhappy.

Mrs. —— rejoiced at our Misery, and now, with a very religious Air, tells me Mr. *C*——*y* was engaged, possibly married, to one who loved him, and had been beloved by him; that I should rob this Lady of her Lover and her Life, if I continued to see him, and that Friendship alone made her reveal this. How was I surprized with different Passions, Love, Fear, Shame, and Compassion for the Lady I thought I had injured, whom she artfully praised and pitied!

Poor Mr. *C*——*y* all this time while dream'd he was fortunate, that Love meant to crown his Wishes. But how was he grieved and surprized to find me cold, angry and changed; at last, sadly and sincerely, I told him what I had heard. Kneeling he confessed some Part, that he had loved this Lady; but his Heart was now strongly charm'd to me, whom he must to Death adore; that he would act with Honour to her, though not Passion. But I had determin'd even to part with this beloved Lover, rather than injure another; therefore resolved to see him no more. Weeping I left him to return the Vows he seemed to forget; but to no Purpose. He returned with no Warmth thither; she languished and died unbeloved. But alas I was far from rejoicing at this Absence, and Justice had defaced some of that Passion, which sure was never deeply rooted in my Soul. Never did I feel those Pains and Pleasures my lovely Master can give me every Hour.

Without dying, I tore myself from this Lover. Mrs. *P*—— triumphed in her Malice, and to this Moment Mr. *C*——*y* still hates her for it. He married a Lady some Years after, of a large Fortune, and has been happy in every Thing but Love. He still remembers me with Passion; but, oh! I can have none, but for the ever-adored *Hillarius.* I am most devotedly and religiously his, with all the Affections of my Soul.

> *If all Mankind were plac'd before my Eyes,*
> *The present, past, and all that shall hereafter rise,*
> *With noble Scorn I'd look whole Nations o'er,*
> *And only fix on him I now adore.*
> *All that is charming in his Face appears,*
> *Sweet Wisdom in the Bloom of sprightly Years.*
> *For Adoration every Feature made,*
> *Oh! how they charm! oh! God, how they persuade.*

With awful Wonder I approach their Charms
With bending, trembling Knees, and longing Arms,
With Extacies that ne'er can be express'd,
But by my dying Eyes, where my fond Soul's confess'd.

Behold me, my lovely Angel, half free, and wishing to be entirely so, from the ungentle Soul of my young Lover, who only used the blessed Moments Love had lent him, to make himself disagreeable to me. But we had Intervals of Tenderness, when my Pity prevailed over my Pride, by his most humble Submissions.

We often went abroad together, my Lady would not move without me to any Diversions, and indeed I received many Proofs of her Favour. We were invited to pass some Months at the old Lord *Stafford's*, where the Hours passed agreeably enough. There were some Company who had known the World and Courts. Amongst the rest, a Relation of my *Strephon's*, formerly a Maid to King *James's* Queen; she used to furnish my lonely Hours with Books, I found one wrote by Mr. *Bond;* some Things in it pleased my Humour, and I wrote in an empty Leaf my Thoughts of it; which he very obligingly answered. Thus began the Letters, you have honoured with your Praises, which alone makes me proud of them. Alas! I was not then inspired by your divine Beauties, nor by Love, I only was taught by Fancy, and by Solitude and Nature. Oh! survey the tender Things my Passion has sigh'd to you, and confess, oh! lovely Ungrateful, the Difference between cold Friendship and raging Love, between my adorable Lover, and my unknown Friend.

After some Time I returned to *Fulham* again, where Love soon found a new Amusement for me. A Gentleman and his Wife came to lodge at Mr. *Cenny's*, whom I had before some little Knowledge of, and now was often with. They seemed a good, happy, dull Pair, and I little thought in the Husband to find a Lover, for I then wished for none, but a Rest from Passion.

To avoid the Impertinence of Mr. *G*——, I often withdrew hither, where I was treated with all possible Respect, and intreated still to be. We danc'd, play'd at Cards, and diverted ourselves and the Hours, till Mr. *T*——*ds* grew suddenly melancholy, which I imputed to Lowness of Spirits and much Study; I knew not his inward Anguish, nor its tender Cause. His Wife complained of his Change of Temper, and I endeavoured to console her. Neither I, says she, nor his Children are dear to him, his Health and Rest is lost. I pitied her Grief, and tried to divert him. I heard him sigh, and saw him disordered, but little thought myself the Occasion. I advis'd them to leave that Place, and feared Retirement had bred this Melancholy; they resolved at last on going, but it was on Condition I would accompany them for some Time in Town; which they forc'd me to promise I would, after a thousand Intreaties not to be refused. But I delayed it as long as I could, not caring to receive such Civilities from Strangers; and indeed hating to give Mr. G—— so much pain. The Design of my going had reduced him sometime to the utmost Despair; sometimes to such Outrages that I could not suffer, and which drove me from him, sooner than I cared to go, and left him a Prey to his own rude Passion. A Sigh or a Tear would have retarded me, but Commands and Curses I despised.

In fine, I went with my new Friends, who seemed transported they had me safe, from the Violence of my young Lover. But I had not been many Days in Town, when I perceived an unexpected Coldness in Mrs. *T*——, which wakened my Apprehension, till I observed whence it proceeded. I then found Love too plainly wrote in the Husband's Face and Actions; he was eternally near me, nor could he indure a Chair should divide us.

Not dreaming this would end in Love, I had used myself to be pleased with his Company, and grieved to see I must soon lose it. I always avoided being alone with him, not caring to give Pain. He sought as much to speak with me, and silently with his Eyes complained of my Coldness. One Day I was turning over *Chaucer*, a Book he was very fond of, and there I found my Name with a Complaint beneath it; and some Days after he dropped a Letter, a too tender one, into my Bosom; at last, few Hours past without some Instance of his Passion, then in its most violent Fury.

One Day I was dressing my Head, and much surprized to see Mr. *T*—— behind me, in the Glass, where I observ'd his Face pale. I started, and turned round, equally disordered; he pressed my Hand with a most passionate Look, and a Sigh which spoke for him, and dropped a Letter at my Feet. His Hand felt rather like Death than Love. I feared to hear him speak. Retire, says I, for God's Sake; if you are seen here it will create some Uneasiness to us all. He bow'd and left me, but with a Trouble Words can ill define; but my Heart has well understood since, from those adorable Charms of yours. The poor Wife grew every Day more uneasy, and the Husband more in Love, therefore I resolved to leave the Place, in hopes both his Passion and her Jealousy would die. But they were not so easily put to death. I let him know my Resolution of leaving his House, where I gave such Pain. He implored, if I would go, to suffer him only to speak to me, and to convey me where I meant to go, if I valued his Life. I left Mrs. *T*—— as civilly as I could; but he watched my going, at some Place in the

Neighbourhood, and flew after the Coach, and leaped into it with more Love than Discretion. We were no sooner out of his Neighbourhood, but he burst into a Flood of Tears; we drove an Hour, hoping he would recover himself, but in vain; he sigh'd and wept still more, and at that Moment I believe he endured all the Love and Sorrow his Soul could sustain.

My Concern, tho' it did not flow into my Eyes, was not less sincere. I implored him to be comforted, and assured him, by leaving his House, I meant not to leave the Friendship I had for him, but to make his Family easy. Oh God! says he, lovely *Clio,* do you prefer their Rest to mine? how can I live without you? Love and Grief would not permit more Words. I ordered the Coach to stop, and left my poor Lover sad as Death. The next Morning, by Eight o'Clock, he returned, and from that Day, for some Weeks, was twice or thrice every Day with me. But that Hour in the Coach was the only one I ever past alone with him. The Concern I saw him in, made some tender Impressions on my Soul, and I grew to like him more than I wished. The Hours passed on very pleasingly, and he continued his Regard, till some Evenings ere I left *London,* instead of his Visits, I received a Letter or two of Excuses for Absence. These, however sincere, did not agree with the Pride and Tenderness of my Soul, which was never deeply engaged, and now resolved to appear itself. I considered the Anguish our conversing, though so innocently, gave his Wife, and that he was not blessed with any shining Merit to deserve me. Therefore I left him, and *London,* with but few Sighs.

Oh! my Adorable, say, was this Love, was this like your tender, faithful *Clio,* who has sought you as she would Life, or as the Vulgar would Interest! Who has suffered Absence, Excuses, and appearing Neglect; and still burns with increasing Passion, and must to the last Hour of her Life.

I returned to *Fulham;* but found my young Lover almost Raving; he had made a fine Story from my being at Mr. T—— House, and behaved himself so ill, I could no longer be his Friend. In every Action he discovered his Folly and Meanness. He reproached, he swore, and treated every body near him with the Air of a Tyrant. I could not receive any Company in Quiet for him, which obliged me to think of a Way of removing him, for the whole Family was in an everlasting Storm; therefore, I intreated the People of the House, if they wished to keep me, to give them Warning, which, at last, they did, to my Joy, and my Lady and her Son left the House, where I had been too long a Slave. This Parting inraged Mr. G——, and still removed him further from my Tenderness; but ere long we ceased to be open Enemies, unless Wine sometimes blew up his Resentment. I sometimes went to visit my Lady, but often parted in Anger, when Love broke out into ill Manners. I grew truly weary of this Kind of Life, and resolved, some Way, to free myself from this Tyranny. When Love, more ingenious than I, in Pity, presented me a Cordial, one infinitely sweet to my Soul, and still grateful to my Memory.

Some Friends of mine came to pay me a Visit at *Fulham,* and brought with them a young Gentleman, whose Person was agreeable to my Wishes, though not adorned with those adorable Features, nor shining with your immortal Spirit. He had a peculiar Sweetness in his Form and Manner, which I never found till that Moment. His Face was spread over with Love and Softness. I have often thought him like some rosy Bed, which invites the Traveller to rest. From the Moment I saw him, I was inspired with an uncommon Tenderness for him, as he was with a respectful Passion for me. When he went I could not forget him, nor be easy till I saw him again. My Thoughts were filled with him, and I found my Soul aching with a pleasing Anguish, which no Diversion could remove. From that Day he began to write me tender Letters, to improve himself in my Heart.

I began to fear I loved, indeed, or something like it, but the sweet Object was more mine than I could wish. His Soul, his Time, his Wishes were devoted to me, and he only lived in beholding me; never were two Hearts more sweetly joined. If they were not raised to the divine Transports I have since tasted, they, in Return, had none of the bitter Anguish of Love, none of those cruel Torments that now sink me to the Earth, and make my Misery outweigh my Joy. He had none of those exalted Views that now tear my divine *Hillarius* from me; but was all Love, and Tenderness, and mine. To the Devotion of his Love, he offered up his Interest, his very Soul, and in return I gave him mine. Never did two Lovers live a more harmonious Life. It was a Kind of Heaven we possessed, our Hearts wore no mean Disguise, but seemed made for one another. But oh receive this divine Truth from my Soul. The Passion that inspired it then, was far below what I now find; it was only a Preparative for the glorious Flame I am now glowing with, which almost extinguishes the Memory of any other. It is Adoration, rather than Love, I now burn with; oh! receive it, sweet Sovereign of my Soul.

With what Transport could I dwell on this Difference, but my Time presses me to return and finish.

My Fate would not let me rest on this happy Shore, where I meant to have finished my Life. But all my Friends combine against me, and press me to exchange my sweet Lover, my darling Books, and all my Blessings for Marriage, whose Chains I ever dreaded.

My Brother assails me with Mr. S——. And Mr. G——, whom I have not mentioned some time, with his Visits and his Clamours helped to make me uneasy, and to push me against this Rock, on which I now lie bound. Fortune presented herself to me, and promised me I should have it in my Power to smile on the Distressed, and to relieve them. I had always a Passion for giving, and my Soul had languished under Restraint; this Prospect alone made me venture into this gloomy Part of Life, in whose Shadow I must for ever pine. I had a thousand Agonies of Heart ere I could resolve on this Change, so dreadful to me.

I saw the Person I held most dear on Earth, bound to another; and then fearing ere long to leave me. Had he been free, I own I should have preferred him openly, as my Heart then did in private to all Things. I consulted with him, and found his poor Heart torn between Love and Friendship, he knew not what to advise. My Brother eternally perplexed me about it, who preferred my Interest to the Quiet of my Heart. At last I leaped down this Precipice, nor did I find the Fall so much then. Noise and new Friends drowned the Miseries of it.

My Hurry in this Change of Life a little amused me; my Days were passed in new Diversions. The World courted me, and everything was gay and pleasing; even Mr. S——, whose Fortune had given Smiles to his Face, and new Complaisance to his Mind. We were seemingly happy, or, rather had not Leisure to find ourselves otherwise. These Chambers were never empty, crowded with the Fortunate and Civil. I was treated like a Goddess, and could not turn round without new Adorers. Mr. —— had many Friends, and they all paid their Devotion to me, but religiously I protest without Success. They were forced to live on cold Civility. Amongst the rest, there was one more agreeable to me than the Crowd; his Good-humour and extreme Respect for me, made me distinguish him from the rest. I past a great many pleasant Hours with him; he had Wit, Mirth, and Love.

But I appear, I fear, inconstant, till I return to my melancholy Lover, which I soon did, and endeavoured to console him for my Loss; and from that Time I gave him all my Leisure, which, indeed, was due to his Truth and Passion. Now, my Adorable, I began to live again. Our Tenderness seemed rather increased by this little

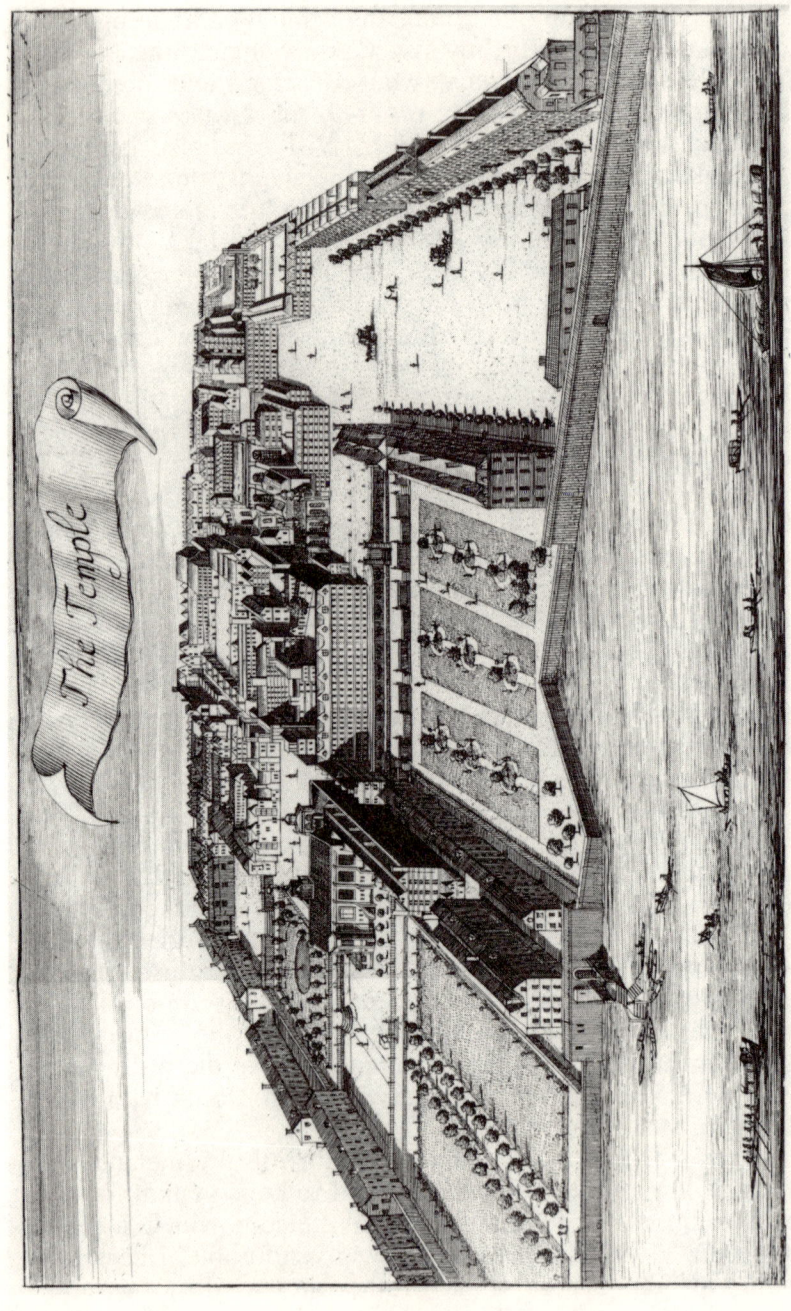

The Temple, from John Stow's *Survey of London*, ed. Strype (1720). The Temple was an Inn of Court where students of the law, practicing attorneys and barristers and other residents studied, worked, and lived. Fowke's husband, Arnold Sansom, and many of her other friends were associated with the Temple. (Courtesy of the Lilly Library, Indiana University, Bloomington, Indiana.)

Parting. We were as often together, as Prudence and Duty would suffer us: though I had a thousand Amusements offered me, I despised them all, to be with Mr. *H*——.

Almost every Day presented me that Happiness, which I blessed it for. Never were two Hearts more tender or more faithful; the Noise and Bustle of the World had made him dearer to me. Oh! I even then saw there was no Blessing but Love. I possessed this Dream of Happiness a great while; and what heightened the last Scene of it, was your adorable Letters. I read them with Adoration and Wonder, yet no Inconstancy; and had the foolish Virtue to resolve never to approach nearer than the Playhouse, while Mr. *H*—— continued in *England*. I looked upon you as a Miracle above my Hopes, and designed rather to be wondered at than possessed. I never before was sensible of Admiration; it was all reserved for you, the Spirit of all Perfection.

While I was charm'd, or rather happy with my favourite Lover, both Love and Fortune withdrew their Favours for some Time: the gay Prospect of Life set before me began to vanish every Day, and I found myself sink amongst the Crowd; yet I will affirm for my Soul, it bore it with no ill Grace, nor found a real Pang, but in losing Mr. *H*——, who was now obliged to leave *England*.

We parted with a thousand Tears on both Sides. Never was Sorrow more sincere, I devoted myself to it, till my Health languished, and Love took Pity on me. I retired into the Country to mourn, which I did sincerely, and was long ere I could receive any Consolation; the first, and only, were your divine Letters, which were glowing with a thousand Beauties. What I had before only wondered at, now began to inflame my Soul, and Love lay in every Line.

> *Not Solitude nor Grief could guard my Heart,*
> *With all its Floods, from the invading Dart.*
> *I sigh'd and languish'd o'er thy charming Strains,*
> *And felt already Life-consuming Pains.*
> *From Admiration I to Passion pass'd;*
> *Oh God, how short! the Passages how fast!*
> *Oh! how unlike those little Tours I made,*
> *Where I had gaz'd, and smil'd, but never staid.*
> *From hence, by Heaven, I never will remove,*
> *No Chance, no Time, no Death, shall end My Love.*
> *Beneath thy Coldness my poor Life may pine,*
> *But not my Passion, that is all divine,*
> *As the bright Eyes from whence it took its Shine.*

> *Here close my Life, the rest is all thy own,*
> *Its Joys depending on thy Smiles alone,*
> *How long 'twill last, is all to me unknown.*

Friday Night, the last Night of my Life or Happiness; disappointed in seeing you.

Oh! would to Heaven, ever-most-charming *Hillarius,* would to Heaven and you, I were here to end my Life; never was I fonder of resigning it; never was I more unable to support it; your Absence kills me. Oh! I am undone without you, and more miserable than Envy can wish me. I am lost to myself, and to the World, nor am I of much value to you. What would inrich another is no Treasure to you; yet can you not restore it, nor can I take it back. My Soul is sweetly lost in your dear Bosom, nor can ever find itself again; the God that created it, will, I hope, never divide it from you, whatsoever becomes of this miserable Body which loves to Adoration. When it lies down in Dust, sigh your Pity over it; and give it one of those Moments I now languish for; sure I shall be proud in Death, and happy.

I now flatter myself I have not long to live; 'tis the only Thought that affords me Comfort; it is kinder than the absent *Hillarius,* and bids me sweetly hope. Sure there are gentle Slumbers in the Grave, for those that die of Love; I long to dream there of the adored *Hillarius;* his divine Beauties will still glow in every Atom of this poor Body. Never was any Heart so enamoured as this which now sighs for you; oh! have Pity on it the little Time it must stay here; and sometimes give a Tear to this faithful Picture of my Soul. Be tender of its Faults, or rather do not see them; let only the Adoration I have for you appear to shadow every Blemish, or rather to enlighten the whole. Nothing can be more beautiful than my Love, but my divine Lover, who is all perfect.

Oh! my heavenly Lover, I am sad to Death, even whilst I think of your Perfections; think then how miserable I am grown, and what I still must be without you; oh! let your sweet Letters pour Health and Life into my dying Bosom, if you wish them me; or you will soon lose in Death, most lovely of Mortals,

Your adoring

CLIO.

Temple,
October, 1723.

A SONG.

1.

Foolish Eyes, thy Streams give over,
Wine, not Water, binds the Lover,
At the Table then be shining,
Gay Coquet, and all designing.
To th' addressing Foplings bowing,
And thy Smile, or Hand, allowing.
Whine no more thy sacred Passion,
Out of Nature, out of Fashion.

2.

Let him disappointed find thee,
False as he, nor dream to bind thee.
While he breaks all tender Measures,
Murdering Love, and all its Pleasures.
Shall a Look or Word deceive thee,
Which he once an Age will give thee?
Oh! no more, no more, excuse him,
Like a dull Deserter use him.

To my Soul's only Desire.

1.

Oh! that I had no Time to tell
    My Passion, or thy Power,
For oh! I love so very well,
    'Tis Death to part an Hour.

2.

In vain my Friends Amusements bring,
    Or what they fancy so,
The flowing Glass, and speaking String;
    My Soul is fallen too low.

3.

Rais'd high before, by thy sweet Breath,
    How steepy is its Fall,
It sinks into the Shades of Death,
    Till waken'd by thy Call.

A SONG

To my Unkind, but ever Charming.

Oh ye tender Thoughts that throng
My Soul, and tremble on my Tongue,
To ador'd *Hillarius* move,
And inflame his Heart with Love.
Oh! leave him not till you have shown
How miserable I am grown.

Tell him, the Wretch that naked stands,
In the *North*'s Blast, or *Africk*'s Sands,
Tho' the Heat melts the burning Veins,
Feels not his hapless *Clio*'s Pains.
Above all dull Comparisons they grow,
The perfect Extract of all human Woe.

To my Angel, on my Jealousy.

Pardon my tender Jealousies,
　　That rage when you depart,
They know, when absent from your Eyes,
　　The Weakness of my Heart.
How can I wise, sweet Charmer, be,
My Soul and Judgment flies with thee.

Oh what remains to guard my Breast
　　From those distracting Fears!
I lose my Colour and my Rest,
　　And drown my Sight in Tears.
Oh of what Service can it be,
Deny'd the Joy of seeing thee!

To my Soul's Adoration.

Every Blessing Heaven can give,
With my lovely Lover live!
Fortune, as my Heart, be kind
To thy noble thinking Mind!
Fortune, to thy Genius bend,
All thy great Designs attend;
Love already is thy Friend.
In thy charming Face he shines,
In thy Soul-commanding Lines,
On thy Love-inspiring Tongue
Are a Train of *Cupids* hung;
Every Word conveys a Dart,

Through the Ear, into the Heart;
Every Feature gives Desire,
Every Breath blows up the Fire,
Every Motion charms the Sight;
Oh! thou Heav'n of all Delight.
From all coarse Alloy refin'd,
Thy Body is a perfect Mind.
Ev'ry bright, transparent Vein,
Surely does a Soul contain;
Mine, at least, is there I'm sure,
From the Transports I endure.
Wonder not if every Part,
My Lips, my Eyes, and heaving Heart,
To thy dear Breast with Transport strain,
To take their Spirit back again.
All my Frame trembles with Delight,
And thy Charms swim before my Sight.
Sweet Extacy from Earth calcin'd,
Oh! heav'nly Transport of the Mind,
Then dull Mortality retires,
Mean Interest, and low Desires,
They all to mightly Love resign,
And leave my burning Wishes thine.
How little and how low appears
All my past Hopes, and mortal Fears,
To the new Heaven that I possess,
In thy exalted Tenderness!
And by those lovely Arms embrac'd,
I'm far above all Troubles plac'd.
Malice and Envy trembling stand,
Kept distant by thy noble Hand.
All Things grow sacred you protect,
And shining by your Passion deck'd,
Your Passion can a lasting Passport give
To future times, and make your Favourites live.

To the adored Hillarius.

Where will my rising Admiration end!
Oh! to what Heights will my Desires ascend!
When will the Time arrive that I shall be,
Oh! Soul of Sweetness, satisfy'd with thee!
Let those dear Lips some soft Relief impart,
And bathe the Flames of my dissolving Heart.
Too eagerly they burn, with lavish Haste,
And as they rise, I feel my Spirits waste;
Beneath my World of Love my Life declines,

But, as it fades, my Passion brighter shines;
Thy Absence, to this raging Fever join'd;
Will leave thy *Clio* nothing, but her Mind,
Thy Life-inspiring Arms with Haste restore,
And chear me with the Beauties I adore.

To my heavenly Charmer.

My poor expecting Heart beats for thy Breast,
In ev'ry Pulse, and will not let me rest;
A thousand dear Desires are waking there,
Whose Softness will not a Description bear,
Oh! let me pour them to thy lovely Eyes,
And catch their tender Meanings as they rise.
My ev'ry Feature with my Passion glows
In ev'ry Thought and Look it overflows.
Too noble and too strong for all Disguise,
It rushes from my Love-discov'ring Eyes.
Nor Rules nor Reason can my Love restrain;
Its godlike Tide runs high in ev'ry Vein.
To the whole World my Tenderness be known,
What is the World to her, who lives for thee alone?

To the Charmer of all my Wishes.

Why sinks my Heart within its little Cell?
Hillarius loves, and all Things should be well.
Does not his heav'nly Tongue charm all thy Fears?
Does not his lovely Lips drink up thy Tears?
Does not his Eyes with Pity overflow?
Does not his Soul dissolve to hear thy Woe?
Does not he weep when thy poor Muse complains?
Does not he bless her tender, trembling Strains?
And does he not his own sweet Passion tell?
Then chear thy Griefs, and let thy Soul be well.
  What Health, what Life, what Joy for me remains?
Tho' Fame and Fortune join to chant my Strains.
If the whole World should languish at my Feet,
And I were powerful, rich, ador'd and great,
In Heav'n itself my Wishes would repine,
Unless my Soul could call *Hillarius* mine;
Unless my Eyes his Beauties could survey,
And press them to my Soul the live-long Day.
My Transports then my every Verse should tell,
And all Things in my Bosom wou'd be well.
Now from my Arms how often is he torn,
And my charm'd Wishes for their Master mourn!

A SONG

No Comfort, no Amusement they can take,
But droop and languish for his lovely Sake.
With folded Arms, and Earth-bent-Eyes I stand,
Nor feel the Pressure of the Lover's Hand.
Lost to the World, and to myself I grow,
And nothing but his thousand Beauties know.
To Heav'n and Earth my raging Love I tell,
And ev'ry Eye can read my Soul's unwell;
All meaner Passions from my Mem'ry flown;
Oh! sweet *Hillarius*, I am all thy own.
Not Nature loves her mighty Maker more,
Who does her Beauties, and her Life restore.
To thee with ardent Fondness I incline,
My Hopes, my Muse, my Hours, my Life are thine:
No dull Reserves, like vulgar Hearts, I have,
Bounteous as Heav'n I ev'ry Blessing gave,
That all my Actions, Words, and Thoughts may tell
I love to Death.—Oh God! I love too well.
Oh! thou who charms my waking Wishes so,
For whom my Heart thus beats and Eyes o'erflow,
Let no new Object to thy Soul be dear,
Add not to Absence such a killing Fear;
Let thy dear Memory my Looks retain,
And think o'er all my Tenderness again.
If any Beauty to thy Sight appears,
Recall my Sighs, and agonizing Fears,
And to the World thy noble Passion tell,
She shall not love in vain, who loves so well.
  When to the Theatre my Conqueror goes,
The Treasurer of all my Heart's Repose,
Remember my poor Life all trembling lies,
In ev'ry Look of those transporting Eyes;
Oh! let them not on transient Beauty stay,
Nor deal the Blessings of my Soul away.
For when I next survey'd thy heav'nly Face,
My jealous Eye would miss the lavish'd Grace
For I can all thy thousand Beauties tell,
And know the Magazine of Charms too well.
With heav'nly Wisdom the soft Scenes survey,
Mind not the gaudy Players, but the Play;
Or if they should thy Admiration call,
To Art and Ornament impute it all.
Think, so adorned, how *Clio* would attract,
Who feels the Passions, which they only act.
And when some noble, very moving Part,
Wakes all the Fondness of thy gen'rous Heart,

A SONG

> Then let thy Hand which moves with godlike Grace,
> Shadow the sacred Sorrows of thy Face.
> Ev'ry sweet Tear the God of Love will bring,
> My Lips shall sip them from his dewy Wing.
> Oh! how my Heart will joy when he shall tell
> Its soft Desires, my Charmer loves so well.

Oh! most lovely, most beloved *Hillarius,* say, in what Manner shall I approach the Charmer of my Soul? what tender Titles shall I use to kindle up thy Flame and make it bright as mine? Oh! let me go back to all I have said that's dear and moving, let me collect all my Sighs and Tears, and pour them out again upon thy Bosom. Oh! let my Eyes remember every Look, that had the Blessing to express my Love, or to inspire thine. Let sweet Sincerity and artless Passion flow from my Tongue, and shine upon my Face; for there are Charms in Truth which Falsehood cannot wear, and Art is but a Shadow of its godlike Beauty.

> How sweet, how soft, how noble, and how bright
> Is perfect Love? how lovely to the Sight?
> Contentment lies upon its faithful Breast,
> And charms its tender Wishes into Rest,
> How ardent, yet how modest is the Fire
> Of a respectful Love, unstain'd with rude Desire!
> How faithful and how humble it appears!
> How musical its Sighs! how sweet its Tears!
> How tenderly in Absence it complains,
> And trembling breathes its Heart-distracting Pains!
> In Silence mourns, or else with Fear implores,
> Dreading to grieve the Bosom it adores.
> The noisy World it all regardless flies,
> And seeks the Grove with melancholy Eyes.
> From Friends, and Fame, and Fortune it retires,
> To breathe to the cold Floods its fond Desires.
> Dead to all Joy it lies with folded Arms,
> Conversing with the Mem'ry of thy Charms;
> Repeating all thy matchless Beauties o'er,
> Fanning the Flames that rag'd too high before.
> This is a Picture of a Love refin'd,
> Drawn from the noble Passion of my Mind.

Full of divine Hillarius, *and killing Jealousy.*

Oh divine *Hillarius,* what Ages of Pain have I suffered since I last saw you! The Fear of losing you has made me poor, old, and miserable. I cannot look forward to any Happiness without you, who are the End and Business of all my Desires.

Could I be so mean to imagine there could be Transport on Earth, but in your Bosom, I should hate my Dullness; rather let me still possess my discerning Misery, which is just to your Beauties, and knows you are the Master of all Perfection, the most perfect Resemblance of Heaven; your Wisdom, your Sweetness, your Modesty, your Loveliness, (oh! would to God I could say your Truth!) all convince me there is nothing but *Hillarius*.

The World cannot give me another Blessing, nor Heav'n itself make me happy without this; never will I descend from your Brightness to dull Mortality, but preserve amidst all the Agonies of Disappointments and Absence, the Memory of the adored *Hillarius*.

To live and die yours will be the only Pride of my Soul, which I will bear with me after Death. My Bosom is so sweetly inflamed, the Grave cannot chill its Passion; I shall even there languish for my adored *Hillarius*, my Heart cannot part with his sweet Image.

> Oh! to adore thee but a few short Years,
> To my unbounded Flame too mean appears.
> To all Eternity I must be thine,
> Nor Death shall interrupt my grand Design.
> Let the World languish, and its Sun expire,
> The Moon dissolve in Tears, and Stars retire,
> Still shall my Soul retain its more immortal Fire.

FRIDAY EVENING,
Heaven bless it for giving me adored Hillarius.

> Sweet Inchanter of my Thought,
> Hear the Wonders thou hast wrought;
> Hear thy godlike Power confest,
> And see thy Triumphs in my Breast.
> Gay and light and unconfin'd
> Were once the wishes of my Mind;
> No real Passion it sustain'd,
> Not truly pleas'd, nor truly pain'd;
> My airy Muse, like me, was wild,
> And there she sung, and here she smil'd.
> To Love and Tenderness unknown,
> Thy Eyes converted has alone,
> And to my Soul a Softness gave,
> Which made, and keeps it still thy Slave.
> No other Flame it entertains,
> No other Name adorns my Strains.
> My Songs, my Life, my Soul, my Arms,
> Are all devoted to thy Charms.
> In my Blood thy Beauty reigns,
> *Hillarius* beats in all my Veins.

A SONG

From the low World my Heart retires
To talk to its own fond Desires,
Unheeding what is said or done,
Musick, and Mirth, and Wit I shun;
And whatsoe'er the Subject be
That others choose, I speak of thee.
My Lips turn pale with angry Shame,
If they are forc'd from thy dear Name;
Charm'd with the Sound, I cannot part
With the sweet Letters, for my Heart.
By Love I swear, I love thee so,
That I could Flattery forgo.
For I'm so nobly and so wholly thine,
Thy Praise is sweeter to my Ear than mine.
if wisely any Tongue would flatter me,
Let it address my Soul with praising thee.

To my Heaven, Hillarius.

Let my warm Heart its heav'nly Charmer bless,
And pour out something of its Love's Excess.
Fed by thy Beauty's everlasting Flow,
My deathless Fondness can no Ebbing know.
Could I express what now I feel for thee,
'Twere like a Drop from the high-swelling Sea.
A thousand soft Desires would fill its Place,
One Touch of thine, or Look from that dear Face;
One soft Embrace from all that I adore,
Would swell my Soul and makes its Tide run o'er.

To the Godlike Hillarius.

My Life is treasur'd in thy Eyes,
And absent from thee *Clio* dies,
No Joy then visits my sad Heart,
There Mem'ry racks with cruel Art,
And all thy Beauties I survey,
And sigh my very Soul away.
What tender Wishes fill my Breast,
Which sweetly steal away my Rest!
But, oh! thy very Shadow grows
Dearer to me than all Repose;
And Misery which flows from thee,
Or, even Death would lovely be.
For oh! a noble Pride I take
In being wretched for thy Sake.

A SONG

Thou art all Heaven to my Thought,
And cannot be too dearly bought.

*On the Fear of losing all that is lovely
and dear to me.*

Let me employ each Love-devoted Leaf
To sacred Passion, or approaching Grief,
Say sable Shades where folds your shadowy Wings,
That I may dip my Pen while Sorrow sings.
No joyous Hours my sad Reflection wrong,
No impious Mirth prophane my solemn Song;
Of Love and painful Absence let me speak,
Broken my Voice, and pale my dying Cheek;
My Hair to every furious Wind unbound,
Mourning for thee, and scatter'd on the Ground.
No more let my proud Hand its Beauties bless,
Let it thy Absence and my Flame confess.
The Locks once honour'd by thy sacred Care,
No mean Design, no common Praise can bear.
Nor shall my Fingers condescend to play,
When my Soul's heav'nly Mover is away;
Or if they do, thy Absence they shall mourn,
And pierce the Hearers with my deep Concern;
Their corresponding Tears with mine shall flow,
And sacrifice to thee obedient Woe.
My Friends, my Lyre, thy Empire shall confess,
And all Things weep with *Clio*'s Tenderness.
The God of Love shall to his Favourite tell
None ever lov'd so long, none lov'd so well;
Of all my Words he shall Accountant be,
And pierce my Soul again, when it loves ought but thee.
If e'er my Eyes, or Lips, or Hands impart
Any kind Message from my faithful Heart,
May I, oh! dreadful Wish, thy Passion lose,
And angry Heav'n my parting Breath refuse.

To my overflowing Heart.

Poor Bankrupt Heart, canst thou do nothing more,
To shew thy Flame, than others have before?
When mine, be Witness Heaven, is greater far
Than any past, or all the present are;
So fierce, so lasting, and so tender too,
No History can show, no Lover knew.
For sure no Lover e'er could charm like thee,

And none was ever charm'd so much as me.
Oh! can I, but with dying Eyes, confess
When thou art near, my mighty Tenderness!
Can I but tremble at thy sacred Feet,
And fault'ring cry, oh! heav'nly, dear and sweet;
While Extacies too high to be exprest
Charm ev'ry Sense, and labour in my Breast.
Why has my Eyes no Language to impart
The soft Desires of my imploring Heart?
Why has my Lips no Eloquence to move,
Why dumb and pale when they should plead for Love?
There, lovely charmers, all the Roses keep,
And sure they bloom the more, the more I weep,
And would in all their native Colour lie,
Tho' Death should still my Voice and close my Eye.
For oh! they know not that I love so well,
How should they know, what I can never tell?
Charm'd with the Sweets of ev'ry heav'nly Touch,
I can but fainting say, I love too much.
Oh God! from whence this deathless Passion sprung,
Give soft Perswasion to my trembling Tongue;
On ev'ry Feature Eloquence bestow,
Let my Eyes sparkle with my Passion's Glow.
Let ev'ry tender Thought be there exprest,
And dart itself into his lovely Breast,
Till all its cruel Coldness it resign,
And burns, and loves, and languishes like mine.
Let me for Love, sweet Heav'n, do something more,
Than ever any Mortal did before.

To the all-lovely Hillarius.

Oh! let the Fulness of this Book impart
A little Emblem of my crowded Heart;
Where thy immortal Beauties press as near,
As Love has plac'd the tender Letters here,
'Tis all writ o'er by thy transporting Eyes,
No Blank appears, all full of thee it lies.
There is no Room for any other Name,
Nobly employ'd in one superior Flame.

To the all-conquering Hillarius.

All Time, my Adorable, appears lost but this, divinely employed on my Love. I should be more than blest could I paint its Beauties to you; then should I hear those heav'nly Lips confess, none knows of Love but *Clio*, whose Passion grows every Hour more immortal. I can think of nothing but the inchanting *Hillarius;* all my Senses are yours, and my Life itself only of your allowing. Would it were happy enough to bless you! would it were passed with you, my Angel, and I should ask no other Heaven! how should I be eternally adoring you to my last Moment! Oh I am more than assured by Love himself, that if any thing could increase my Passion, it would be to be always with you; there is a Million of your Beauties not discerned at this Distance; yet I see enough to inslave me for ever, to keep my Soul in perpetual Adoration.

> Be witness ye sad Hours that creep along,
> That hear my beating Heart, and tender Song,
> If any but his ever-sacred Name,
> Can give my Muse or Love-sick Measures Flame;
> If any little Conquest I have wrought
> Ever returns to my innobled Thought.
> My Life I only date from that sweet Hour,
> When I gave up its Freedom to thy Pow'r.

> *To the inhuman World.*

> Oh! cruel World, what Sacrifice I make,
> When I resign all Treasure for thy Sake?
> When to thy dull Demands my Soul I give,
> And that dear Breast, in which my Wishes live?
> Will ye not, in Return, my World resign,
> And let my Charmer be entirely mine?
> Ungentle Business, let us make a Truce;
> Oh! break not on my Joys with an Excuse!
> Call not *Hillarius* from my longing Breast!
> Of human Kind I yield thee all the rest;
> The Warrior and the Statesman take to thee,
> But leave the Conqueror of Hearts to me.
> The God of Love will soft Employment find,
> And these fond Arms shall the sweet Pris'ner bind.
> Ah! set him once from thy hard Fetters free,
> And Love will leave no Time to think of thee.

> *On the sad Thought of Parting.*

> Scarce can my Soul the killing Fear sustain,
>   Of the sad Death its Joys must quickly die,
> The Days and Nights of never-ceasing Pain,
>   When absent from thy Life-inspiring Eye,
> When smiling Hope which soft Relief bestows,
> Will leave me to the Deluge of my Woes.

A SONG

Methinks I feel like the lost lavish Heir,
    Who sees the last of his declining Store,
And ev'ry Morning wakes to new Despair,
    And starts at the sad Thought of being poor.
But ah! the Simile is far below
The noble Misery I undergoe.

To some new Scene the Bankrupt may remove,
    And court again the Favour of his Fate,
But all my Treasure is in tender Love,
    Spring of my Life, and my Soul's sole Estate,
Without thee I should languish on a Throne,
And, crowded by the World, be still alone.

Oh sweet Companion! finish'd to my Mind,
    Ev'ry Perfection in thy Person shines,
Wise as a God, as melting Mercy kind,
    Sweet in thy Looks, transporting in thy Lines.
Oh! Soul of Beauty, Nature wond'ring stands
At her great Work, and blesses her own Hands.

Happy for me if I had ne'er survey'd
    The fatal Treasurer of all her Charms,
Insensible this bosom might have laid,
    Dully contented in cold lawful Arms,
Nor dream'd, encharm'd by those dear Eyes of thine,
Of heav'nly Riches that can ne'er be mine.

The happy Villager contented seems,
    To all the fine Desires of Life unknown,
He unrepining drinks the cooling Streams,
    Talks to the Groves, nor knows he is alone.
But thou, alas! are Nectar to my Heart,
And I must sink in Death, whene'er we part.

To my adorable Hillarius.

See how the hasty Paper slides away,
And yet my Soul has ev'ry thing to say,
Full of thy flowing Beauties I remain,
And strive to breathe my soft Desires in vain;
Still some new Charm breaks in upon my Mind,
And stops the tender Closure I design'd.
    What way shall I escape thy Excellence;
Oh! lovely Conqueror of ev'ry Sense!
Blindness itself would be a weak Defence.

A SONG

'T wou'd leave my Hearing to attend thee more,
And show some Grace I had not found before
In thy dear Voice, whence ev'ry Sweetness flows,
And gently steals away the Soul's Repose.
How have I blest the ever-charming Sound!
How have I list'ned till my Feet were bound!
How have I wonder'd at the Moments flight,
And unperceiv'd lost half the flying Night!
Ev'ry sweet Accent with such Pow'r is fraught,
That it pours Heaven itself upon the Thought.
We die away, but know not by what Grace,
If by the Voice, or Shape, or killing Face;
To what Perfection are thy Features form'd!
With what angelic Glow their Sweetness warm'd!
The sparkling Soul, whose Lustre I adore,
Breaking like new-born Day thro' ev'ry Pore.
When to the Earth thy lovely Eyes are bent,
Their Brightness veil'd with tender Discontent,
How soft their Langour, how divinely sweet,
When my Tears pour themselves before thy Feet!
When some kind Fear by tender Passion wrought,
Folds thy dear Arms, and dashes o'er thy Thought,
Who can the Beauties of thy Fondness paint,
Thy lovely Sadness, and thy dear Complaint.
The Lute is not with Half thy Softness crown'd,
When it awakes the sleeping Ecchoes round,
The bubbling Springs that lull the love-sick Swain,
May learn of thee new Music to complain.
Ev'n Grief is hush'd by gazing on thy Eye,
And furious Anger all enamour'd dies.
While I behold thee, I forget to grieve,
Nor my approaching Misery perceive.
All I have suffer'd, all I must sustain,
Clasp'd in thy Arms, attack my Breast in vain.
But oh! when from these Transports I descend,
How many Deaths will the vast Fall attend!
When from the Summer of thy Sight I part
What Floods of Grief will break upon my Heart!
Pale Fear presents them to my trembling View,
What, my sweet parting Treasure, shall I do?
Thy Resolution on my Griefs bestow,
While I implore thee, they outrageous grow.
Oh my best Life, while Love and Time allows,
Confirm my Soul with thy inspiring Vows;
Such heav'nly Comfort to my Wishes give,

That I the Pangs of Parting may outlive;
Say, nothing shall thy Tenderness remove,
Thy well establish'd, thy increasing Love.
To godlike Truth the softest Flattery join,
And swear thou wilt beyond the Grave be mine;
Then let a Tear these sweet Expressions seal:
Balm to my Mind, how thou can'st pain or heal?
Now force me from thy Bosom, for I know,
Nor Love, nor Life, will suffer me to go.
Part with my Eyes after this last Embrace,
Their Strings are fasten'd to thy lovely Face,
Oh quick my pale and dying Lips resign,
Or my charm'd Soul will breath itself to thine.
See how my struggling Arms inchain thee fast?
Can Life these bitter Agonies outlast!
Oh! no, I feel the brittle Blast decline;
Now, cruel Duty, this cold Clay is thine.

I have faintly essayed, oh divine *Hillarius,* to paint the Pangs of Parting; but sure it is impossible; even the Fear of it cannot be expressed, how terrible then must be the Reality! Oh shade me from these Thoughts which oppress me to Death. How happy are you, adored *Hillarius,* whose Business defends you from them, or whose Mind refuses these tender Impressions! I see it does, I remark your Easiness, and know you can live in Absence; it is possible you can be happy, even in the long Absence of Death. When I recall my everlasting Disappointments, I am more than sure of this, and would, if possible, restrain the Fondness of my Soul; but too, too late, it has overflowed in this little Book, and must do so till Death; all my Passions flow down this immortal Stream, and bear even Life along with them.

Adieu *Hillarius,* lovely, sweet and wise,
Take this fond Off'ring of my flowing Eyes,
And read with Rev'rence what my Soul has writ,
Where Love and Truth attones the Loss of Wit.
Above its little Flashes I became,
I nobly trusted to my ardent Flame,
And courted thy sweet Wishes more than Fame.
With ease I could have charm'd the Reader's Ear,
But was not dull enough to study here.
Let the unwounded, and the Heart at rest,
Seek vain Applause, but I am too unblest.
When my ador'd *Hillarius* is unkind,
Let not the Bay, but mournful Cypress bind,

A SONG

To Mirth and rosy Chaplets ah! Farewel,
No more I will aspire, no more excell,
The Pains of Absence I will only tell.
When my poor Muse and I together mourn,
And move the God of Midnight with Concern,
Do thou *Hillarius* from thy Friends depart,
And read the Anguish of my breaking Heart.
If Sickness should arrest my tender Lays,
Do thou imagine all my Passion says,
Let thy kind Fancy bear thee to my Bed,
To charm my Pulse, or bind my burning Head.
Our meeting Souls will some soft Way contrive
To keep the Fervour of our Flames alive.
But I forget, alas! thou art unkind,
Let Death and Cypress my cold Temples bind.
   Love is a Vapour quickly disappears,
And leaves the Soul in Solitude and Tears;
To the cold Tomb it leads the short-liv'd Days,
Consumes the Life, and on the Spirit preys.
Oh, faithless Guide, I perish by thy Hand,
My Glass now drops the last remaining Sand;
The God of Love now swims before my Eyes,
And in my Breast his Dart all broken lies.

   My Last Will. To the immortal Hillarius.

If she can dye, made glorious by thy Praise,
Hear what her Heart in Death's cold Ague says.
Thy Image on her tender Mem'ry glows,
And in the Shade of Death a Warmth bestows.
Oh! dearer to me than the Life that stays,
To yield thee, sweet Executor, my Lays,
My Soul will not retire till it has given
Itself once more to thee; thou sure art Heav'n;
Or wilt preserve for it that happy Place,
And make it worthy of its God's Embrace.
A thousand noble Ways you may improve,
But cannot add to its immortal Love.
To thy sweet Memory my Joys I give,
The tender Hours when I did more than live.
Let them not from thy gentle Mem'ry go,
By other Objects, or Time's restless flow,
My Sighs and Tears now for thy Sorrow keep,
Sigh o'er my Sighs, let thy own calmly sleep;
For oh! I love so well, I would not be
Rais'd to new Life, with any Pain to thee.

Oh! if you sorrow, let it not be much,
Pain not my Ashes, which thy Tears would touch,
Nor hasten to me, let my Passion wait,
No Hour at Death's cold Mansion is too late.
When Age has gazed thy shining Beauties o'er,
And ravish'd some from the luxuriant Store,
Then let it give thee to my faithful Arms,
And bless my Grave with thy remaining Charms.
Till then let Heav'n my lovely Lover bless,
Health to his Mind and more than wish'd Success;
Such Friends, whose Services and Love may be
Enough to recompence the Loss of me.
But lest this heav'nly Cordial may decline,
Let me present thy Soul with one of mine;
Next to thyself most noble and sincere,
The second Jewel in my Journey here.
Oh! let me recommend him to thy Care,
To soften Pains, and make Misfortunes fair.
Can I a nobler Character impart?
Oh place this Blessing in thy godlike Heart!
He knew my Passion, and he sweetly knew
To keep its Brightness, yet to sooth it too;
His Youth and undesigning Breast defend,
And wear to Death itself this valued Friend.
No more, what have I else intitled mine,
My Life, my Soul, my Muse, my Friend, are thine.
To thee I make my only Treasures o'er,
Yet if you grieve, am richer than before.

FINIS.

Explanatory Notes

Works frequently cited have been identified by the following abbreviations:

Clio and Strephon	Fowke, Martha, and William Bond. *The Epistles of Clio and Strephon, being a Collection of Letters.* . . . London: Printed for J. Hooke, F. Gyles, and W. Boreham, 1720.
DNB	*Dictionary of National Biography.*
Highfill	Highfill, Philip H., Jr., Kalman A. Burnim, and Edward A. Langhans. *A Biographical Dictionary of Actors, Actresses, Musicians, Dancers, Managers, and Other Stage Personnel in London, 1660–1800.* Carbondale and Edwardsville: Southern Illinois University Press, 1982.
HMC	*Historical Manuscripts Commission.*
London Stage	*The London Stage, 1660–1800. Part 2, 1700–1729.* Ed. E. L. Avery. 2 vols. Carbondale: Southern Illinois University Press, 1960–68.
Lonsdale	*Eighteenth-Century Women Poets*, ed. Roger Lonsdale. Oxford and New York: Oxford University Press, 1989.
Miscellany	Anthony Hammond, ed. *A New Miscellany of Original Poems, Translations, and Imitations.* London: Printed for T. Jauncey at the Angel, without Temple Bar, 1720.
OED	*Oxford English Dictionary.*
VCH	*Victoria County Histories.*

55 **Clio:** Martha Fowke's poetic name, first used in *Clio and Strephon,* was probably chosen to link her to the famous Greek woman poet Sappho; Clio was supposed to be Sappho's daughter (Edward Phillips, *Theatrum Poetarum* [London, 1675], cited in Germaine Greer et al., eds., *Kissing the Rod: An Anthology of Seventeenth-Century Women's Verse* [London: Virago, 1988], 265). The poetic self-portrait of Fowke is earlier than her autobiography; it was first printed in *A New Miscellany,* ed. Anthony Hammond (London, 1720). The version in *Clio* differs significantly, suggesting that the *Miscellany* version might have been edited. The Hammond text was reprinted in *Clio and Strephon: being the Second and Last Part of The Platonic Lovers* (London: Printed for E. Curll, 1732). The poem may have been inserted in *Clio,* either by Fowke herself or by Hill or by the publisher, as a substitute for the customary frontispiece portrait. It

has been partially reprinted in Lonsdale, 86–87. Although Fowke's poem ends by inviting Hammond to draw her picture, she actually preempts him, presenting her own image artfully controlled. A similar self-presentation, "To Strephon," figures in *Clio and Strephon,* 1–4.

55 **Line 1—Hamond:** Anthony Hammond (1668–1738), politician and man of letters, edited and was the major contributor to *A New Miscellany* (London, 1720), in which this poem was first printed, together with several other poems by Fowke. Hammond may have met Thomas Fowke, Martha's brother, while Hammond was deputy paymaster of the British forces in Spain; he noted in an account book for 1713 that he spent "the greatest part of the year in Minorca" (Bodleian MSS Rawl D1207). Thomas jr. was serving with the British Army there. A poem by Thomas Fowke to Hammond, dated circa 1714 from Minorca, is in *Miscellany,* 119–20. In a prose letter to "Strephon" (William Bond) Martha Fowke notes that her brother was "a fine Person with fine Sense, and the greatest good Nature" (*Clio and Strephon,* 76). Thomas jr. prospered, becoming Governor of Gibraltar, until an unfortunate misinterpretation of orders led to his being cashiered in 1756.

55 **Lines 4–5—Lawrels . . . bays:** The bay or laurel (*Laurus nobilis*) was in classical times a symbol of poetic achievement. Here Fowke seems to associate the laurel with military success while the bays are associated with poetry. The *Miscellany* text reads "let the sweet bays . . . ," probably an editorial change to avoid repetition of "Oh."

55 **Line 10—olive:** Eliza Haywood's savage attack in *Memoirs of a Certain Island* (London, 1725), reprinted in appendix B, describes "Gloatitia" (Fowke) as a "big-bon'd, buxom, brown Woman"; Fowke's father was also dark, as were most of the Fowkes of Gunston, according to the testimony of their cousin Gerard Fowke in his manuscript genealogy (Bodleian MS Rawl B130). The "s" after the apostrophe seems to have dropped out.

55 **Line 14—Poetry's:** *Miscellany* reads less colloquially, "*Poesie* is called": the rhyme "Mind/join'd" reflects a common early-eighteenth-century pronunciation.

55 **Line 19:** *Miscellany* text reads "no Wound they made."

55 **Line 20:** *Miscellany* gives "circling" for "arching."

55 **Line 24—the faithful lover:** *Miscellany* gives "her faithful lover," possibly referring to "art"; alternatively an editorial slip.

55 **Lines 27–28—little Cause for smiling:** Fowke's father was murdered by one of his servants in 1708; see the introduction. Martha's mother had died a few years before her husband. At the time this poem was written Martha's brother had been away on military service for at least seven years (*Clio and Strephon,* 85). "Friends" was often used for relations. The death of Fowke's father before she was twenty was extremely traumatic for her; she discusses her reaction later in her autobiography, and the

murder is also noted in a footnote to the reprint of this poem in *Clio and Strephon: being the Second and Last Part of The Platonic Lovers* (London: Printed for E. Curll, 1732).

55 **Line 35—Ducela:** *Miscellany* gives "Bucelia"; Lonsdale's annotation suggest a playful personification of "buckle."

55 **Line 39—when Dress and I are Friends:** Fowke is contrasting her informal attire and long loose hair, with the formal dress and hairstyle required for social appearances. Early-eighteenth-century women generally dressed elaborately for dinner in the early afternoon.

55 **Lines 40–41:** *Miscellany* has "darling white." Fowke's handkerchief of fine thin linen (lawn) suggests both modesty and lack of pretension.

56 **Lines 44–45:** Fowke disclaims any particular visual beauty for her hands but claims they captivate the listener's ear when she plays the harpsichord. Fowke's interest in music, noted frequently in her autobiography, may have been one of the bonds that linked her to Hill, himself an appreciative connoisseur who had written librettos for Handel among others. *Miscellany* reads "speaking Cord," but "tender" is a favorite word of Fowke's.

56 **Line 49—not a German:** Corsets of the German fashion had been introduced by the ladies of the Hanoverian court who accompanied George I to Britain. Lady Cowper's diary records a comment by the Countess of Buckenburgh: "Foreigners hold up their Heads and hold out their Breasts, and make themselves as great and stately as they can." Lady Deloraine made the tart rejoinder: "We show our Quality by our Birth and Titles, Madam, and not by sticking out our Bosoms" (*The Diary of Mary, Countess Cowper, Lady of the Bedchamber to the Princess of Wales, 1714–1720* [London: John Murray, 1864], 102). *Miscellany* replaces these lines with a less personal couplet that describes her tears: "Again they press to wrong this artless Draught, / Brib'd by my Fate to ruin every Thought."

56 **Line 51—Isaac:** Mr. Isaac, choreographer and dancing master (fl.1631?–1716), taught Queen Anne and was acknowledged the "Prime Master in England for 40 years together" (Highfill). *Miscellany* gives the incorrect "Isiah." Fowke had the "best masters" for both music and dancing; see *Clio,* 000.

58 **Hillarius:** Poetic version of Aaron Hill's name. For Hill, see the introduction.

58 **tender letters:** Some of Hill's letters to Fowke can be identified from internal evidence; they were published in Hill's *Works* and *Dramatic Works* and are reprinted in appendix A.

58 **Julius:** Julius Caesar was a favorite historical character for Hill, who wrote an unpublished tragedy on the subject, and even named his only son Julius Caesar. It seems likely that Fowke and Hill first met at a performance of Shakespeare's *Julius Caesar* around 1721 (see appendix A).

60	**my Grandfather:** Thomas Fowke, Martha's father, was the fourth son of John and Joyce Fowke of Gunston, Staffordshire. The extended family was large; John's father, Roger, had nineteen children. See the extensive manuscript genealogy by Gerard Fowke c. 1677 (Bodleian Library, MS Rawl B130). The family derived their ancestry from the Normans and was moderately prosperous, although suffering in the Civil War which divided the family (see Staffordshire Visitation, *Harleian Society,* ser. lxii, 95; *VCH Staffordshire,* 5:32; Burke's *Peerage* [1949], 789). Family connections of Thomas Fowke linked him with an extensive network of gentry, lawyers, merchants, and divines in England, Ireland, and America.
60	**Revolution . . . his Royal Master:** After James II was forced to leave the throne in the Glorious Revolution of 1688, Thomas Fowke resigned his army command rather than swear allegiance to the new sovereigns, William and Mary, although he later conformed in order to return to the army.
60	**my mother had a good Jointure:** Martha's mother, Mary Chandler (née Cullen or Culling?), married Thomas Fowke in London on 4 July 1688 (Foster, Joseph, ed., *London Marriage Licenses, 1521–1869* [London, 1887]). They were both aged 30. She was the widow of Mr. Chandler, a wealthy merchant, noted by Gregory King some years earlier as resident at Apsley Hall, Somerford, Staffordshire, in the immediate neighborhood of the Fowke estate at Gunston (Staffordshire Record Society, *Collections for a History of Staffordshire* [1919], 240–41). Her widow's jointure (her settled estate from her previous marriage) was presumably linked to this part of the country, close to Martha's paternal family.
62	**duke of Marlborough:** John Churchill, Duke of Marlborough (1650–1722), politican and general. Fowke's father would have presumably come in contact with him through his military service. Marlborough's avarice and lack of generosity were common Tory accusations.
62	**the King:** Charles II.
62	**Grandfather:** Thomas Fowke's maternal grandfather was Richard Marche, whose daughter and heir, Joyce, married John Fowke, eldest son of Roger Fowke of Gunston, Staffordshire. Richard Marche was gentleman usher at the courts of Charles I and II, and was store-keeper at the Tower. His estates of 460 pounds per annum were settled on the second, third, and fifth sons of John and Joyce Fowke, omitting Thomas, the fourth son, possibly because he was considered as well-established financially by his marriage. John Fowke may have taken over his father-in-law's position at the Tower, or Fowke is confused. John Fowke, who went to Oxford and was entered at the Inner Temple as a lawyer, died before 1677.
62	**Widow of Sir Antony Vincent:** Anne, eldest daughter of Sir James Austen, and widow of Sir Anthony Vincent, married Thomas Fowke in 1677. Income from her widow's jointure would cease upon her death.
62	**Daughter of Col Codrington:** Colonel Christopher Codrington was captain general of the Leeward Islands. On his death circa 1697 he was succeeded

EXPLANATORY NOTES TO PAGES 63–64   153

in the post by his son Christopher (1668–1710), who was a friend of Steele. The younger Codrington bequeathed his estate to found a college in Barbados and to endow the Codrington Library, All Souls, Oxford.

63 **born the 1st of May:** Hill wrote several poems to Fowke celebrating her birthday; see appendix A. Fowke is somewhat disingenuous here about her date of birth, which was hardly "some years" after the Revolution of 1688. According to the registers in Hertfordshire Record Office, she was baptized on 12 May 1689; her epitaph records her birth as 1690 (see *Gentleman's Magazine* 51 [1782]:22).

63 **Fondness he wanted:** Fondness that he lacked.

63 **we were both born in Hertfordshire:** Thomas Fowke was baptized at Hertingfordbury on 30 April 1690. The estate of Hertingfordbury had been sold by Thomas Keightley, of a Staffordshire family connected in some way to the Fowkes, to John Culling (Cullen) of London, Fowke's uncle, who built a very fair house there, according to Chauncy's *History of Hertfordshire*. Culling married Martha Perle, by whom he had a son John and a daughter Elizabeth; he died in 1687, leaving John his heir under age. After John's death around 1702/3, the estate came to Elizabeth. She features in Manley's scandal-romance *The New Atalantis* (London, 1709), 1:214–29, 231–33; 235–36), as "Louisa," who was enticed into a fake "polygamous" marriage by William, 1st Earl Cowper, bore two children, and died in November 1703. Elizabeth's heirs sold the estate to Spencer Cowper Esq., and the house was pulled down in 1810 (John Edwin Cussans, *History of Hertfordshire* [London, 1870–1881], 2:104). The original owner of the estate, Thomas Keightley, turns up later in Fowke's life as one of her professed admirers.

63 **branches:** chandeliers.

64 **my Mother became a Catholick:** There were a large number of Catholics in the small town of Brewood near the Fowke family home of Gunston because the important local family of Giffard was Catholic (see *VCH Staffordshire,* 5:44). The Fowler family also had a Catholic family chapel at St. Thomas, outside Stafford. Fowke's own Catholic faith seems to have been superficial; her evaluation of herself as not "naturally devout" is comparatively frank for an eighteenth-century woman. Later in her life she speaks of going to the Anglican church, not a Catholic chapel.

64 **breed me a Catholick:** Bring me up in the Catholic faith.

64 **a Closet finely furnished with the best Authors:** The small room or closet attached to a bedroom was often used as a study or private library.

64 **Cassandra and Cleopatra:** La Calprenède's *Cassandre* (1642) was translated into English in 1652; his *Cleopâtre* (1648) was translated 1654. Orondate was the hero of *Cassandra*. The popularity of these romances especially in royalist circles in the second half of the seventeenth century is discussed by Hubert McDermott in *Novel and Romance: The Odyssey*

to Tom Jones (Totowa, N.J.: Barnes & Noble, 1989), 111–31. Among the last bequests of Charles I before his execution was his copy of *Cassandra*.

65 **an inclination to Latin:** Sharing a brother's tutor was one of the few ways in which a woman could gain access to instruction in Latin.

65 **Hugonots:** Huguenots were French Protestants, many of whom fled after the Edict of Nantes (1685) ended religious toleration in France.

65 **such a kind of hand, as this:** Writing was generally taught late in education, if at all for women and the lower classes. Fowke is clearly conscious of the visual appearance of the manuscript she is writing, and the reaction of her reader, Hill.

65 **Cowley and Ovid:** Translations of Ovid's *Heroic Epistles* appeared in Tonson's edition of 1680, primarily the work of Dryden. Abraham Cowley's collection of love poetry, *The Mistress* (1647), went into a number of editions well into the eighteenth century, as did his collected *Works* of 1668.

65 **Miss Patty:** A common nickname for Martha.

65 **my work:** Needlework.

65 **Father Confessor:** Possibly Father Philip Philmot or Philmott, S.J., born in Staffordshire c. 1650s, ordained in 1683, and resident at the College of St. Chad in Staffordshire from 1696 to 1702. He then moved to London and may have gone underground. He died in 1725. See Geoffrey Holt, S.J., *The English Jesuits, 1650–1829: A Biographical Dictionary* (London: Catholic Record Society, 1984), 193–94.

66 **Of the Order of *Jesu*:** A Jesuit.

66 **Pallmall:** Fashionable street near St. James's Palace.

66 **wrote Verses for my brother against his Breakings-up:** Not traced.

67 **Mr. B——:** Unidentified Huguenot landlord of the Fowke family. Note that the sharing of beds by young people of the same sex was common at this period.

67 **the immortal Lewis:** Louis XIV, King of France, responsible for the expulsion of the French Protestants, died in 1715. He is not usually described so positively in English writings at this time, and this may indicate Fowke's political leanings toward Jacobitism.

67 **Albemarle street:** In Mayfair, to the west of Old Bond Street and just north of Piccadilly and St. James, part of a newly built and fashionable area.

67 **A relation of our's:** Possibly her cousin, John Cullen, of Hertingfordbury, who died young in 1702/3; he would have known her from her cradle.

69	**Oronooko, my Favourite:** *Oroonoko, or the Royal Slave,* the 1688 romance by Aphra Behn adapted to the stage by Thomas Southerne in 1695, was revived on 7 July 1702, and was particularly popular in 1703 and 1704, with five Drury Lane performances each year (*London Stage*). Behn's description of Oroonoko in the original may suggest his appeal to Fowke: he possesses "that real greatness of soul, those refined notions of true honour, that absolute generosity, and that softness that was capable of the highest passions of love and gallantry . . . the most illustrious could not have produced a braver man, both for greatness of courage and mind, a judgement more solid, a wit more quick, and a conversation more sweet and diverting." Cited McDermott, *Novel and Romance,* 128–29.
69	**we provided a mask:** Women often wore masks to conceal their identities in public gatherings, and they were commonly worn by prostitutes. For a young girl to appear masked and with no female chaperone was a scandalous violation of propriety. In 1704 Queen Anne ordered that no woman was to presume to wear a vizard mask in either of the theaters (David Green, *Queen Anne* [New York: Scribner's, 1970], 125).
69	**much too nice:** Too scrupulous.
69	**Arlington-street:** A fashionable street parallel to the west of the upper part of St. James's Street; the chapel was probably that of the Envoy of the Catholic Duke of Savoy, who is noted in the Westminster ratebooks for 1710 as resident in Arlington Street. Alternatively, the existence of a Catholic chapel at "My Lord Stafford's House" was noted in 1712 by an informer; see T. G. Holt, "The Embassy Chapels in Eighteenth-Century London," *The London Recusant* 2 (1972): 19. Martha Fowke was visiting Lord Stafford in the country some years later when she wrote her letters in *Clio and Strephon.*
69	**her chair:** Sedan chair.
70	**a Nobleman's Daughter of *Ireland*:** The Fowkes had a number of family connections in Ireland. Her grandfather's brother, a lawyer, moved to Ireland, and had twenty children. Possibly Miss Bellenden is referred to here; see note following.
70	**Sir C—— B——l——n's son:** Probably a cadet branch of the Bellendens. The first Lord Bellenden had received a peerage as a reward for his adherence to the royalist cause, and the second Lord Bellenden married a daughter of Henry Moore, Earl of Drogheda, who was connected to the Fowke family. Lord Bellenden died in 1707. His daughter, Miss Bellenden, was a noted beauty and Maid of Honour, and may be the "nobleman's daughter" mentioned above.
72	**to offer himself:** To suggest himself as a potential husband.
73	**to settle some fortune on me:** Although Mrs. Fowke's jointure would have ceased on her death, she presumably had some additional money now left to her husband. Martha Fowke apparently had enough money settled on her to live comparatively independently even after her father's death.

73	**till my Mourning was out:**	Mourning for a parent involved wearing only black for the first six months, and black, white, or grey for the second six months.
73	**Devonshire-Street:**	Part of a newly built residential area north of High Holborn.
73	**cabinet:**	A case, or small piece of furniture, for the safe custody of jewels or other valuables.
73	**Cousin-German:**	Child of one's uncle or aunt; cousin was used more generally for a range of relationships.
73	**in fine:**	To summarize.
73	**old Gentleman:**	He was then about forty-eight.
74	**a Niece of his own:**	A relation on the Fowke side of the family. This may possibly be the cousin some years older than Martha, the daughter of her aunt Dorothy and Thomas Wroth, a lawyer, who was probably named after her grandmother Joyce. Alternatively she might be Mary Walker, the only child of a rich clergyman. Her mother Sarah, Thomas's sister, had died before 1677, suggesting that her grandmother might have brought her up. However, since Thomas Fowke had nine siblings, there are other candidates.
74	**Spring-Garden:**	A pleasure ground between Whitehall and the Thames, praised for "the solemness of the grove, the warbling of the birds" (*Character of England* [1659], cited in Antony Hamilton, *Memoirs of Count Grammont,* ed. Sir Walter Scott [London, 1889], 2: 132–33).
74	**my cousin's closet:**	It is interesting that Martha's grandmother Joyce Fowke bequeathed her personal library to her granddaughter, Martha's cousin, rather than to her male heirs.
74	**Physician to my Mother. . . . The Physician's Friend:**	Unidentified.
75	**his Family, and Education, but mean:**	Fowke is strongly aware of the class differential between herself and this young merchant of comparatively low social status. Haywood in her attack on Fowke in *Memoirs of a Certain Island* calls him "a young Mechanick," that is, a menial tradesman.
75	**Windsor, and Hampton-Court:**	These royal palaces several miles to the west of London were already tourist attractions, easily accessible by boat on the river Thames.
75	**a Nephew of his own:**	A Fowke cousin of Martha's. Like many of the Fowke family, he was probably involved in merchant enterprises, either in the Turkey or Virginia trades.
76	**would have been more sensible:**	"sensible" has the obsolete meaning of causing intense painful, or pleasurable, emotion.

76	**an old Governess:** The offical governesses of the Princesses Mary and Anne, daughters of King James, were Lady Frances Villiers, wife of Colonel Edward Villiers, and, after her death, Lady Clarendon. However, this governess is likely to have been of lower standing and an actual instructor. The princesses' education was minimal, covering basically reading and writing; special tutors were employed for French, music and dancing, as with Martha Fowke.
77	**I wrote my Complaints on all the Windows:** Inscribing verses on window glass with a diamond was a common practice at the period.
77	**Miss H——d:** Possibly a daughter of Anthony Hammond.
77	**Trafficker:** Trader or merchant, but with negative implications.
77	**Hyde-Park:** The royal park northwest of St. James's Palace.
77	**How was I pleas'd to find myself at Liberty:** A manuscript note in W. Musgrave's copy of *Clio* in the British Library (1418.c.51) dates this as 1706.
78	**He fail'd three Times:** Went bankrupt.
78	**Cousin-German. . . . peevish Beauty:** Unidentified. The episode of the elopement, however, indicates the social and moral attitudes of the people around Fowke at this time.
79	**your looking on it:** Hill's house and extensive garden in Petty France, Westminster, overlooked St. James's Park (Hill, *Works,* 1:53; 251–65).
79	**Fulham:** A village, surrounded by market gardens, to the west of London, on the banks of the Thames, which was popular as a summer retreat. Fowke lodged with the Cenny family, whose gardens and land ran down to the Thames. Steele rented lodgings with the same family (*Correspondence of Sir Richard Steele,* ed. Rae Blanchard [Oxford: Clarendon, 1941], 181).
82	**The Scorpion Haywood:** Eliza Haywood (1690?–1756), novelist and dramatist, initially a friend of Fowke's, viciously attacked her in *Memoirs of a Certain Island,* accusing her of the grossest immorality, and incest with her father (see appendix B and the introduction). Although the work was not published until 1725, it may have circulated earlier in manuscript; Fowke's knowledge seems to be hearsay.
82	**the Murderer was executed:** No account of the trial or execution has been found.
84	**Mr. B——:** Married to a former neighbor and friend of Fowke, probably in Staffordshire, since he seems to indicate knowledge of her grandmother. His offer to elope with her and form a bigamous second marriage ironically echoes the situation of Fowke's cousin, Elizabeth Culling ("Louisa"), de-

ceived by William Cowper (see above). Contemporaneously, Beau Fielding had bigamously married the Duchess of Cleveland, former mistress of Charles II, having been earlier trapped into marriage by a woman who pretended to be a wealthy widow; see Lawrence Stone, *Broken Lives* (Oxford: Oxford University Press, 1993), 60–68.

85 **interest:** Financial prudence.

85 **a very famous Oculist:** Possibly Sir William Read, who was a friend of Steele and mixed in London society, or his brother-in-law and partner Mr. Brinsden, who seems to have moved in Jacobite circles. Alternatively he might be a Mr. Fountain, who lived in Chelsea, and was consulted by Mary Astell for her failing sight (Ruth Perry, *The Celebrated Mary Astell* [Chicago: University of Chicago Press, 1986], 278, 286). No connection with the Fowke family has been discovered for any of these possibilities. Another possibility is William Sydenham, son of the more famous Thomas, although he is not known to have specialized in diseases of the eye; however, he lived in Richmond, not too far from Fulham, and was connected by marriage to one of Fowke's cousins.

85 **Sir William M——y——d:** Sir William Maynard, Bt., died 25 Dec. 1715, and was succeeded by his brother Henry, also a merchant with interests in Turkey.

86 **Mr. Cenny's:** Fowke's Fulham landlord. The Cenny family owned extensive market-gardens and land by the river in Fulham.

88 **Red-Lyon-Square:** A newly built area, a little to the north of Lincoln's Inn Fields.

89 **Bedford-Street:** Runs north from the Strand toward Covent Garden.

89 **He presented, he intreated:** "presented" here seems to be an unusual intransitive form of the verb, either in its meaning of giving a gift, or of appearing in a formal manner (OED).

90 **Bath:** Popular spa town and social center.

91 **Mr. Wicherley:** The playwright William Wycherley (1640?–1716) visited Bath in 1711 and in 1714 and 1715; see Eugene McCarthy, *William Wycherley: A Biography* (Athens: Ohio University Press, 1979). Spence in his *Anecdotes* notes: "He had therefore long resolved to marry in order to make a settlement from the estate, to pay off his debt with his wife's fortune, and to plague his damned nephew" (McCarthy, 238, n.124). In the last months of his life he was cozened by two adventurers who bullied him into a marriage; see Howard P. Vincent, "The Death of William Wycherley," *Harvard Studies and Notes in Philology and Literature* 15 (1933): 219–42.

91 **a Gentleman, young, and not unhandsome:** Not identified.

91	**he threw me on the Bed:** It was not unusual at this time for bedrooms to double as rooms for company.	
91	**Passion:** Any strong emotion, in this case anger.	
92	**Col K———r:** The Honourable Colonel William Ker was a subscriber to Savage's *Miscellaneous Poems* (1726), in which a number of Fowke's poems were printed.	
92	**Oxford:** Fowke may have been staying with relatives; a Peter Fowk or Foulks, of Christ Church, was Proctor in 1705, and lecturer in Rhetoric at Oxford (*Angliae Notitia* [1707], 683).	
92	**Mr. Hally:** Edmond Halley, 1656–1742, mathematician and astronomer, was Savilian professor of geometry at Oxford from 1703 until his appointment as Astronomer Royal in 1721. The DNB describes him as sprightly, vivacious, and genial to his friends.	
92	**King-Street:** A fashionable residential street running from St. James's Square to St. James's Street.	
92	**Sir Harry B———y:** Possibly Sir Henry Berkeley.	
92	**Pyramus and Thisbe:** The lovers in the play within the play in Shakespeare's *Midsummer Night's Dream,* who communicate through a chink in the wall.	
94	**shelves:** Rock ledges, reefs.	
94	**seated:** Resident.	
94	**St. James Street, on the Terrass:** A fashionable street in which to lodge; Steele lodged at Lady Vanderput's in St. James's Street, from 1717 until his wife's death in 1718. The Terrace was a row of houses at the northern end.	
94	**His Grace of B———fort:** Henry Somerset, 2d Duke of Beaufort, 1683?–1714. In his short life he was married three times: to Lady Mary Sackville in 1702, to Rachel Noel in 1706, and to Lady Mary Osborne in 1711. He owned Beaufort House, an extensive estate on the river between Fulham and Chelsea, which after his death was the residence of his aunt, the Duchess of Ormonde, whose Jacobite husband was in exile. He also owned a London house in the newly built Grosvenor Square and extensive estates in the West and in Wales. The Beaufort circle was strongly Tory, if not Jacobite. There was a connection between the Duke of Ormonde and Thomas Keightley, since they both married daughters of Laurence Rochester, Lord Clarendon; and Fowke claimed Keightley as a relation. Eliza Haywood in her *Memoirs,* describing Beaufort as being "never over-nice in his choices," alleges that Fowke was his mistress and had a son by him but she was turned off when the Duke happened to arrive unannounced to find "the most dirty and disagreeable of her footmen in her	

arms." The Key to the *Memoirs* identifies this Duke as Richmond, but the details of Haywood's accusations seem too close to Fowke's own description of Beaufort. Delariviere Manley dedicated the second volume of her *Memoirs of Europe* (1710) to Beaufort, praising him as "a Prince of distinguishing Merit" (1:144–45).

94   **Edmund Smith:** Edmund Smith (1672–1710), son of Edmund Neale and Margaret, daughter of Sir Nicholas Lechmere, was adopted by his uncle Lechmere. In 1705, expelled from Oxford, he went to London, where he was already entered as a student at Inner Temple. He wrote for the Whigs and was friends with Addison and Steele, although he had a wide circle of influential friends. His tragedy *Phaedra* was produced in 1707. Fowke's elegy has not been identified. It seems unlikely to be the Miltonic one in 1712 listed by Foxon, "On the Death of Mr. Edmund Smith," since no other work of Fowke shows the influence of Milton. The Whig John Oldmixon in his attack on Beaufort as "Otho" in *Court Tales: or, A History of the Amours of the Present Nobility* (London, 1717) may be alluding to Fowke as the "She Poet" who made "Fulsome Addresses" to Beaufort, and who "amidst her Lewdness and Infamy, is the greatest Fury of a Zealot" in Britain (85–89). Fowke's connection with Smith is unclear, although she may possibly have met him while staying in Oxford. Smith actually competed with her relative Peter Foulkes for the position of Censor at Christ Church, Oxford (Samuel Johnson, *Lives of the English Poets*, ed. G. B. Hill [Oxford: Clarendon Press, 1905], 2:1–15). In London, Johnson notes, Smith's "way of life connected him with the licentious and dissolute."

94   **Platonick Love:** The elaborated code of courtly love called platonic arose in France and was developed in aristocratic circles in seventeenth-century England. Fowke's association with it can be seen in *Clio and Strephon*, often known by its subtitle as "The Platonick Lovers." Fowke emphasizes the code's intense emotionality and its lack of physicality, portraying "a Love refin'd" founded on tenderness and respect for women: "How ardent, yet how modest is the Fire / Of a respectful Love, unstain'd with rude Desire." That the practice was not necessarily totally ascetic may be indicated by a poem entitled "Platonick Love" in *The Grove: Or A Collection of Original Poems, Translations, &c.* (London: Printed for W. Mears at the *Lamb* without Temple-Bar, 1721), a volume to which Martha Fowke Sansom subscribed: "So Kissing stirs up soft Desire / When grosser Pleasures quench the Fire." However, at the beginning of the eighteenth century, these aristocratic concepts of love were gradually being transformed into a more domestic sentimentality. Fowke's views were mocked by a writer a few years later as "that *stale* concern . . . Fav'rite of wrinkled Nymphs decay'd" ("On Seeing a Lady Reading the Platonick Lovers," *The Scarborough Anthology for the Year 1733* (London, 1734).

94   **quarteridge:** A quarterly allowance or payment; while the Duke is a minor, his small allowance every three months is spent on his grandmother's servant girls, buying their sexual services.

96   **a private Ball:** The episode with Mr. S—— is depicted with considerable

flair and a sense of self-parody. The man involved in this "tragic farce" has not been identified.

97   **left word I should lye in the ———:** Probably The Temple, site of the house or lodgings of the friends of Fowke who trapped her into this misadventure.

97   **adamantine:** Immovable, impregnable.

97   **starv'd:** Chilled, cold.

99   **Love liv'd longer when unconfin'd:** This was a basic tenet of the libertines of the period. Fowke's father was oppressed by the chains of marriage. Richardson's rake, Lovelace, in *Clarissa* argues in the same vein: "It is infinitely better for her and for me, that we should not marry. What a delightful manner of life (O, that I could persuade her to it!) would the life of Honour be with such a woman! The fears, the inquietudes, the uneasy days, the restless nights; all arising from doubts of having disobliged me! Every absence dreaded to be an absence for ever! And then, how amply rewarded, and rewarding, by the rapture-causing return! Such a passion as this, keeps love in a continual fervour; makes it all alive. The happy pair, instead of sitting dozing and nodding at each other in opposite chimney-corners, in a winter-evening, and over a wintry Love, [is] always new to each other, and having always something to say" (Lovelace to Belford, 25 April, [*Clarissa. Or, The History of a Young Lady: Comprehending The most Important Concerns of Private Life,* 3d ed., London, 1751, with a new Introduction by Florian Stuber (New York: AMS Press, 1990), 3:281]).

99   **my beloved Shades:** "Shades" is a poetic expression for a piece of ground overshadowed by trees. Fowke refers to the Cennys' garden in Fulham.

100   **writing Billets. . . . he powder'd for me:** He wrote love letters (*billets-doux*) and dressed himself in formal attire, including a powdered wig, in order to impress Fowke.

100   **glass:** Mirror.

100   **divine *Shakespear*:** Shakespeare's works were popular at this period, having appeared in 1709 in a convenient illustrated octavo edition edited by Nicholas Rowe. There was a revival of stage performances from 1717 to 1725, with 17 percent of all performances being of Shakespearean plays; these were not box office successes and seem to have been often played "At the Request of Ladies"; see Arthur H. Scouten, "The Increase in Popularity of Shakespeare's Plays in the Eighteenth Century: A Caveat for Interpreters of Stage History," *Shakespeare Quarterly* 7 (1953): 189–202. John Dennis the critic complained of the modish nature of the enthusiasm for Shakespeare, and Fowke frequently tends to speak of Shakespeare as her "lover."

101   **a favourite Neighbour:** Unidentified.

EXPLANATORY NOTES TO PAGES 101–106

101 **Cleveland:** Barbara Villiers, Duchess of Cleveland (1641–1709), mistress of Charles II, who gave dukedoms to his three sons by her. She was renowned for her beauty and her extravagance, losing the sum of twenty thousand pounds at cards in a single night. Her affair with John Churchill (later Duke of Marlborough) was said to have been the foundation of his successful career.

101 **Mazarine:** Hortense Mancini, Duchess of Mazarin (1646–1699), the charming, beautiful, and witty niece of Cardinal Mazarin, left her miserable marriage in 1675 and moved to London, where she was prominent at court. Her misfortunes inspired Mary Astell's pamphlets on marriage.

102 **low:** Short.

102 **a son of Eden, a gardener:** Possibly connected in some way with the Rench family, who were notable gardeners with property at Broomhouse Nurseries in Fulham (Charles James Féret, *Fulham Old and New* [London, 1900], 2:132). An alternative candidate is Christopher Gray (1694–1764), of a Fulham family, whose nursery was famous for its extensive range of American plants; the first *Magnolia grandiflora* in England is said to have been grown in his nursery. He knew Philip Miller and Mark Catesby and numbered Horace Walpole among his customers. See E. J. Willson, *West London Nursery Gardens* (Fulham and Hammersmith Historical Society, 1982), 16–20.

102 **worse Figures in the Side-Box:** The enclosed seats beside the stage at the theater were particularly popular with fashionable young men.

102 **excus'd my descent:** Made up for the disparity in social rank.

103 **favoured by the Muses:** Fowke published poems as early as 1711, in *Delights for the Ingenious*. Other work probably remains to be identified.

103 **Duke of B——t:** The Duke of Beaufort died in 1714; thus this period of Fowke's life is approximately 1712 to 1714.

104 **some other who had assumed my name:** Whores often assumed the names of society ladies: "It is the Manner of those Houses to give each other the Names and Titles of such Women of Beauty and Quality, as they resemble in Air, Shape, and Stature; and upon Novices and Foreigners they impose 'em, as the real Persons" (Richard Steele, *The Theatre* 6, cited in Calhoun Winton, *Sir Richard Steele, M.P.* [Baltimore and London: Johns Hopkins Press, 1970], 172, n. 42.

106 **pass'd some Hours at Kensington:** Kensington Palace was a royal residence, surrounded by elegant gardens; nearby was a small village of recently built houses.

106 **The painter and his wife:** Mr. C——, the painter, seems most likely to be Daniel Coning (1668–after 1727), assuming that C——y is a misreading of C——g. He was a portrait painter, who painted Lord King (1720), as well

as ten or so portraits of the Tracy family at Stanway circa 1726. The portrait of Martha Fowke has not been traced.

106 **the favourite Mistress of C——k:** Thomas Coke, M.P., 1674–1717, was appointed Vice-Chamberlain in 1706. His first wife, Lady Mary Stanhope, died in 1704. His involvement with Elizabeth Lawrence and her mother, Mrs. Ryder, is detailed in Manley's 1709 novel of political scandal, *Memoirs of the New Atalantis* (ed. Rosalind Ballaster [London: Penguin, 1992], 100–101). Manley muses ironically on the origins of the wealth demonstrated by the luxurious living conditions of Mrs. Ryder and her attractive widowed daughter: "whence then these fine lodgings, wax lights, card assemblies, nice eating and rich clothes. We lived no longer in an age when fairy kings and queens bring such riches to mortals." Delariviere Manley lived next door to Mrs. Ryder (*Adventures of Rivella* [London, 1714], 31–32), and it is tempting to surmise that Fowke and Manley might have met socially, at one or another card assembly.

107 **Lottery-tickets:** Lotteries, both public and private, were extremely popular at the turn of the century; tickets earned interest as well as being entered for prizes. Fowke's generous unsecured loan of two hundred pounds seems exceedingly naïve and unlikely.

108 **A Man of Fortune and Distinction in Ireland:** Identified in a manuscript note in W. Musgrave's copy of *Clio* in the British Library (1418.c.51), which also corrects the initial R. to K., as "Thomas Knightley, of Hartingfordbury." Knightley, or Keightley, married Lady Frances Hyde, second daughter of Edward 1st Earl of Clarendon; he was separated from her for twenty years. He was appointed vice-treasurer of Ireland in 1686, and was one of the Lord Justices in Ireland in 1702. He died 19 January 1719. His brother-in-law, Clarendon, described him as "a man of very good sense, and of an excellent understanding."

110 **a particular Friend:** The friend and fellow prisoner of Thomas Fowke may be Robert Borrowes of Kildare, second son of Sir Kildare Borrowes. Alternatively, he may be Major Belless of the Earl of Lorain's regiment. Prisoners taken in Spain after the battle of Almanza were exchanged or ransomed in 1713 as negotiations began for the Peace of Utrecht.

113 **Mr. S——:** Arnold Sansom, lawyer, whom Fowke eventually married, after an affair, intimated in the text below and described in detail by Mrs. Haywood: "He was old and infirm, and had occasion for a Nurse, he therefore took her into Keeping, and allow'd her four hundred Crowns a year [one hundred pounds] . . . [which] served to put her into a habit and manner of living, to draw Company more agreable to her Taste; she now cou'd dress, make Entertainments, had handsome Lodgings." (*Memoirs* 1:45) Arnold Sansom was Comptroller of the particular Receivers in the Custom House in 1707 at a salary of five hundred pounds a year. He may be the attorney Mr. Samson or Sampson mentioned frequently by the young law student Dudley Ryder; see *The Diary of Dudley Ryder, 1715–1716*, transcrib. from shorthand and ed. William Matthews (London: Methuen, 1939), 31, 35–36, 125, 172, 190, 258, 266–67, 353, 360, 361, 372.

The date of Fowke's marriage to Samson was probably 1720 or 1721, although no official entry has been found; by the latter year Martha Fowke subscribes to *The Grove* (London, 1721) as Mrs. Sansom. The phrase "pretty gentleman" means a fashionable but not foppish man about town.

115   **Temple:** Fowke may have lived with Sansom in his chambers in the Inner Temple for some years before she married him, as well as afterward. The Inns of Court provided living accommodation for families as well as offices for lawyers; a set of chambers could include a dining-room, bedroom, study, and servants' rooms. Fowke refers to "these chambers" as the place where she is writing her account in 1723. In commendatory verses prefixed to Richardson Pack's *A New Collection of Miscellanies in Prose and Verse* (London, 1724) she gives her address as The Paper Buildings, Inner Temple.

115   **died away:** Fainted.

116   **A little retired house near Windsor:** The painter Antonio Verrio had been employed under Charles II to decorate Windsor Castle, the royal palace some twenty miles to the west of London; while at Windsor he had also painted frescoes of erotic scenes from Ovid on the staircase of Burford House, given by the King to his mistress Nell Gwyn in 1681. Verrio's own house may have been similarly decorated. See Robert R. Tighe and James Edward Davis, *Annals of Windsor* (London, 1858), 2:327.

116–   **a Friend of Mr. S. . . . Mr. A——s:** Possibly John Anstis, 1669–1744, heral-
117   dic writer, member of parliament, and Garter king-of-arms. He was a strong Tory and was arrested in 1715 on charges of Jacobitism. He was admitted to the Inner Temple in 1688 and would have been a contemporary and neighbor of Sansom's in the Temple. He also had a house near Fulham and would thus have been available as a messenger between Sansom and Fowke. Hearne described him as "a Man of a very sweet Temper, very modest, and of excellent Learning" (*The Remains of Thomas Hearne: Reliquiae Hearnianae*, comp. by Dr. John Bliss, rev. John Buchanan-Brown, [Carbondale: Southern Illinois University Press, 1966), 164, 286.

117   **Mrs. Moor:** Possibly Anne, daughter of Digby Foulke, Esq., who married the Hon. William Moore; Anne was connected with the Maynards, who owned Sandford Manor House in Fulham (Féret, *Fulham Old and New*, 3:275).

117   **Richmond:** A pleasant small town on the banks of the Thames to the west of London where the Princess of Wales, later Queen Caroline, spent summers from 1717 onward; it was popular with courtiers, artists, and writers. Richard Savage and James Thomson, members of Fowke's circle, spent time there. It was easily accessible from Fulham by boat.

117   **one Gentleman in it:** This young man who had a serious illness, may be the "Damon" whose two poems to "Mira" describing his love, his fever, and Mira's rebukes were published in *Miscellaneous Poems, Original and Translated, By Several Hands*, ed. Matthew Concanen (London, 1724). In

EXPLANATORY NOTES TO PAGES 119–123   165

Miscellaneous Poems and Translations (1726), ed. Richard Savage, two poems by David Mallet are addressed to Myra, and, in a review of the volume, along with praise of the nine poems contributed by Fowke as "Clio" to the collection (*British Journal*, 24 September 1726), Fowke is noted as having recently changed her poetic name from Clio to "Myra," since the name of Clio "has of late been so abus'd and scandalized." Mrs. Sansom is entered as a subscriber for two copies of Concanen's miscellany. Musgrave's copy of *Clio* has a manuscript note connecting this young man with the officer who, according to Haywood's attack in *Memoirs*, flatly rejected Fowke's amorous advances.

119 **pale as the dying *Adonis*:** In mythology, the young Adomis, loved by the goddess Venus for his beauty, was killed while hunting a boar and was turned by Venus into a flower.

119 **Mother to the present Duchess of Bolton:** Eleanor, daughter of Sir Robert Needham, was mistress to the Duke of Monmouth, illegitimate son of Charles II, who initially went by the name Crofts. Her two children by Monmouth were Henrietta, who became the third wife of the Second Duke of Bolton, and James Crofts, Colonel of the 9th Dragoons in 1719, who died in 1732. Parsons Green was a small hamlet adjoining Fulham.

120 **our mighty Town:** An ironic description of the small village of Fulham.

120 **a Country 'Squire . . . Mr. H——n:** Unidentified.

121 **Durfey:** Thomas D'Urfey (1653–1723) was a voluminous writer of popular plays, translations, satires, burlesques, and songs, the latter appearing in a series of collections between 1683 and 1720. *Wit and Mirth: Or Pills to Purge Melancholy* was a six–volume compilation published 1719–20.

121 **our Corporation:** Playfully suggests the existence of a social group around Fowke, interested in ideas of platonic love.

121 **sola:** Alone.

121 **he was a Swede:** Possibly associated with the Swedish envoy in London, Count Carl von Gyllenborg (1679–1746), who was arrested for involvement in a Jacobite conspiracy in 1717.

122 **A Friend of our Family's:** Unidentified, but might be connected with the Giffard family, neighbours of the Fowkes in Staffordshire. Lodgings at Putney would have been just across the river from Fulham.

123 **A Lady who had lodg'd at *Fulham* . . . Mrs. P——:** One possibility is the so far unidentified Mrs. P——h——r, the identification given in the Key to Haywood's *Memoirs* for a friend of Gloatitia/Fowke called Dalatilla. Another possibility is a Mrs. Lucy Rodd Price, the separated wife of a Judge of the Exchequer, who lived in Gray's Inn. She translated plays from the Spanish, giving one to Richard Savage, which was eventually staged by the actor Bullock as *Woman's A Riddle*. Another play from the

Spanish, probably translated by Mrs. Price, was printed by Savage as *Love in a Veil* (1719); it brought him the acquaintanceship of Steele. See Clarence Tracy, *The Artificial Bastard: A Biography of Richard Savage* (Cambridge: Harvard University Press, 1953), 38–39.

123 **Mr. C——y:** Unidentified.

125 **the old Lord Stafford's:** The earldom of Stafford had been revived by James II; the "old" earl, a Catholic and Jacobite supporter, married to but separated from the daughter of the Count de Gramont, died in April 1719 and was succeeded by his nephew William.

125 **a Relation of my Strephon's:** The Strephon of *Clio and Strephon* was William Bond (169?–1735), the nephew of Lady Gage of Hengrave, Suffolk, whose father (Bond's grandfather) had been controller of the household of Queen Henrietta Maria. William Bond was a Catholic and active in the Jacobite cause (*HMC Stuart Papers* 8:287). He inherited little money and had to make his way in the world of letters. The book which occasioned Fowke's correspondence with "Strephon" was volume 5 of the *Spectator*, Bond's continuation of Addison and Steele's periodical.

125 **A Gentleman . . . . Mr. T——ds:** Lewis Theobald, lawyer, dramatist, translator, and periodical writer, was later better known as the editor of Shakespeare and a victim of Pope's satire in the *Dunciad Variorum* (1729). Theobald's poem praising Clio at her cottage in Fulham appears in *The Grove*. Theobald was a Tory and possibly a Jacobite, dedicating *The Persian Princess* in 1717 to the Duchess of Ormonde. He also was the lawyer for both Wycherley's widow and her lover who foisted her on the dying dramatist; this suggests the close-knit web of relationships in Fowke's world. Theobald may have looked back fondly to his interchange with Fowke; he wrote fifteen years later to Warburton about his eagerness to receive a letter: "You bring back to my mind the time of a love-correspondence; and the expectation of every fresh letter from you is the joy of a mistress to me. But when I am growing wanton it is time I should break off abruptly" (John Nichols, *Illustrations of the Literary History of the Eighteenth Century*, 2:257). Theobald was an enthusiastic reader of Shakespeare, as can be seen in his periodical *The Censor* (1715, 1717), although no particular interest in Chaucer has been documented.

126 **dressing my Head:** Arranging hair in an elaborate formal style.

128 **young Gentleman, whose Person was agreeable to my Wishes:** Mr. H——, who is "bound to another" and about to leave Britain, fits the situation in the poems, probably by Fowke, published a dozen years later in the *Barbados Gazette;* he has not yet been identified, although if the initial is a printing error, Jonathan Blenman, a law student and writer of pamphlets, is a possibility.

128 **those exalted views:** Hill was continually involved in projects, including pressing oil from beech mast, planting vineyards, and providing timber from Scotland for the navy. He also was active as a manager in the theater.

EXPLANATORY NOTES TO PAGES 129-148

129 **My Brother assails me:** In acknowledging her brother's influence in urging her to marry Sansom, Fowke provides another view of the facts interpreted by Haywood: "her Brother . . . being instructed by his Sister, in the Humour and Disposition of *Rutho* [Sansom], instead of suffering him to do himself Justice in discarding a Woman who had been so false to him, forced him to marry her: since that, she does what she pleases, goes where she pleases" (*Memoirs* 1:46).

131 **your adorable Letters:** Aaron Hill wrote to Fowke praising her work (see appendix A). They were aware of each other's presence at the theater on several occasions but did not formally meet till later.

131 **I found myself sink among the Crowd:** Possibly an allusion to the economic crash of the South Sea Bubble in 1720, when the gay prospect of prosperity vanished for many fashionable investors as the stock market dropped dramatically.

135 **calcin'd:** Reduced by burning to an essence, purified of the grosser part.

137 **tell:** Count, reckon up.

137 **Magazine:** Store house.

142 **the Fulness of this Book:** An indication that Fowke is coming to the end of the bound book in which she is writing; she fills the last pages with these fragmentary poems to make it an emblem of her heart, which is filled with thoughts of Hill.

148 **The second jewel in my Journey here:** A printed note in the original identifies this as "Mr. D——r." John Dyer (1700?-1757), poet and painter, came to London from Wales in 1720 or early 1721 to study law, but on the death of his father, he abandoned his legal studies in favor of poetry and painting. He and Fowke exchanged verses; see Dyer's "The Country Walk" and "The Inquiry" ("Sad is the shepherd while Clio is gone") and Fowke's "To Mr. Dyer," Richard Savage, ed., *Miscellaneous Poems and Translations* (London, 1726), 48, 44, 209. Dyer also painted her portrait (untraced), an event commemorated in verse by both Savage and Hill. Dyer went to Rome in 1724, continuing to write poems to Fowke from there, but on his return from Rome he seems to have severed the relationship about 1726, feeling apparently that their close friendship was inappropriate in view of Fowke's marriage. Dyer eventually became a clergyman.

Appendix A: Letters and Poems of Aaron Hill to Martha Fowke Sansom

THE following five letters come from two sources:
1. *The Works of the late Aaron Hill, Esq; in Four Volumes,* 2d ed. (London: Printed for the Benefit of the Family, MDCCIIV [misprint for 1754]), abbreviated as *Works*. The first edition of 1753 seems to have been hastily put together and the contents and pagination differ in the second edition. In this appendix obvious misprints have been corrected.
2. *The Dramatic Works of the Late Aaron Hill, Esq.,* 2 vols. (London: Printed for the Benefit of the Family, 1760), abbreviated as *Dramatic Works*. Vol. 2 contains a section of love letters, some to Hill's wife and three to Martha Fowke Sansom, the latter identified from internal evidence.

1.
                              June 11, 1721.
   Madam,
I consider the honour of your friendship, and that inexpressible pleasure, which I receive from your correspondence, as two of the greatest happinesses, I have met with in life. I wear with pride, the noble title, you adorn me with, of your friend; and you will not wonder at the transport which it gives me, when you reflect, as you once did, thus divinely,

> "How few in all the tour of life, we find,
> "Who either can *improve*—or *charm* the Mind!
> "Scarce can my thought, in all the boasted crowd,
> "Recal *one friend,* to make my mem'ry proud.

But you add immediately after,

> "That much of *flattery* your *youth* has prov'd,
> "For you have been, what others call belov'd."

APPENDIX A   169

You will forgive me, Madam, if I observe, that the *last* of these two charming lines, is not a more self-evident and infallible truth, than the *first* is a natural impossibility. We could not flatter C—— were we never so inclinable: One might say perhaps a thousand things, which C—— wou'd think *flattery*—but C—— would, in that, as in most other points, find nobody, who thought like her.

How rapturous is that glow of fancy, which distinguishes your writings! But you temper your muse's fire, like that of your eyes, with a gentle air of sweetness, which divinely softens the radiance; I say, *divinely,* because it puts one naturally in mind, of what is said of the *divinity,* in the original of our 104th Psalm.

> The *god-grac'd presence* hov'ring *angels* fill,
>   *Angels!* fit heralds of the *Almighty*'s will.
> Ten thousand fiery *lightnings* sweep his way,
>   Nimble couriers of his sway;
> And round his *temples,* hissing swift, in blue *meanders* play.
>   Yet, gracious, *man*'s unequal eye to screen,
>   Wisely, he shades the too resplendent scene,
> And, like a curtain widely drawn, spreads out *whole heaven*
>   between.

I should never have done, if I allow'd myself to speak of *you,* till I had nothing *new* to say in your praise. I must therefore, check the zeal of my inclination, as *coach-men* chain a wheel, when they descend a steep hill, that, by preventing it from turning at all, they may be sure of its not turning too violently. It is impossible to tell you, with how much respect and admiration, I am,
                    Madam,
                        Your most obedient
                        Humble Servant,
                        A. Hill.

Works, 1:33–35. (In 1st ed., 1:22–24, with date of June 21, 1721).

Note: The use of the name "Mira" in the following letters and poems probably reflects later editorial intervention, since Fowke was "new-christened" by Mallet in 1726, after the attacks on her by Haywood.

2.

   Madam,
   I had just finish'd the inclosed verses, when I had the honour of

receiving yours, dated yesterday; I am scarce more amaz'd at the prodigious force of your genius, than at the sweetness of your nature; reflecting, with compassion, on the certain influence of your charms, you temper the pain you give, by a mixture of condescension.

I came to the house [i.e., playhouse], before you, with design to sit conceal'd, and feast my eyes on your loveliness; as my soul had been often entertain'd with your excellence; I thought the bench wou'd hold but three—and when I saw three Ladies enter, neither of which was the Lady whose idea my mind shone with, I felt a melancholy weight at the disappointment, which fled, immediately upon your entrance, like a mist, before the sunbeams.

I believ'd myself unknown, 'till at the end of the play, I had the honour to salute you. The reason you have given for discovering me sooner has almost drawn me to a vanity; which, however, unapt I am to fall into, it was, on this occasion, scarce possible to resist. I own I feel some pride in the very imagination, that you guessed at me.—Not to appear disagreeable in the eyes of a MIRA, is all the personal merit, which it becomes a man to wish for.

It is impossible to describe you, either in your mind, or your person. One may do it in idea—but words give way, like quicksand, beneath too weighty a pile of building. One may *see* you for ever, unwearied, and admiring; but to speak you, is as impossible, as to excell you!

It were the business of an age, to read the learning of your eyes! They let out more meanings, than they take in objects! And to study the occult sciences, which may be learnt from their perusal, will teach me tomorrow night, the most enchanting philosophy.

>   I am,
> With the profoundest respect,
>   and admiration,
>   Madam!
> your most humble and most obedient servant,
>   A. Hill.

*To the never enough admir'd Mrs.——, after seeing her
at* Julius Caesar.

> Pleas'd to be plac'd, unknown, in MIRA's view,
> I gave my eyes free loose, and gaz'd you through;
> Watch'd your unguarded looks, each motion weigh'd,
> And, unsuspected, lurk'd, in ambuscade:

But, if, unsure, my sympathetic heart,
Felt you, thro' distance, with ideal smart,
How shall I point the strong, the sweet, surprize,
To see you stand, confess'd, and bless my eyes!
Happy, mean while that those doubt-wand'ring beams,
Spread random fires, nor shot collected streams,
Scarce I sustain'd her charms' diffusive shine,
While gilding every form, they glanc'd o'er mine,
But, ah! what power unguess'd cou'd then protect,
When their whole force, contracted, darts, direct.
Soft are her features, and her air is sweet,
High majesty and melting languor meet!
Round her pleas'd mouth impatient Cupids throng,
To snatch th'inspiring music from her tongue:
Thick, thro her sparkling eyes, break unconfin'd,
The wing'd ideas of her crowded mind;
A mind! that burning with inferior glow,
Does her whole form with lustre overflow!
Still as she speaks—or looks—or moves—new rays
Scatter fresh beauties, in eternal blaze;
Lost in excess of wonder, we retire,
Find words too weak, and silently admire.
Judge then, O Muse! thus aweful, in thy charms,
How my soul labour'd with its late alarms;
To see you near—to see you so divine!
Was joy to others' eyes—was pain to mine!
Dubious, perplex'd, with interrupted gaze,
I turn'd my varied looks a thousand ways.
Reduc'd at length, to one forc'd choice, of two,
To look on Caesar's murder, or on you;
Slow, my reluctant eyes to disengage,
I bent 'em, tingling, on the bloody stage!
'Tis hard—I sigh'd—to see my fav'rite bleed,
But, 'tis more hard to die, in Caesar's stead.

To the adorable Mrs. ——, in excuse for not answering immediately one of her letters.

    Can heavenly MIRA easily forgive!
But why do I that needless query make;
Pity, and she, like twin-born sisters, live,
    And their sweet union, death alone can break.

    Speak then O guilty Muse, with humble sound,
Softly approach—and whisper in her ear;
As criminal thou art, it will be found,

She caus'd thy crime, whose power now moves thy fear.

Tho', I confess my thanks too long delay'd,
My thanks for blessings, which impoverish thought,
Yet if she calls compassion to her aid,
She'll save the guilty penitent she taught.

Ere I beheld her face, with ease I writ,
With ease cou'd float on passion's troubled roll;
But, since her eyes have reinforc'd her wit,
Th'unconquer'd fire consumes my burning soul.

So generals, not yet near enough to fight,
Fearless dispatch light parties far and nigh,
But when the foes whole army comes in sight,
Slow they draw back, and in close silence lie.

Dramatic Works, 2:389–92.

3.

1721.

Madam,

There are so many shining beauties, in the verses, and the letter, which I had last the honour to receive from you; that 'tis impossible to praise them, as they ought to be praised, without writing a comment on every line, and taking more pains on your excellence, than Madam *D'acier* did, on *Homer*'s. Yet, there is one part, so blameable, that not even the zealous partiality, with which I consider your vast merit, can enable me to defend it. I must, therefore, give you up to the critics, for prophaning your *sublime*, with a mixture of *ironical*.

You are guilty of this charge, in that agreeable air of pleasantry, with which you undertake to persuade me, that you were not at the *Play*, when I can demonstrate, that you sat with me all the evening: You were not, indeed, in that very *box*, which you appeared in, before.—But you were in the front boxes, in the side boxes, in the pit, on the stage,—you came with me—went home with me, and whatever you know, or think you know, to the contrary, I have never parted with you since.

Such is th' attractive *C*——'s magic skill,
That *once* to see her, is to see her *still:*
Such her soft *sounds,* that their *delightful* strain
Murmurs, for ever, in the echoing *brain!*

APPENDIX A 173

> Such her sweet *looks,* that, from her piercing *eye,*
> Th'immortal *glance,* once *shot,* can never *die.*
> Proud, the pleas'd *memory* strong impression takes,
> And, but in *death's* dark shade, its *hold forsakes.*

You complain of a kind of inactivity, which you sometimes feel, and are so free with yourself as to call it a laziness. This proceeds but from a temporary *absence* of your *soul,* which you may be sure is *abroad,* inspiring *mine,* and inflaming it with a thousand *ideas* of your *loveliness.* I will give you an example, how perpetually I am haunted, by this charming busy spirit, from a description of a lonely walk, which I took, the other evening.

Going out of the *Park,* by *Buckingham-house gate,* while my eyes glided negligently over the form of the fabrick—it was whispered in my ear, by some unseen divinity—with how much ravishing *softness,* mixed with *fire* and *energy,* has the soul-charming C—— praised the lines, which *Strephon* writ, on this building!

I left the town, at once, behind me, and found myself enclosed, by the green hedges of a lane, on this side *Chelsea.*—I was about to reflect on the *coolness,* the *sweetness,* the *innocence,* the *quiet,* of a country *retirement;* but, before I had formed the first ideas of contemplation, the same busy *whisperer* was interrupting me again, with the following *simile:*

> As neighb'ring here, the noisy *city* swarms,
> And, here, the *country* spreads her silent charms;
> Ev'n so, it said, can *C*——'s tow'ring *mind,*
> Stoop, sudden, from the *awful* to the *kind!*
> Form'd for *magnificence,* and widely *will'd,*
> Bid with vast *wishes,* and with *grandeur* fill'd!
> So, can it *sink* to *nature's* cooler shade,
> And seem for *softness,* and sweet *pity* made!
> Smoothly *forgetful* of its *native* heat,
> Stay and be *hid,* in *fancy's* mild retreat.

Passing on, without so much as designing whither to go, I found myself in a lane, betwixt gardens, leading out of the *Willow-walk,* that goes up to *Tothil-Fields.* The *Ditches* on each side, were adorned with double *hedges,* and thick-planted with *trees:* they were arched over-head, and scarce admitted the sun-beams, which struggled, as it were, through them, with a kind of quivering lustre. The whistling of a breeze played delightful among the boughs, with a musical murmur. The birds shook the air, with the melody of their warblings, and the leaves seemed to dance, as if sensible of the harmony. The whole lane was unfrequented, and full of short windings; at every corner of which, some new scene of industry saluted my eye, with great variety of prospects. The fruit trees budded thick.—The garden beds sprung green, and a lively intermixture of red, blue, white, and yellow, in the flowers which surrounded me, glowed with silent emulation. The bean blossoms wafted, a perfume to my smell, and every sense was feasted on the luxury of nature.

In so charming a situation, I was sinking to the indolence of despising *ambition*. I was beginning to envy the safe content of the *humble*.—How blessed, said I, are they, whom no proud *hopes* mislead! whom no *danger* threatens! whom *quiet, ease,* and *plenty* conspire conspire to make *happy!*—I was going on at this rate, when one of the *warblers* in the hedge, seem'd to sing in distinct and articulate notes.—*It was in just such a garden, as that on the right, that C*——, *for some years, blessed the neighbourhood of* Fulham, *and made her* COTTAGE *immortal!*

I started from my amusement, and traced the turnings of the lane, 'till it opened, at last, on the very *point of Milbank,* at the *mouth of Chelsea Reach.* The sudden *change* of prospect, to so noble an enlargement, was agreeably surprizing. The bosom of the *Thames,* hardly ruffled by the breeze, flow'd majestically *glassy;* the deep-loaded *barges* drove on, slowly, with the *stream,* and the *stateliness* of their *motion* was set off, by its opposite, in the nimble *glide* of the *wherries,* which crossed each other with a *swiftness* and irregularity, not easily conceivable. The curling track of those *eddies,* which they formed by their passing, broke the reflection of the *sun-beams* into sparkling *showers of lustre.* And I was wandering into *commerce,* and the benefits of *navigation,* when I found my *thoughts,* of a sudden, drawn *aside,* to this reflection:

> *Deep,* smooth, and *clear,* as this *fam'd rivers* tide,
> Does our inspiring *C*——'s genius glide!
> Thus, as her *judgment,* in full *depth,* moves slow,
> Strongly *serene,* with mild, but forceful *flow:*
> Bright, on the *surface,* her gay *fancy* plays,
> And shoots on every side, its sparkling blaze.

I reclined myself at length, against the side of the *bank,* and went to *sea,* with the *river.* I met with *whirlwinds* and *hurricans,* and was so tossed from shore to shore, that *day-light* died away, during the *voyage of my fancy.* I recollected myself, and walked homeward, in the brownness of the night, which had shadowed over the fields, with a melancholy streakiness, from the paleness of the *moonshine*. Yet, the *stars* seemed to burn with a more than *usual lustre;* and the *milky way* lay open, with uncommon breadth of *radiance*.—How like are the *charms* of C——, thought I, as I walked on, and her *bright* and extensive *genius,* to that *profusion* of *mixed luminaries!* The number, and the force, of all those millions of blazing worlds, is almost *lost* in their *distance*. Could we count them distinctly, each prodigious individual were too vast for our comprehension.—How impossible then, to describe them, while we see them so remotely!

I have troubled you, Madam, with the particulars of a *walk,* that may have *tired* you.—But, by the *influence* of your spirit, which you find, was always *near* me, I leave you to judge how little *reason* you had to *assert,* that I did not *see* you at the *play,* because you knew you were not *present*. It is not, you see, in your *power* to deprive me of your *company,* since my soul is become so conversant, that it boasts the *honour* of an *intimacy,* which you are not consenting to.—I am, with an admiration that glows with your excellence,

Madam,
Your most faithful and obedient Servant,
A. Hill.

Works, 2d ed., 1:39–45; 1st ed., 2:180 ff.

4.

Madam,

The language of your heart declines all hearers, but the object of its tenderness: and, since I never see you, alone, (but when my dreams are kinder than your lodgings) you must give this paper leave to tell you, what I cannot—that the admiration, which I long since found your due, now only serves to dignify a warmer passion: for it became impossible again to see and hear you, without effects that soften'd friendship into wishes of a dearer nature.

To converse with you, and yet be patient under these necessities of often leaving you, is to be wretched, within view of transport.— A man, who has never once seen you, might live happy in his ignorance: but far from such a happiness is he, who, after having learn'd from your accomplishments indifference for all your sex besides, is tortur'd by restraints, and distance, and lives separated from the soul you rob him of.

I will not aim at a description of my sentiments.—They must

have been unworthy their inspirer, if words cou'd have the power to make her comprehend them.—Respectful, soft, endearing years of life, devoted to your taste, and acting for your happiness, might do, perhaps, some little justice to the passion you impress me with; but writing is by far too faint, and distance too incapable, to give ideas of your influence.

Receive me therefore, ever yours,—or, be so generous to save me from this growth of your attraction.—Condemn me never to behold you more; or let me never be depriv'd of seeing you.—All repetitions of such pleasures, as my heart is filled with, when I sit and listen to your sweetness, are succeeded by new pains, which you can never rightly judge of, because there is no man as worthy your esteem, as you are of mankind's in general.—I carry with me, from your gentle conversation, a thousand inexpressible remembrances, of words, looks, movements, softnesses and graces;—which, compared with the gay female world, make all things tasteless in it, but the image of that single loveliness, where all those excellencies center.

Since I must gather, from the consequence of this confession of my wish, what rank my happiness may hold in yours,—and since it cannot be a difficulty to convey your sentiments, where they will be sacred to my bosom only,—be so divinely good, as, (with a frankness, fit for generous minds, like yours) to let me be instructed—how far I may presume to hope, your heart's dear confidence (once tastelessly rewarded) has the courage to believe again; and trust the influence of your power—which I was born to feel the force of,—on the soul of,
  Madam,
   your now happy, or unbless'd, but always
    your most faithfully devoted servant,
     A. Hill.

Dramatic Works, 2:392–93.

5.

 Madam,
Every new time I see you, every new letter I have the blessing to receive from you, I gather still new proofs, in justice to the sex you honour, that all their softest and most amiable virtues may consist with all their elevated, and most thoughtful.

You look, and write, and act, with such an equal likeness to yourself, and such a sweet superiority to all the world beside, that friendship is too cold a passion, to do justice to your influence; and love too bold a wisher, when it wou'd aspire to hope your tenderness.

I know not how to disobey you, since my soul is in your custody;—yet, do not use your power, to the prevention of my future peace.—I can, I must forbear to press you,—if you will insist upon that sacrifice!—but I must never think of happiness, after such proof of your indifference.

Why, Madam, are you so unjust, in your opinion of your own fine mind? Why so insensible to its angelic covering?—In all the world, but in yourself, you are the first to find accomplishments!—Why do you speak of Time? It has but heightened your attractions.—Tho' you were always form'd as now, you were not always so supremely perfect!—Time has robb'd you of no beauties, in attending you from spring to summer.—'Tis to that profitable change, your fine sense owes its title to the fruits of this compleater season.—Why shou'd you, with this delicate unconsciousness, do such injustice to your loveliness?—You have every thing of gayety, but its light flutter, and its vanities; and you have every thing of wisdom, but its sowerness and its gravity.

Divinely modest, and judicious, as you are, you recommend refinement, as a bound to my esteem; and speak of happiness as lost, if carried farther.—But surely! all esteem for you, must, of necessity, be a refin'd one:—for, while its growth is from your personal charms, it has its root in your dear virtues.—there is indeed a happiness, that may be sometimes lost in finding: but, it is the fate of rash and unweigh'd passions.—I have long been charm'd with, long reflected on my present wish:—I have felt you at my heart, and held, and press'd you to my reason.—I have been the lover of your mind and body; and, it is as impossible to sense, that one, of your inspiring eyes, shou'd cloud the lustre of the other, as that a heart, which you have touch'd, as you have mine, shou'd grow less conscious of your dearness, because bless'd with your possession.

If therefore you insist (which Heaven forbid!) on my obedience to your hard injunction, you can have but one just reason for your doing so;—and I must find it in my own unworthiness.—As for my friendship, which you do such honour to, when you declare it worth your keeping,—That must be yours, by double claim, when I am also blessed with being so.—When did you ever think, that light was less refin'd, because it had some warmth mix'd in it? Why then shou'd such a love, as you inspire, be less refin'd than friendship? Why, rather, not join'd with it, both to strengthen, and enliven it?

But, what are all these reasonings, if oppos'd to your felicity! I love, with too devoted an attachment, to be happy, while you seem to doubt it.—I had rather see myself for years, unbless'd, than you a day uneasy.—Continue then your generous frankness: It so charmingly becomes you, that it raises your idea, even above your other greatnesses!—Inform me with it,—if there is not yet some stronger reason than you have express'd?—If it is so, I will prefer your quiet, to my own.—I will shew you the refinement of my love, by the submission (wou'd I cou'd add suppression!) of my wishes.—But, if your apprehension of the common consequences of unsteady and ill-grounded passion, is the only motive of your cold, yet kind advice,—conclude it an impossibility, to any weighed, or rational affection; and, therefore, never capable of finding the least room, in the devoted heart you animate.

Your dear invaluable letter came (as all mine do) directly to my hand.—The postmen bring me several at once; and, if I am from home, they are all put together in a little box I keep for that purpose.—Your heavenly image, in my heart, is not securer of a sacred privacy, than every thing you write, is sure of, in your letters.—And it is with purpose that my own shou'd find their way to your view only, that I thus inclose 'em, in such others, as are fit for any eye you please; these being taken out, and honour'd with a happier disposition.

I cannot be at rest, nor dare indulge myself, in the wished joy to meet your eyes, 'till you remove this painful doubt, in which your last (all goodness as 'twas meant!) has left the heart, of,
   Madam,
    your unchangeably devoted,
     and (from his soul) your faithful,
      humble servant,
      A. Hill.

Dramatic Works, 2:394–96.

The following poems by Aaron Hill are addressed to Martha Fowke Sansom. Hill's eccentric punctuation and italics have been preserved. Obvious misprints have been corrected.

To C——o.

 Snar'd, in intangling mazes of thy charms,

Teach me to shake these *silky chains* away;
Slow, thy *sweet* force, my *stubborn* mind disarms,
  'Till ev'n *ambition* bends, beneath thy sway.

What shall I do, to free my struggling soul,
  Bow'd, to the soft'ning *biass* of thy song?
As circling *straws,* in whirlwinds, driving roll,
  So are my hurry'd *passions,* swept along.

Fool, as I was!—I felt thy distant *fire,*
  E're from those *eyes,* it flash'd undying flame;
Yet, sure, said I—for once—I may aspire,
  And view *that heav'n,* whence all this brightness came.

So, the light *cork,* that on the *Thame's* smooth side,
  Embay'd, glides *buoyant* and just *skims* the shore,
Edges, ambitious, to the rapid tide,
  And rushing down the stream, returns no more.

Late my free *thoughts,* unbounded, as the *air,*
  Could, with an eye-beam's swiftness, scale the sky;
Wander, in *starry* worlds, and busy'd there,
  From human *cares,* and human *passions* fly.

Down to dark *earth's* deep *center,* could I roam,
  And, thro' her *chasmy lab'rinths,* wind my way;
See *Gold* unripen'd, in its dusky *home,*
  And mark how *springs,* in *veiny bendings,* stray.

Oft as th'alarming *trumpet* struck my *ear,*
  Or the big *drum's* dead *beat* hoarse-thund'ring rose,
My summon'd *soul* sprung out to *war's* wish'd sphere,
And plung'd me in the ranks of *fancy'd foes.*

Wide as unmeasur'd *nature's* trackless space,
  Untir'd *imagination* restless flew;
Disdain'd to fix on *object,* or on *place,*
  And every moment, some *fresh* labour knew.

C——o was *then,* unseen, unread, unknown;—
  Now, lovely tyrant, she usurps my mind;
Devoted fancy vows itself her own:
  And my *whole* thought is, to *one theme,* confin'd.

Yet, *pow'rful* as she is—she *doubts* her *lays;*
  Blind, like the *sun,* to her own blazing flame,

Transports the list'ning soul—engrosses praise;
    Yet humbly wishes—an immortal name.

Oh! that I could but *live,* 'till that late day,
    When *C*—'s unremember'd name shall die!
Then should I hope, full leisure to *display*
    Those unborn *deeds,* which in my *bosom* lie.

But, as it is, our fleeting sands so fast
    Ebb to their *end,* and lead us to *decay;*
That e're we learn to *see,* our daylight's past,
    And like a melting *mist,* life shrinks away.

Works, 3:6–8.

The MUSE'S EXPOSTULATION, *with a* LADY, *who denied herself the Freedom of* FRIENDSHIP, *from too delicate an Apprehension of the* WORLD'S MISTAKEN CENSURE.

O Born to *pity* woes, yet form'd to *give,*
Shut from whose *presence,* 'twere a *pain,* to *live!*
Who make all *converse* tedious, but your *own;*
And, *that* with-held, leave the forsaken none.
Urg'd by what motives, would you *wish* to shun
The *sight,* and *voice,* of him, whose *soul* you won?
On what false fears does this cold *flight* depend?
What fancy'd *foe* does *prudence* apprehend?

   When *bodies* only are to *bodies* dear,
The danger there consists in being *near;*
And, when the *fair,* the soft contagion spy,
Discretion calls 'em——and 'tis wise, to *fly.*
But, where associate *spirits* catch the *flame,*
Flight is a cruel, and a fruitless *aim.*
Souls have no *sexes;* and if *minds* agree,
Parting is dying, to set fancy free.

   Nor let mistaken *virtue* wrong the breast,
That opens kindly to so sweet a guest:
Not saints, in heav'n a purer warmth express,
Than *reason* feels, when touch'd by *tenderness.*
Relenting *wisdom* dignifies *desire,*
And rais'd *ideas* fan the bright'ning fire;
'Till the white *flame,* ascending to the sky,
Spreads its low *smoak,* in *envy's* darken'd eye.

   Whence grew society, so wish'd an *art,*

If the *mind*'s elegance betrays the *heart?*
Were it a *crime* in flashing souls, to rise,
And strike each other thro' the meeting eyes?
Those op'ning *windows* had not let in light,
Nor stream'd ideas out, to *voice* the sight.

   Why are you form'd so *pow'rful,* in your *charms,*
If *beauty* ought to *fly* the wish, it *warms?*
Vainly did *heav'n* inspire that tuneful *tongue,*
With *notes* more sweet, than ever *seraph* sung!
If, justly, all that *harmony* you hide,
Your *musick* useless, and its pow'r untry'd.
Have *wit* and *eloquence* in vain, conspir'd,
And giv'n you *brightness,* but to *shine* retir'd?
Must you be *loveliest,* yet be never *shown?*
Than *all* be wiser, yet be heard, by *none?*
Oh! 'tis too delicate!—'tis falsely nice,
To bar the *heart* against the *mind's* advice.

   But, you will say, that *honour's* call, you hear;
That *fame* is tender—*reputation,* dear:
That, from the *world's* malignant blast you fly,
Fear the *fool's tongue,* and the discerner's *eye.*
The spleen of disappointed wishes *dread,*
Or envy's *whispers,* by detraction spread?
Alas! what *bounds* can limit your *retreat?*
Where will sought *safety* rest your flying feet?
Is there a *corner,* in the globe, so *new,*
That *malice* will not find, as sure as *you?*
The very flight, that shuns, attracts the *wrong;*
And every censure fear'd, you force along.
"There's *cause,* no doubt, for her *retreat,* they'll say,
"A fearless *innocence* had dar'd to *stay!*"
Scandal has, either way, an edge, to strike,
And wounds *distinction* every where *alike:*
Superior *excellence* is doom'd, to bear
The *slings* of sland'rous *hate,* and rash *despair:*
'Tis the due *tax,* your rated merit pays,
And ev'ry judging *ear* will call it *praise.*

   Think—and be kind—convert this fruitless pain
To a fix'd *firmness,* and a calm *disdain.*
Since *cautious absence* can no more be free,
From false *reproach,* than *present smiles* will be,
Diffuse those *gifts,* which heav'n design'd should bless,
Nor let their *greatness* make their *pity* less.

Indulging *freedom,* ev'ry *fear* disarm,
And, with a conscious scorn of slander, *charm.*
Bold, in your guarded *strength,* your *heart* unbind,
And, to be *safe*—suppose yourself *all mind.*

Yet, needless that! since such respect you draw,
That ev'n your *tenderness* is arm'd with *awe:*
Permitted *love,* would silently admire,
And a soft *rev'rence* tremble, thro' *desire,*
The warmest *wishes,* when inspir'd by *you,*
Strike, but as *heav'nly inspirations* do.
The op'ning *heart* makes room for *joys* refin'd,
And ev'ry *gross idea* shrinks behind.

You need not then, the gentle sound reject,
Shou'd *Love's* fear'd *name* be giv'n to soft respect:
When ill distinguish'd *meanings* are the same,
How poor the *diff'rence,* which they draw from *name!*
There are, in *love,* th'extremes of touch'd *desire,*
The noblest *brightness,* or the coarsest *fire!*
In vulgar *bosoms,* vulgar *wishes* move;
Nature guides *choice,* and as men *think,* they *love.*
But, when a pow'r, like *yours,* impels the *wound,*
Like the clear *cause,* the bright *effect* is found.
In the loose *passion,* men profane the *name,*
Mistake the *purpose,* and pollute the *flame:*
In nobler bosoms, friendship's *form* it takes,
And *sex* alone, the lovely *diff'rence* makes.
Love's generous warmth does *reason's* pow'r display,
And fills *desire,* as light *embodies* day.

Love is, to *life,* what *colour* is, to form:
Plain drawings oft are *just,* but never *warm.*
Love, in a blaze of *tints,* his *light'ning* throws;
Then the form *quickens,* and the figure *glows.*
Works, 3:26–31.

The CHANGE;
To the Lovely Cause of it.

Sweet enslaver! can you tell,
E're I learnt to *love* so well,
How my *hours* had wings to move,
All unbusied by my *love!*
'Tis amazement, *now,* to me,
What could *then* a pleasure be!
But *you,* like *God,* new sense can give,

And now, indeed, I feel, I live.

Oh! what *pangs* his breast alarm,
Whom soul and body, *join,* to charm!
Endless transports dance along,
Sweetly soft! or nobly strong!
Flaming fancy! cool reflection!
Fierce desire! and aw'd subjection!
Aking hope! and fear encreasing!
Struggling passions, never ceasing!
Wishing! trembling! soul-adoring!
Ever blest, and still imploring.

Let the dull, the cold, and tame,
All those dear disorders blame;
Tell 'em, that, in *honour's* race,
Charm'd by some such heav'nly face,
Lovers always *foremost* ran;
Love's a second *soul* to *man.*
Ease is languid, low, and base;
Love excites a generous chase:
Glory! Wealth! Ambition! Wit!
Thought, for boundless empire, fit!
All, at Love's approach are fir'd,
Bent more strong, and never tir'd,
He, who feels not Love's sweet pain,
Lives at *ease*—but lives in vain.

Little dream you, what is due,
Angel form! to Love, and you!
'Tis from *you,* I *joy* possess!
'Tis by *you,* my grief grows less!
Sadly *pensive,* when alone,
I the *shades* of life bemoan;
If some *voice* your *name* impart,
Care lies lighten'd, at my *heart;*
Ev'ry *woe* disarms its *sting,*
And I look down on *Britain*'s king!

When my fancy brings to view
Works, which *wealth* and *pow'r* can do;
All my spurr'd excitements wake,
And *fortune* charms me, for your sake!
Oh! I cry—'twere *heaven* possest
To make her *great,* who made me *blest.*

In the *morning,* when I *rise,*
If the *sun-shine* strikes my eyes,
All that *pleases,* in his view,
Is, my *hope,* to look on *you!*

When the sable sweep of *night*
Drowns *distinction,* from my *sight,*
I no *inward darkness* find;
You are *day-light* to my mind!

All my *dreams* are *lives* of joy,
Which, in *waking,* I destroy*:*
You, a slave to custom made,
Are of *forms,* and *rules,* afraid:
But your happier *image,* free
From fantastic tyranny;
Independent, kind, and wise.
Scorns *restraint,* and knows no *ties.*
Oh! the dear, the racking pain;
Who that *sleeps* thus, wou'd *wake* again!

Works, 3:34–39 [37].

On CLIO's *Birth-Day*

O'er the blue *violet,* while the amorous wind
    Bends, and perfumes his wings, to fan this day;
Why has pale sickness winter'd o'er my mind,
    And, with chill *agues,* check'd the warmth of *May?*

Is it not CLIO's *birth-day?*—Toil of thought!
    Height, beyond all, that e'er ambition trod.
Sum of refin'd desire! by *angels* taught,
    To look, and think, and act, a *female god!*

Oh! my rapt *soul,* sits trembling in my *eyes,*
    Starting, impatient, at her pow'rful *name:*
Dearer, than *life,* to that sweet sound it flies,
    And *health* rides rosy, on the living *flame.*

Wak'd into sudden strength, I blaze again,
    Love, the restorer, dress'd in *Clio*'s smile,
Triumph'd o'er *nature,* gave delight to *pain,*
    Sweeten'd *affliction,* and could *death* beguile.

May *joys* un-number'd, as the charmer's *sweets,*
    Bless this revolving day's eternal round;

'Till the proud *world* its *dawn*, with rapture *greets*,
   Conscious of *her*, who made it first renown'd.

Long—let 'em say—long, e're our father's day,
Three thousand years ago, on this sweet day,
That *Clio,* whom contending nations praise,
Embloom'd, by her sweet birth, the first of *May.*

Britain, illustrious by the starry *lot*,
   Far, in the *north*, distinguish'd island, lies,
Now known by later names—oh! envy'd spot!
   Why did she not in our warm climates rise?

Sure, she was heav'nly grac'd! for, to this hour,
   After such length of ages roll'd away!
Fame of her *charms,* augments her sex'd pow'r,
   And her thought's *lustre* give our *wits,* their sway.
                          Works, 3:41–43.

   To a Lady, desiring her Letters might not been expos'd.

No! thou best soul, that e'er this body knew,
Unhappy I may be, but not *untrue!*
Blest, or unblest, my *love* can ne'er *decay*,
Nor could I, where I could not love, *betray.*
Cold, and unjust, the shocking caution kills,
And, in one meaning, spots me o'er with *ills.*
Silent, as sacred *lamps,* in bury'd *urns*,
The conscious flame of lovers inward burns:
Life should be torn, and *racks* be stretch'd in vain,
And varied *tortures* tire their fruitless *pain,*
E're but a *thought of mine* shou'd do thee *wrong*,
Or spread thy *beauties* on the *public tongue.*

   Yet, thou can'st fear me——oh! be lost the *shame*,
Nor heap *dishonour* on my future name!
Have I been never *lov'd?*—yet, cruel, tell,
Whom I betray'd to *thee,* tho' lov'd so well?
Take thy sweet *mischief* back, their *charms* erase,
Oh! leave me *poor*, but never think me *base.*
Not e'en, when *death* shall veil thy starry eyes,
Shall thy dear *letters*, from my *ashes*, rise;
Fix'd to my *heart*, the grave shall give 'em *room*
To charm my waking *soul*, in worlds *to come.*
While in my *verse,* with far more faint *essay,*
Thy *wonders,* I to *after times* convey;

Tell thy vast *heav'n of sweets*, and sing thy *name*,
'Till fir'd by *thee*, whole *kingdoms* catch thy *flame*.
     Savage, ed.. *Miscellaneous Poems*, 280–81; *Works*,
                 3:43–44.

To Mr. DYER; *on his attempting* CLIO's *Picture.*

 Soul of your honour'd *art!* what man *can* do,
In copying *nature,* may be reach'd by *you:*
Your *peopling* pencil a new *world* can give,
And, like *Deucalion,* teach the *stones* to live,
From your creating hand, a *war* may flow;
And your warm strokes, with breathing action, glow:
But, from that *angel form,* to catch the *grace,*
And kindle up your *ivory,* with her *face.*
All, unconsum'd, to snatch the *living fire,*
And *limn* th'*ideas,* which those eyes inspire;
Strong, to your burning *circle,* to confine
That *awe-mix'd sweetness,* and that *air* divine;
That sparkling *soul,* which *lightens,* from *within!*
And breaks, in unspoke *meanings,* thro' her *skin.*
This, if you can—hard task and yet unprov'd!
Then, shall you be *adorn'd,* as now *belov'd.*
Then, shall your high-aspiring *colours* find
The art, to picture *thought* and paint the *wind.*
Then, shall you give *air* SHAPE, imprison *space,*
And mount the *painter* to the *maker's* place.
                Works, 3:45–46.

WHITEHALL STAIRS

From *Whitehall Stairs,* whence oft, with distant view,
I've gazed whole *moon-shine* hours, on hours away,
Blest but to see those *roofs,* which cover'd *you,*
And watch'd beneath what *star,* you sleeping, lay.

 Launch'd on the smiling *stream,* which felt my *hope,*
And danc'd, and quiver'd, round my gliding *boat,*
I came, this day to give my tongue free scope,
And vent the *passion,* which my *looks* denote.

 To tell my dear, my soul-disturbing muse,
(But that's a *name,* can speak but half her charms)
How my full *heart* does my *pen's* aid refuse,
And bids my *voice* describe my *soul's* alarms.
To tell what *transports* your last *letter* gave,
What *heav'ns* were open'd, in your soft complaint,

APPENDIX A

    To tell!—what *pride* I take, to be your *slave,*
And how triumphant *love* disdains restraint.

    But, when I miss'd you, and took *boat* again,
The sympathetic *sun* condol'd my *woe;*
Drew in his *beams,* to mourn my pity'd *pain,*
And bid the shadow'd *stream* benighted flow.

    Sudden, the weeping *skies* unsluic'd their *store,*
And torrents of big *tears* unceasing shed;
Sad, I drove downward, to a flooded *shore,*
And, disappointed, hung my *dripping head.*

    Landed, at length, I sable *coffee* drink,
And, ill surrounded, by a *noisy tribe,*
Scornful of what *they* do, or say, or think,
I, rapt in *your* dear *heav'n,* my *loss* describe.
                                                    Works, 3:46–47.

Note: From Whitehall Stairs, an embarkation point near to Hill's house in Westminster, it would have been possible both to see the Inner Temple, where Martha Fowke Sansom lived, and to take a boat to visit her.

        To the Same [i.e. Martha Fowke Sansom]

Yes—now 'tis time to *die*——*despair* comes on;
Who keeps the *body,* when the *soul* is gone?
She *sets*—fair *light,* that shew'd me all my joy,
And, like the *sun's,* her absence must *destroy.*
She, who *once* wept my *fancy'd* loss of breath,
Now, crimeless murd'rer! gives me *real* death.

    Yet, have a care, touch'd *heart,* nor sigh one *thought,*
That stains such *goodness* with a *purpos'd fault.*
Soft, as her *tears,* her gentle *meanings* move;
Her *soul* sheds *sweetness,* tho' her *look* is *love.*
Her *voice* is *musick,* tun'd to *heav'n's* low note;
Her *touch* bids *transport,* thro' each art'ry, float;
Her step is *dignity,* but *pity* checkt;
At once, she fans *desire,* and plants *respect.*
Unconscious of her *charms,* she dreams of *none,*
And doubling *other's* praises, shuns *her own.*
Modest, in *pow'r,* as kneeling *angels* pray,
Noiseless, as *night's* soft shade, tho' bright, as *day.*
Wise, unassumingly; serenely *deep,*

Easy as *air,* and innocent as *sleep:*
Blooming, like *beauty,* when adorn'd for *sin,*
Yet, like the *bud,* unblown, *all blush* within.

O! 'tis impossible, to quit such *bliss!*
Yet live, superior to a loss, like this!
Where will she, next, her thousand conquests make?
On what *new climate* will her *sun-shine* break?
Where will she next, (sweet *tasker* of my *care!*)
Teach our charm'd sex, to hope, to wish, to dare?
Far from her fruitless *guardian's* watchful *eye,*
What may she hear! what *answer!* oh! I'll *die.*
Bless'd by her *sight*—time's race were one short stage;
She *gone*—one widow'd *moment* were an *age.*

Works, 3:48–49.

A SONG

Clio! smiling, soul-invader!
   Soft amuser of my days,
Be my silent *passion's* aider,
   Teach my *tongue,* to speak thy *praise.*

Thou, like *heroes,* scarr'd all over,
   Wanting room, to suffer more;
Pil'd with *praise,* canst hear no *lover*
   Tell the[e] ought, untold before.

Truth, with modest *bounds,* contented,
   Rightly praising *thee,* must say,
More than *falsehood* e'er invented,
   When the widest went astray.

Works, 3:50.

MAY-DAY

Welcome, dear dawn of *summer*'s rising sway,
Fair *fav'rite* of the year! soul-soft'ning *May!*
Late, have I learnt, by *love's* sweet *Queen,* inspir'd,
Why, from my youth, *this* day my bosom *fir'd;*
'Twas for her *birth,* that blooming nature sprung,
'Twas in her *notes,* the sky's soft rangers sung!
The breeze blew soft, to sigh her soul's sweet frame,
And the boughs bent, in *homage* to her name.
Thick shot the *meads,* to paint her fruitful mind,
And flow'rs, that roll'd her *breath,* enrich'd the wind.
For *her,* the *sun* wake'd out, to bless our isle,

And lighted up half heav'n, to *paint* her *smile;*
Oh! we are *lovers* all! our *Celia* reigns.
And the warm'd world is sick, with my sweet pains.
                                    Works, 3:315–16.

Note: Although this poem is addressed to "Celia," May 1st was Fowke's birthday, and Hill has other poems commemorating this day as Clio's birthday.

To CELIA

Oh! thou *eclipse,* and *glory,* of thy kind!
Thou *vast o'erwhelmer* of the drowning mind!
Bid me not *write* my thoughts, or *speak* my pain,
'Till thou hast giv'n me back my soul, again:
As well might *ship-wreck'd* slaves, who *floating,* lie,
Swim, through the *billowy storms,* which *sweep* the sky,
And my poor *sighing* breast its *torments* show,
And paint, in *cool* description, *burning* woe.
Lost to *sense, mem'ry, meaning*—all, but *thee!*
I *drag on* life's dull load, in *misery.*
Absent, from those dear eye's *destructive* shine,
I pant, methinks, to tell thee, why I *pine.*
But, when I touch my *pen,* my flaming *heart*
Burns up, at once, and *dazzles* trembling art.
Love's scatt'ring *sparks,* on my *full* bosom, fall,
And, kindling wild reflection, blows up all.
                                    Works, 3:327–28.

See note to preceding poem for "Celia."

To CLIO:
On her praising Mr D——R, and shewing me some of his
Verses.

Matchless inspirer of my muse and me,
Thou heaven, of blended smiles, and Majesty!
Thou, by whose light, all *others* worth is shown,
While thou art *dark,* as midnight, to thy *own:*
Praising desert, like *his,* you charm *me,* too,
And, for your blessing *him,* my thanks are *due.*
Mean are the *minds,* who but their *own* possess,
And reap no joy, from *other's* happiness.
I *groan,* beneath *their* pains, whom *sorrow* wrings,
And, when *their hope* is rising, *mine* has wings.

APPENDIX A

O *Clio!* to *deserve* such praise from *thee,*
Points out *thy* friend, a bosom one, for *me,*
My sympathetic soul *reveres* his name,
Sweet are his *thoughts,* and soft, as *evening air;*
Joy gilds his *smiles,*——his *sighs* invite *despair:*
Strong is his *sense,* and his *reflection* deep,
Wide, as his *prospects*——as his mountains *steep;*
Oh! may he still be *blest,* with thy *esteem,*
Oh! may thy *charms,* forever, be his *theme!*

Vast is my *wonder,* at his *Fancy's* flight,
   Till I remember, *whence* his *store* was drawn;
Clio, the inspirer *Clio!* lent him *light,*
   And spread soft *influence,* o'er his wid'ning *dawn:*
Warm'd, by th'enliv'ning *lustre* of her *beams,*
   His rip'ning *reason* burnt with conscious *glow;*
Blaz'd, in the radiant *charmer's* starry streams,
   And shed diffusive *heav'n* on all, *below:*
Oh! thou soft *sun* of *wit,* and *love's* gay clime!
   Point but *one ray* of thy *broad shine,* on *me,*
Then, shall my kindled *soul* flame out sublime,
   And glitter proudly, with thy *friend* and *thee.*

Works, 4:96–98.

Appendix B: Eliza Haywood's Attack on Martha Fowke in *Memoirs of a Certain Island Adjacent to the Kingdom of Utopia* (2d ed. [London: 1726], 1:43–49; 183–86).

[AFTER discussing "Flirtillaria" (Mrs. George Hill, sister-in-law of Aaron Hill), and describing her as mercenary, malicious, and sexually promiscuous, Haywood attacks Martha Fowke Sansom, under the name of "Gloatitia." The Key published with the second edition identified those attacked.]

Behold another of much the same Character, in every thing as ridiculous, in some more vile—that big-bone'd, buxom, brown Woman, who is now talking to her;—the Conformity of Manners, join'd to the Fondness both of them have for new Acquaintance, have made them very intimate—her Name is *Gloatitia* [Key identifies as Mrs. S——n——m], Daughter of the Chevalier *Del Gloatus* [Key identifies Major F——e].—Some say it was from him she learn'd those deluding Arts, she has since practis'd, to the Ruin of as many Women as she could get acquainted with their Lovers or Husbands.—Whether this Report be true, I will not pretend to determine; for my pure and hallow'd Fires would sicken at a sight so horrible, so shocking as an Act of Incest: but this is certain, that they scrupled not to be seen in the same Bed together, and the old Goat would run into luscious Encomiums on the Beauties of her Limbs to all the young *Chevaliers* who came to his Levee. When she was about the Age of Sixteen, he was about to marry her to a young Mechanick, but the Fellow's good Stars directed him to avoid so great an Evil; an intimate Acquaintance of his, one of those to whom already she had been liberal of her Favours, made a timely discovery of her Humour, and to confirm the Veracity of his Words, produc'd some Letters he had receiv'd from her, containing an acknowledgement of all that had pass'd between them. This broke the Match, but she had, however, the good fortune to please a certain Duke [Key gives D. of R——d, probably meant as

Richmond] who never was over-nice in his Choice—he had a Son by her, and allow'd her a handsome Subsistence, till happening to come at an hour she did not expect him in, he found the most dirty and disagreeable of all his Footmen in her Arms.—'Tis not to be imagin'd but that the ocular Demonstration of a Falshood like this, would oblige him to quit her.—After this she fell into great Extremities, and, shunn'd by all who had the power to serve her, rang'd the Town for a miserable Maintenance, was common even to the meanest Rank of Men, and at last despis'd by the vilest, and most profligate.—Who that sees her now, dress'd in her rich Brocade, Diamonds in her Hair and Breast, and a handsome Equipage to attend her, would believe she had been accustom'd to trudge the Streets with scarce a Shoe, and been transported at the Invitation of a Blue-apron Gallant, who charitably feasted her on the Remnants of those Treats, made for more fortunate Ladies of the same Vocation? Yet all this has been her Case for many Years together, and still would have been so, if *Rutho* [Key gives Mr. S———n———m] had not chang'd the Scene: he was, perhaps, the only Man in the world who wou'd have thought her worth retrieving; but he never had an intrigue with any thing but a common Woman, and they say, has suffer'd sufficiently for his Pleasures that way.

He was old and infirm, and had occasion for a Nurse, he therefore took her into Keeping, and allow'd her four hundred Crowns a year; a vast Income for a Creature who had liv'd for a long time without seeing the thousandth part of such a Sum of her own—but it is not in this Wretch's Nature to be grateful or constant, and she regarded the Man who had preserv'd her from perishing, no otherwise than to make him her Property.—the Money she receiv'd from him, served to put her into a habit and manner of living, to draw Company more agreeable to her Taste; she now cou'd dress, make Entertainments, had handsome Lodgings, and it was an advantage to her, that having been known before by few but those of the meaner sort, the extreme vileness of her Character reach'd not the ears of those Persons she was now in a condition to converse with. Everybody knew she had been Mistress to the Duke *Dubarbe,* and believing it was he that debauch'd her, and considering her as an unfortunate Gentlewoman (for *Del Gloatus* was really of a good Family, and had an honourable post in the Army) pity'd a Fault, they believ'd, she had been but ensnar'd to commit. She was visited by several Persons of good Fashion, and some of tolerable Reputation scrupled not to be seen in her Company. *Rutho* had taken lodgings [Key identifies as a Gardener's House at Fulham] for her in a Place perfectly pleasant, it was in the Country, but so near the City, that whenever she pleas'd to go to it, she might be there in an hour's time; and indeed it was there she pass'd most of her days and nights, seldom being at home but when she expected her old Gallant, still continuing her former manner of living, tho' with more Privacy, and better Company. The amorous Stealths she took were not, however, so secret, but that *Rutho* at last had intelligence of them, and was about to turn her off, when her Brother, who had been absent from the Island some years, return'd; and being instructed by his Sister, in the Humour and Disposition of *Rutho,* and how to behave, instead of suffering him to do himself Justice, in discarding a Woman who had been so false to him, forced him to marry her: since that, she does what she pleases, goes where she pleases,—her Husband is in too much Awe of the young *Chevalier,* to dare to discover how much he is dissatisfy'd.— Her Actions now plainly demonstrate to the World, it was not *Poverty* alone which had obliged her to those Courses he would have taken her from;—her Inclinations now appear bare-faced, and so monstrous impudent is she in pursuing the gratification of them, that she waits not for being address'd, nor thinks it beneath her to make the first application.—Two or three indigent Persons, whose Consciences are complaisant enough to yield to any thing for Interest, are maintain'd by her, for no other Service, than to procure her a variety of those Pleasures she most delights in.—The best Wine, and Conversation with the handsomest Men, are all the Heaven she wishes, and having an absolute command of the unhappy browbeat *Rutho*'s Purse, is resolv'd to want nothing that she thinks essential to her happiness;—from one scene of Debauchery she hurries to another, and scarce a day passes, without being Witness of some new Crime as extravagant as shameless.—Of all the Gods there is none she acknowledges but *Phoebus,* him she frequently implores for assistance, to charm her Lovers with the Spirit of *Poetry;* but he had receiv'd a Check from *Jupiter,* for inspiring the Genius of a sometime since deceas'd Nobleman [i.e., Rochester], too severe, to dare to aid the Sentiments of this Wanton.—She pretends, however, to have an intimate acquaintance with the Muses—has judgment enough to know that *ease* and *please* make a *Rhyme,* and to count ten Syllables on her Fingers.— This is the Stock with which she sets up for a Wit, and among some ignorant Wretches passes for such; but with People of true Understanding, nothing affords more Subject of ridicule, than that incoherent Stuff which she calls Verses.—She brib'd, with all the Favours she is capable of conferring, a Bookseller (famous for publishing soft things) [Edmund Curll, though not identified in the Key] to print some of her Works, on which she is not a little vain: tho' she might very well have spared herself the trouble. Few Men, of any rank whatsoever, but have been honour'd with the receipt of some of her Letters both in Prose and Measure—few Coffee-Houses but have been the Repository of them—she daily hears the upbraidings of one Lover for her discover'd Addresses to another; but she can bear it without blushing, and is not of a humour to make herself uneasy at any thing that is said to her, or of her.— The greatest mortification that, perhaps, ever happen'd to her, was, that after having taken the pains to dress herself in the most exact manner she cou'd, in order to charm a young Officer, brought him into her Bed-chamber, dismiss'd her Attendants, and invited him to her Arms with all the tempting languishments of loose Desire, he remain'd insensible!—he was not to be provoked!—he was not to be mov'd!—cold as a *Greenland* Rock, not all her Fire cou'd melt him! in vain her swimming Eyes declared what 'twas she wish'd—in vain her Robe thrown by, disclos'd her naked heaving Breasts rise swelling to be press'd—in vain her glowing trembling Hands grasp'd his, and gently stole themselves into his Bosom— in vain her longing, her expecting Soul, seem'd to evaporate in Sighs—in vain she fainted, dy'd away before him—all her Blandishments were lost on him—not that his reserve was owing to his Virtue, or to a Frigidity of Nature; in the whole Island, there was not a Man who had less a Notion of the one, nor a greater Warmth of the other; but Favours offer'd in a manner so free, so unsought, so unthought of, instead of gently touching the Passion she endeavour'd to raise, quell'd all the motions of Desire, and shock'd the Soul.—In a Scene like this, there was no possibility of a Medium; he must have been extremely *delighted,* if he had not been extremely *disgusted,* and, as he was the latter, pretending a sudden Indisposition, he took his leave before it was consistent with good Manners.—Judge with what Confusion a Woman of her Temper must receive such a Baulk, but resolving not to be wholly disappointed, call'd for her Man *Johannes;* he was a tall, well-made young Fellow, of good Features, and a sanguine Complexion, and from that time, was ever ready to afford his Lady consolation.— She had not Gratitude, however, long to be sensible of the Obligations she had to him, but for some little Negligence of Behaviour, either in publick or private, incens'd his Master against him, and got him turn'd away.—In his place there is now another, whom she seems much more to approve of, and has given him a Diamond-Ring, and a Locket of her Hair—But I shou'd wear out the day, to recount the thousandth part of her various Amours, or the unnumber'd Changes of her roving Inclinations;—nor does a History, such as hers, become me to relate.—I wou'd have pass'd both hers and *Flirtillaria*'s in silence, if the signaliz'd Airs of these Coquets had not oblig'd you to remark them—but by the little I have said concerning them, 'tis easy for you to believe they are Objects of detestation to every heavenly Power, and to me in particular, whose Name they every hour blaspheme, and call to witness of the most abhorr'd Falsities.—I shall only add this of *Gloatitia,* that she has lately been deliver'd of a Child which must heir the unhappy *Rutho*'s Estate, tho' to which of her *Enamorato's* the little Compound does with most right belong, even the omnipotent *Jupiter,* who breath'd the Breath of Life into it, can scarce determine.

Memoirs of a Certain Island (London, 1726), 1:43-49.

[Later in Haywood's roman à clef, she gives the story of Riverius (Richard Savage) and adds to it a further attack on Fowke:]

Not inconsiderable are the number of Friends which his Genius [for poetry] this way has gain'd him—and had he not been unhappily introduc'd to the acquaintance of a vile Woman, a Pretender to that Art, he might have deserv'd many more than he has found; but led by her Insinuations, and perhaps instigated by a belief, that complying with her Humour might be of some advantage to his Fortune, he has been sway'd not only to mean Actions, but such also as are unjust and wicked.—The Wretch being married to a Gentleman well deserving a more worthy Wife, is not content he should endure the load of Infamy, which taking to his honourable Embraces a Woman who brought for her Dower three base begotten Children, has pressed his Reputation down with, continues to encrease the Burthen, by sinning with as many as her now almost antiquated Charms have power to seduce; I grieve to think how often my young Favourite has been betray'd by her Wiles, to further her leud Designs on those of his Acquaintance who appeared amiable in her Eyes.—Nor was this Office, shameful and scandalous as in all Ages it has been esteem'd, the worst he has unwarily been drawn into; the Monster whose Soul is wholly compos'd of Hypocrisy, Envy, and Lust, can ill endure another Woman should be esteem'd Mistress of those Virtues she has acted with too barefaced an Impudence to pretend to, and is never so happy as when by some horrid Strategem she finds the means to traduce and blast the Character of the Worthy: To assist a Disposition therefore so near of kin, and so pleasing to the infernal Potentate, a thousand busy Fiends are always at her Call to furnish Mischief, and new-point Invention; but notwithstanding her Propensity to malice, Dissimulation, of which she is a perfect Mistress, makes her not insensible that the surest way of hurting a Reputation, is to speak of it with an affected Candor——No body in Conversation seems to have more Softness and Gentleness, she boasts of no good quality so much as good-nature, and under that Cover, when ever she does speak a severe thing against any one, 'tis with the more ease believ'd; but it is but seldom she attempts it, 'tis enough for her to lay the Scheme of Mischief, the *executing* it she leaves to others, who if detected, must bear the Blame; while she perhaps shall be the first to *condemn* what she has been the sole occasion of. With how much readiness the easily deceiv'd *Riverius* has obliged her in spreading those Reports, coin'd in the hellish Mint of her own Brain, I am sorry to say: but as his adhering too much to the Interest of so detestable a Creature, has been the only Crime he has hitherto been guilty of, 'tis to be hoped his good Sense will in a short time get the better of her Infatuations——It cannot be doubted but that he has lost many Friends on her account, in particular one there was [i.e., Haywood herself] who bore him a singular Respect, tho' no otherways capacitated to serve him than by good Wishes.—This Person receiv'd a more than common Injury from him, thro' the Instigations of that female Fury; but yet continuing to acknowledge his good Qualities, and pitying his falling into the contrary, took no other Revenge than writing a little Satire, which his having publish'd some admirable fine things in the praise of Friendship and Honour, gave a handsome opportunity for—The Poem consists of but a few Lines, which because the Character of this unfortunate Youth is fully, tho' briefly comprehended in them, I will recite.

To the Ingenious RIVERIUS, on his writing in the Praise of Friendship.

> *Throng'd with the Plaudits of a Croud of* Friends,
> *'Tis nobler Pleasure when a* Foe *commends:*
> *When from my injur'd Soul thy moving Lays*
> *Extort Delight, and force unwilling Praise,*
> *The World must own the Justice of the Theme,*
> *And those thy* Folly *wrong'd, thy* Wit *esteem!*
> *While with such Force thou plead'st in* Friendship's *Cause,*
> *We wonder whence thy Muse th'*Idea *draws:*

Or how so well the Theory *thou know'st*
Of virtues, which thy Practice *cannot boast.*
In budding Youth too much to Mischief prone,
In vile Thersites' *Mind might'st paint thy own!*
                    Memoirs of a Certain Island, 1:183–86.

Bibliography

Armstrong, Nancy. *Desire and Domestic Fiction: A Political History of the Novel.* Oxford: Oxford University Press, 1987.

Baine, Rodney. *Defoe and the Supernatural.* Athens: University of Georgia Press, 1968.

Ballaster, Ros. *Seductive Forms: Women's Amatory Fiction from 1684 to 1740.* Oxford: Clarendon Press, 1992.

Barker-Benfield, G. J. *The Culture of Sensibility: Sex and Society in Eighteenth-Century England.* Chicago: University of Chicago Press, 1992.

Behn, Aphra. *The Works of Aphra Behn.* 4 vols. Ed. Janet Todd. Columbus: Ohio State University Press, 1992–94.

Benstock, Shari, ed. *The Private Self: Theory and Practice of Women's Autobiographical Writings.* Chapel Hill: University of North Carolina, 1988.

Blodgett, Harriet. *Centuries of Female Days: Englishwomen's Private Diaries.* New Brunswick, N.J.: Rutgers University Press, 1988.

Blouch, Christine. "Eliza Haywood and the Romance of Obscurity," *Studies in English Literature* 31 (1991): 535–51.

Bonfield, Lloyd. *Marriage Settlements, 1601–1740.* Cambridge, 1984.

Bowyer, John Wilson. *The Celebrated Mrs. Centlivre.* Durham, N.C.: Duke University Press, 1952.

Brewster, Dorothy. *Aaron Hill: Poet, Dramatist, Projector.* New York, 1913.

Brodski, Bella, and Celeste Schenck, eds. *Life/Lines: Theorizing Women's Autobiography.* Ithaca and London: Cornell University Press, 1988.

Brophy, Elizabeth Bergen. *Women's Lives and the Eighteenth-Century English Novel.* Tampa: University of South Florida Press, 1991.

A Calendar of the Inner Temple Records. Ed. F. A. Inderwick. Vol. 3. 12 Charles II (1660)–12 Anne (1714). London, 1901.

Caribbeana, containing Letters and Dissertations, together with Poetical Essays, on Various Subjects and Occasions. 2 vols. London: Printed for T. Osborne, in Gray's Inn; J. Clarke, at the Royal Exchange; G. Hawkins, at Temple-Bar; R. Dodsley, in Pall-Mall, and W. Lewis, in Covent Garden, 1741.

Chetwood, W. R. *A General History of the Stage . . . from its Original in Greece down to the Present Time.* London: Printed for W. Owen, 1749.

Chudleigh, Mary, Lady. *The Poems and Prose of Mary, Lady Chudleigh.* Ed. Margaret J. M. Ezell. New York; Oxford: Oxford University Press, 1993.

Concanen, Matthew. *Miscellaneous Poems, Original and Translated, By Several Hands. Published by Mr. Concanen.* London: Printed for J. Peele, at Locke's Head in Pater-Noster-Row, 1724.

Cowper, Mary. *The Diary of Mary, Countess Cowper, Lady of the Bedchamber to the Princess of Wales, 1714–1720.* London: John Murray, 1864.

The Cupid. A Collection of Love Songs, in Twelve Parts. Suited to Twelve Different Sorts of Lovers. 2d ed. London: Printed for J. Osborn, 1739.

Cussans, John Edwin. *History of Hertfordshire.* London, 1870–1881.

Davis, Karen. "Martha Fowke: 'A Lady Once Too Well Known'." *English Language Notes* 23, no. 3 (1986): 32–36.

Delany, Mary Granville Pendarves. *The Autobiography and Correspondence of Mary Granville, Mrs. Delany.* Ed. Lady Llanover. 6 vols. London: 1861–62.

Dennis, John. *Original Letters, Familiar, Moral and Critical.* 2 vols. London: Printed for W. Mears, at the Lamb without Temple-Bar, 1721.

Duffy, Maureen. *The Passionate Shepherdess: Aphra Behn, 1640–89.* London: Methuen, 1989.

Earle, Peter. *The Making of the English Middle Class: Business, Society, and Family Life in London, 1660–1730.* Berkeley and Los Angeles: University of California Press, 1989.

Eaves, T. C. Duncan, and Ben D. Kimpel. *Samuel Richardson: A Biography.* Oxford: Clarendon Press, 1971.

Egmont, Earl of. *Historical Manuscripts Commission: Manuscripts of the Earl of Egmont. Diary of Viscount Percival, Afterwards First Earl of Egmont.* 3 vols. London: His Majesty's Stationery Office, 1920–23.

Ezell, Margaret. "Elizabeth Delaval's Spiritual Heroine: Thoughts on Redefining Manuscript Texts by Early Women Writers." *English Manuscript Studies, 1100–1700* 3 (1992): 216–37.

———. *Writing Women's Literary History.* Baltimore and London: Johns Hopkins University Press, 1993.

The Feminist Companion to Literature in English: Women Writers from the Middle Ages to the Present. Ed. Virginia Blain, Patricia Clements, and Isobel Grundy. New Haven: Yale University Press, 1990.

Féret, Charles James. *Fulham Old and New.* 3 vols. London, 1900.

Firmager, Gabrielle. "Eliza Haywood: Some Further Light on her Background," *Notes and Queries* 236 (June 1991): 181–83.

Foster, Joseph, ed. *London Marriage Licenses, 1521–1869.* London, 1887.

Fowke, Gerard. Manuscript Genealogy of Fowke Family. Bodleian Library MS Rawl B130.

Fowke, Martha. *Clio: or, A Secret History of the Life and Amours of the Late Celebrated Mrs. S——N——M.* London: Printed for M. Cooper, 1752.

———, and William Bond. *The Epistles of Clio and Strephon, being a Collection of Letters that passed between an English Lady, and an English Gentleman in France.* London: Printed for J. Hooke, F. Gyles, and W. Boreham, 1720. 2d ed., with same title. London: Printed for J. Hooke, 1729. 3d ed. (actually a reissue of the 1729 edition with new title page), titled *The Platonic Lovers, consisting of Original Letters, that pass'd between an English Lady, and an English Gentleman in France.* London: Printed for John Wilford; and Richard Chandler, 1732. Reprint edition, titled *A Critical Essay, Containing some Remarks upon the Nature of Epistolary and Elegiac Poetry,* by John Porter. New York: Garland, 1971.

———. *Epistles and Poems by Clio and Strephon.* London: E. Curll, 1729. 2d ed., titled *Clio and Strephon: being the Second and Last Part of the Platonic Lovers*. London: Printed for E. Curll, 1732.

Gallagher, Catherine. *Nobody's Story: The Vanishing Acts of Women Writers in the Marketplace, 1670–1820*. Berkeley and Los Angeles: University of California Press, 1994.

Gilbert, Sandra and Susan Gubar. *The Madwoman in the Attic*. New Haven: Yale University Press, 1979.

Graham, Elspeth, et al., eds. *Her Own Life: Autobiographical Writings by Seventeenth-Century Englishwomen*. London and New York: Routledge, 1989.

Green, David. *Queen Anne*. New York: Scribner's, 1970.

Greer, Germaine, et al., eds. *Kissing the Rod: An Anthology of Seventeenth-Century Women's Verse*. London: Virago, 1988.

The Grove; or a Collection of Original Poems, Translations &c. Comp. by Lewis Theobald. London: Printed for W. Mears, 1721.

Grundy, Isobel, and Susan Wiseman, eds. *Women, Writing, History: 1640–1740*. Athens: University of Georgia Press, 1992.

Guilhamet, Leon. *The Sincere Ideal: Studies on Sincerity in Eighteenth-Century English Literature*. Montreal and London: McGill-Queen's University Press, 1974.

Hagstrum, Jean H. *Sex and Sensibility: Ideal and Erotic Love from Milton to Mozart*. Chicago: University of Chicago Press, 1980.

Hammond, Anthony. Notes of 1713. Bodleian Library MSS Rawl 1207.

———, ed. *A New Miscellany of Original Poems, Translations, and Imitations*. London: Printed for T. Jauncey at the Angel, without Temple Bar, 1720.

Hatton, Edward. *A New View of London*. 2 vols. London, 1708.

Haywood, Eliza. *The Injur'd Husband; or, the Mistaken Resentment*. London: Printed for D. Brown, jun.; W. Chetwood, and J. Woodman; and S. Chapman, 1723.

———. *Letters from a Lady of Quality to a Chevalier*. London: Printed for William Chetwood, 1721. 2d ed. London: Printed for D. Browne junr. at the Black-Swan, without Temple-Bar, and S. Chapman, at the Angel in Pall Mall, 1724.

———. *Love Letters on all Occasions lately pass'd between Persons of Distinction. Collected by Mrs. Eliza Haywood*. London: Printed for and sold by John Brindley; Robert Willock; John Jackson; John Penn; Francis Cogan, 1730.

———. *Memoirs of a Certain Island Adjacent to the Kingdom of Utopia*. 2 vols. London: Printed and Sold by the Booksellers of London and Westminster, 1725–26. 2d ed. of vol. 1, 1726.

———. *A Spy upon the Conjurer; or, a Collection of Surprising Stories, with Names, Places, and Particular Circumstances relating to Mr. Duncan Campbell*. London: Sold by Mr. Campbell; and at Burton's Coffee-House, Charing-Cross, 1724.

———. *The Works of Mrs. Eliza Haywood; Consisting of Novels, Letters, Poems, and Plays*. 4 vols. London: Printed for Dan Browne jun., and Sam. Chapman at the Angel in Pallmall, 1724.

Heilbrun, Carolyn G. "Women's Autobiographical Writings, New Forms." *Prose Studies* 8, 2 (1985): 14–28.

Highfill, Philip H., Jr., Kalman A. Burnim, and Edward A. Langhans. *A Bio-*

graphical Dictionary of Actors, Actresses, Musicians, Dancers, Managers, and Other Stage Personnel in London, 1660–1800. Carbondale and Edwardsville: Southern Illinois University Press, 1982.

Hill, Aaron. *The Dramatic Works of Aaron Hill, Esq.* 2 vols. London: Printed for the Benefit of the Family, 1760.

———. "Letters to Richard Savage." *The European Magazine* 6 (1784): 189–94; 277–82.

———. *The Works of the Late Aaron Hill Esq; in Four Volumes.* London: Printed for the Benefit of the Family, 1753. 2d ed., with different arrangement and contents, 1754.

Hill, Aaron, and William Bond, eds. *The Plain Dealer; being Select Essays on Several Curious Subjects . . . Publish'd originally in the Year 1724.* London: Printed for S. Richardson and A. Wilde, 1730.

Holt, Geoffrey, S. J. *The English Jesuits, 1650–1829: A Biographical Dictionary.* London: Catholic Record Society, 1984.

Holt, T. G. "The Embassy Chapels in Eighteenth-Century London." *The London Recusant* 2 (1971): 19–37.

Holmes, Richard. *Dr. Johnson and Mr. Savage.* London: Hodder and Stoughton, 1993.

Hunter, J. Paul. *Before Novels: The Cultural Contexts of Eighteenth-Century English Fiction.* New York: Norton, 1990.

———. "The Loneliness of the Long Distance Reader." *Genre* 10 (1977): 455–84.

[Jacob, Giles]. *The Poetical Register: or the Lives and Characters of the English Dramatick Poets. With an Account of their Writing.* 2 vols. London: Printed for E. Curll in Pater-Noster-Row, 1719–1720; facsimile edition, New York: Garland Publishing, 1970.

———. *Human Happiness. A Poem. Adapted to the Present Times, With Several Other Miscellaneous Poems.* London: Printed for T. Jauncey, and J. Roberts, 1721.

Jelinek, Estelle C. *The Tradition of Women's Autobiography from Antiquity to the Present.* Boston: Twayne Publishers, 1986.

Johnson, Samuel. *Lives of the English Poets.* Ed. G. B. Hill. Oxford: Clarendon Press, 1905.

Jones, Vivien, ed. *Women in the Eighteenth Century: Constructions of Femininity.* London; New York: Routledge, 1990.

Kauffman, Linda. *Discourses of Desire: Gender, Genre, and Epistolary Fiction.* Ithaca: Cornell University Press, 1986.

Kropf, C. R. "William Popple: Dramatist, Critic, and Diplomat." *Restoration,* 2d ser. 1 (1986): 1–17.

Lipking, Lawrence. *Abandoned Women and Poetic Tradition.* Chicago: University of Chicago Press, 1988.

Loftis, John, ed. *The Memoirs of Anne, Lady Halkett, and Ann, Lady Fanshawe.* Oxford: Clarendon Press, 1979.

The London Stage, 1660–1800. Part 2, 1700–1729. Ed. E. L. Avery. 2 vols. Carbondale: Southern Illinois University Press, 1960–68.

Longstaffe, William Hylton. "Notes respecting the Life and Family of John Dyer, the Poet," *The Patrician* 4 (1847): 420–26.

Lonsdale, Roger, ed. *Eighteenth-Century Women Poets.* Oxford: Oxford University Press, 1989.

———. *The New Oxford Book of Eighteenth-Century Verse.* Oxford: Oxford University Press, 1987.

Manley, Delarivier. *Mrs. Manley's History of her Own Life and Times. Publish'd from her Original Manuscript.* 4th ed. London: Printed for E. Curll, 1725. First printed as *The Adventures of Rivella* (London, 1714).

———. *Memoirs of the New Atalantis.* 1709. Ed. Rosalind Ballaster. London: Penguin, 1992.

Marcus, Laura. *Autŏiographical Discourses: Theory, Criticism, Practice.* Manchester and New York: Manchester University Press, 1994.

McCarthy, Eugene. *William Wycherley: A Biography.* Athens: Ohio University Press, 1979.

McDermott, Hubert. *Novel and Romance: The Odyssey to Tom Jones.* Totowa, N.J.: Barnes & Noble, 1989.

McKeon, Michael. *The Origins of the English Novel, 1600–1740.* Baltimore: Johns Hopkins University Press, 1987.

Miscellaneous Poems. By Several Hands. . . . Publish'd by Mr. Ralph. London: Printed by C. Akers, for W. Meadows; J. Batley; T. Cox; S. Billingsley; R. Hett; and J. Gray, 1729.

A Miscellany of Poems by Several Hands. Publish'd by J. Husbands. Oxford: Printed by Leon. Lichfield, 1731.

Mitchell, Joseph. *Poems on Several Occasions.* London: Printed for the Author, and sold by L. Gilliver, 1729.

Mr. Campbell's Packet for the Entertainment of Gentlemen and Ladies. London: Printed for T. Bickerton, at the Crown in Pater-Noster-Row, 1720.

Mullan, John. *Sentiment and Sociability: The Language of Feeling in the Eighteenth Century.* Oxford: Clarendon Press; New York: Oxford University Press, 1988.

Nichols, John. *Illustrations of the Literary History of the Eighteenth Century, Consisting of Authentic Memoirs and Original Letters of Eminent Persons.* 8 vols. London: Printed for the author by Nichols, Son and Bentley, 1817–58.

———. *Literary Anecdotes of the Eighteenth Century.* 9 vols. London: Printed for the author, by Nichols, Son, and Bentley, 1812–16.

Nussbaum, Felicity A. *The Autobiographical Subject: Gender and Ideology in Eighteenth-Century England.* Baltimore and London: Johns Hopkins University Press, 1989.

Oldmixon, John. *Court Tales: or, A History of the Amours of the Present Nobility.* London: Printed for J. Roberts, 1717.

Otten, Charlotte F., ed. *English Women's Voices, 1540–1700.* Miami: Florida International University Press; Gainesville: University Presses of Florida, 1992.

Pack, Richardson. *A New Collection of Miscellanies in Prose and Verse.* London: Printed for E. Curll, 1725.

Perry, Ruth. *The Celebrated Mary Astell.* Chicago: University of Chicago Press, 1986.

———. *Women, Letters, and the Novel.* New York: AMS Press, 1980.

Philips, Katherine. *Letters from Orinda to Poliarchus.* London: Printed by W. B. for Bernard Lintot, 1705.

Pomerleau, Cynthia S. "The Emergence of Women's Autobiography in England." In *Women's Autobiography: Essays in Criticism.* Ed. Estelle C. Jelinek. Bloomington and London: Indiana University Press, 1980.

Pope, Alexander. *Epistles to Several Persons.* Ed. F. W. Bateson. London: Methuen, 1951.

Rogers, Katherine M. *Feminism in Eighteenth-Century England.* Urbana: University of Illinois Press, 1982.

Rogers, Pat. *Grub Street: Studies in a Subculture.* London: Methuen, 1972.

Rumbold, Valerie. *Women's Place in Pope's World.* Cambridge: Cambridge University Press, 1989.

Ryder, Dudley. *The Diary of Dudley Ryder, 1715–1716.* Transcr. from shorthand and ed. William Matthews. London: Methuen, 1939.

Sansom, Martha. See Fowke, Martha.

Savage, Richard. *The Poetical Works of Richard Savage.* Ed. Clarence Tracy. Cambridge: Cambridge University Press, 1962.

Savage, Richard, ed. *Miscellaneous Poems and Translations.* London: Printed for Samuel Chapman, 1726.

The Scarborough Miscellany for the Year 1733. London: Printed for J. Wilford, 1734.

Scouten, Arthur H. "The Increase in Popularity of Shakespeare's Plays in the Eighteenth Century: A Caveat for Interpreters of Stage History." *Shakespeare Quarterly* 7 (1953): 189–202.

Shevelow, Kathryn A. *Women in Print Culture: The Construction of Femininity in the Early Periodical.* London: Routledge, 1989.

Smith, Hilda. *Reason's Disciples: Seventeenth-Century English Feminists.* Urbana: University of Illinois Press, 1982.

Smith, Sidonie. *A Poetics of Women's Autobiography.* Bloomington: Indiana University Press, 1987.

Spacks, Patricia Meyer. "'Ev'ry Woman is at Heart a Rake." *Eighteenth-Century Studies* 8 (1974): 27–46.

———. "Female Rhetorics." In *The Private Self: Theory and Practice of Women's Autobiographical Writing.* Ed. Shari Benstock. Chapel Hill: University of North Carolina Press, 1988.

———. *Imagining a Self: Autobiography and Novel in Eighteenth- Century England.* Cambridge: Harvard University Press, 1976.

Stanton, Domna C., ed. *The Female Autograph: Theory and Practice from the Tenth to the Twentieth Century.* Chicago: University of Chicago Press, 1987. [Originally published in *The New York Literary Forum,* vols. 12–13, 1984.]

Steele, Richard. *The Correspondence of Richard Steele.* Ed. Rae Blanchard. Oxford: Clarendon Press, 1941.

Stone, Lawrence. *Broken Lives: Separation and Divorce in England, 1660–1875.* Oxford: Oxford University Press, 1993.

———. *The Family, Sex and Marriage in England, 1500–1800.* New York: Harper and Row, 1977.

Straus, Ralph. *The Unspeakable Curll: Being Some Account of Edmund Curll Bookseller: to which is Added a Full List of his Books.* London: Chapman and Hall, 1927.

Tighe, Robert R., and James Edward Davis. *Annals of Windsor.* 2 vols. London, 1858.

Todd, Janet. *The Sign of Angellica: Women, Writing and Fiction, 1660–1800.* London: Virago, 1989.

———, ed. *A Dictionary of British and American Women Writers, 1600–1800.* London: Methuen, 1987.

Thielbaux, Michelle. "Foucault's Fantasia for Feminists: The Woman Reading." In *Theory and Practice of Feminist Literary Criticism.* Ed. G. Mora and K. s. Van Hooft. Ypsilanti: Bilingual Press, 1982.

Thomas, Elizabeth. *Pylades and Corinna: or, Memoirs of the Lives, Amours, and Writings of Richard Gwinnett Esq: . . . and Mrs. Elizabeth Thomas Junr. . . . Containing, the Letters and Other Miscellaneous Pieces, . . . Which passed between them during a Courtship of above Sixteen Years. . . . To which is prefixed, The Life of Corinna. Written by her Self.* 2 vols. London: Printed in the year, 1731–32.

Thomson, James. *James Thomson [1700–1748]: Letters and Documents.* Ed. Alan D. McKillop. Lawrence: University of Kansas Press, 1958.

To Sylvia, a Poem. Occasion'd by her Commending the Epistles of the Platonick Lovers, Clio and Strephon. London: Printed in the year, 1738.

Tracy, Clarence. *The Artificial Bastard: A Biography of Richard Savage.* Cambridge: Harvard University Press, 1953.

Turner, Cheryl. *Living by the Pen: Women Writers in the Eighteenth Century.* London; New York: Routledge, 1992.

Turner, James Grantham. "The Libertine Sublime: Love and Death in Restoration England." *Studies in Eighteenth-Century Culture* 19. Ed. Leslie Ellen Brown and Patricia Craddock. Lansing: Colleagues Press, for ASECS, 1989.

Victor, Benjamin. *The History of the Theatres of London and Dublin, from the Year 1730 to the Present Time.* 2 vols. London: Printed for T. Davies; R. Griffiths, T. Becket, and P. A. de Hondt; G. Woodfall; J. Coote; and G. Kearsley, 1761.

Vincent, Howard P. "The Death of William Wycherley." *Harvard Studies and Notes in Philology and Literature* 15 (1933): 219–42.

Warburton, G. D. *Memoir of the Earl of Peterborough.* 2 vols. London, 1853.

Waterhouse, Ellis. *Painting in Britain, 1530–1790.* Baltimore: Penguin, 1953.

Whicher, George Frisbie. *The Life and Romances of Mrs. Eliza Haywood.* New York: Columbia University Press, 1915.

Williams, Ralph M. *Poet, Painter, Parson: The Life of John Dyer.* New York: Bookman Associates, 1956.

Williamson, John Bruce. *The History of the Temple, London.* London: John Murray, 1924.

Willson, E. J. *West London Nursery Gardens.* The Fulham and Hammersmith Historical Society, 1982.

Winton, Calhoun. *Captain Steele: The Early Career of Richard Steele.* Baltimore: Johns Hopkins Press, 1964.

———. *Sir Richard Steele, M.P.: The Later Career.* Baltimore and London: Johns Hopkins Press, 1970.

Index

Addison, Joseph, 27
Adultery, 28
Adventures of Rivella (Manley), 18, 163
Albemarle-Street (London), 67
Anstis, John, 116–17, 164
Arlington Street, Westminster, 69, 155
A———s, Mr., 117. *See also* Anstis, John
Astell, Mary, 158, 162
Austen, Sir James, 19
Autobiography: as genre, 18, 42–43

B———, Mr. (married to Fowke's friend), 82–85
B———, Mr. (unidentified Huguenot landlord), 66–67, 154
Ballaster, Ros, 17
Barbados Gazette, 15, 166
Bath (English spa town), 24, 90–92, 93, 94
Beaufort, Duke of: and Fowke, 94, 96, 103, 104–5, 159–60; connections of, 159; death, 162; Manley's praise of, 160; Oldmixon's attack on, 160
Bedford-Street, London, 89, 158
Behn, Aphra, 15, 16, 23
Bellenden, Lord, 155
Bellenden, Miss, 155
Belless, Major, 163
Berkeley, Sir Henry, 159
Blenman, Jonathan, 166
Blindness, 85–86
Blount, Martha, 31
Blount sisters, 26
B———l———n, Mr., Sir C———'s son, 69–72, 155
Boarding school, 38, 62, 76–77
Bolton, Duchess of, 165
Bond, William ("Strephon"), 15, 24, 34, 125, 150, 166
Books: deprivation of, 65, 73; entertaining, 64, 74; feed sorrow, 82; Fowke's love of, 66, 70, 72, 76, 81, 129; gifts of, 91, 113; loans of, 67, 125; lover abandons, 122
Borrowes, Robert, 163
Boyer, Abel, 42
Brinsden, Mr., 158
B———s, Mr. (friend of brother), 163
B———y, Sir Harry, 92, 159

Calprenède, la, 21, 153
Campbell, Duncan, 24, 28, 30
Cassandra (la Calprenède), 21, 64, 153, 154
Catholicism, 64, 65–66, 70, 73, 153, 154, 155
Cenny, Mr. and Mrs. (landlords at Fulham), 23, 86, 102, 113, 125, 158
Censor (ed. Theobald), 166
Centlivre, Susanna, 24
Chambers, in Inns of Court, 117, 129
Chandler, Mary. *See* Fowke, Mary
Charles II, King, 62, 152
Chaucer, Geoffrey, 126
Chudleigh, Lady Mary, 15
Churchill, John. *See* Marlborough, Duke of
Cibber, Colley, 34
Cibber, Theophilus, 34
Clarissa (Richardson), 161
Cleopatra (la Calprenède), 21, 64, 153
"Cleora," 34
Cleveland, Duchess of (Barbara Villiers), 101, 158, 162
Clio and Strephon: being the Second and Last Part of the Platonic Lovers, 149
"Clio" (pseudonym for Fowke, Martha), 18, 149
"Clio's Picture", 32, 55–56, 149–50
Closet, 64, 74, 106, 153, 156
Codrington, Christopher (son), 62, 153
Codrington, Colonel Christopher, 62–63, 152–53

205

Codrington, Miss (Thomas Fowke's 2d wife), 62–63
Coke, Thomas, 106, 163
Coning, Daniel, 162–63
Cottage, 23, 166, 174
Cowley, Abraham, 21, 65, 66, 154
Cowper, Lady, 151
Crofts, Mr., 120
Crofts, Mrs., (mistress of the Duke of Monmouth), 119–20
Cullen (or Culling), Elizabeth ("Louisa"), 153
Cullen (or Culling), John (cousin), 153, 154
Cullen, John (Fowke's uncle), 63, 153
Curll, Edmund, 24, 42, 149, 151, 193–94
C——y, Mr. (painter), 106–8
C——y, Mr. (young engaged gentleman), 123–24

Dacier, Madame, 15
"Damon," 164
Dancing, 21, 22, 65, 96, 105
Deaths: of father, 20, 81; of mother, 19, 72; of Thomas Keightley, 109–10
Delights for the Ingenious, 15, 162
Dennis, John, 42, 161
Devonshire Street, 73, 156
Donne, John, 15
Dress: corsets, 151; formal, 55, 161; informal, 151
Dunciad, 166
D'Urfey, Thomas, 165
Dyer, John: emotional relationship with Fowke, 25, 37, 148, 167, 189; literary relationship with Fowke, 21, 24, 167, 189; portrait of Fowke by, 25, 174

Education: at boarding school, 76–77; criticism of lovers', 75, 94, 114; Fowke's, 21, 64–65, 72, 76–77
Egmont, Earl of, 38
Epistles of Clio and Strephon, 15, 32, 125, 149–50, 224, 234
Epitaph, 39

Fanshawe, Lady, 18
Fornication, 28
Fountain, Mr., 158
Fowk (Foulks), Peter, 159, 160
Fowke, Gerard, 19

Fowke, John (grandfather), 62, 152
Fowke, Joyce, née Marche (grandmother): family connections, 152, 156; brings up Fowke's cousins, 75; Fowke family's residence with, 64; library of, 74, 156; maxims of, 84
Fowke, Martha: ambition, 15–16, 20–21; attitude to marriage, 38, 75, 114, 129; book subscriptions, as Mrs. Sansom, 160, 165; children, 29, 31, 37, 195; education, 21, 64–65, 72, 76–77; epitaph, 39; family, 19, 60; and Haywood, 28–31; and Hill, 31–37; literary connections, 24–25, 34; marriage to Arnold Sansom, 29, 30–31, 37–38, 129. See also *Barbados Gazette, The Epistles of Clio and Strephon, Miscellaneous Poems and Translations, New Miscellany of Original Poems and Translations,* and Lovers
Fowke, Thomas (brother of Martha): army service, 72; birth of, 19, 63; financial affairs of, 107, 108; Fowke writes verse for, 66; Fowke's praise of, 60, 63, 110; friends with Hammond, 51, 150; in Ireland, 74, 82, 89, 108; sends portrait to Fowke by friend, 110; in Spain, 110; in Staffordshire, 64; urges marriage with Maynard, 89–90; urges marriage with Sansom, 129; writes Fowke's epitaph, 39
Fowke, Thomas (father of Martha): army service, 60, 72, 152; attitude to marriage, 19, 38, 62; description of, 19, 60, 62; disapproves of Fowke's lovers, 67, 75, 76, 77–78; encourages daughter's writing, 20–21, 65, 66; family of, 19, 152; in France, 62; Haywood's attack on, 28; involvement in Fowke's education, 65, 76–77; murder of, 20, 81–82, 150–51; wives of, 62–63, 152
Fowke, Mary (mother): approves of suitors, 67, 70; books of, 64, 67; converts to Catholicism, 64, 153; death of, 19, 72, 152; discourages reading and writing, 21, 65; fondness of, 64; jointure of, 60, 72, 152, 155; first mar-

riage, 152; physician to, 74; unhappy marriage of, 19, 63
France, 19, 62
Freedom: loss of, 73, 76–77, 143; love of, 23, 81, 106, 113, 123; sexual, 26–27
French: language, 21, 65, 66; literature, 21, 43
Frenchman (Mr. B———), 66–67
Fulham, 90, 157, 164; Fowke's residence in, 23, 24, 79–105, 109–11, 117–24, 125, 127–29; visits to, 106, 113, 114

G., Mr. (young gentleman of nineteen), 122–23, 125, 126, 127–28
Gardener, 102, 162
Gardens: Hill's, 39–40, 157, 161; at Fulham, 79, 81, 109, 110, 157; Spring Gardens, 74, 156
Gentry, 19, 24, 30
Giffard family, 153, 165
"Gloatitia" (Haywood's pseudonym for Fowke), 30
Governess, 76, 77, 157
Grandmother. *See* Fowke, Joyce
Gray, Christopher (gardener), 162
Grove: Or A Collection of Original Poems, Translations, &c., 160, 166
Guilhamet, Leon, 35
Gunston, Staffordshire, 19, 150, 152
Gyllenborg, Count Carl von (Swedish envoy), 165

H., Mr. (young gentleman), 128–31, 166
Halkett, Lady, 18
Halley (Hally), Edmond, 92, 159
Hammond, Anthony, 24, 32, 149, 150, 157
Hampstead, London, 119
Handel, George Frederick, 34
Harwich, 38
Haywood, Eliza, 24, 34, 39; attacks on Fowke, 17, 21, 29, 30, 81–82, 157, 191–97; description of Fowke by, 19; jealousy, 30; love for Aaron Hill, 30; relations with Fowke, 28–31
H———d, Miss, 77, 157
Hertfordshire, 63, 64, 153
Hertingfordbury, Hertfordshire, 63–64, 153, 154
Hill, Aaron: cultural interests of, 32– 35, 151, 166; description of, 34; and Haywood, 30; letters of, 35, 42; letters to Fowke, 168–78; letters to women, 35; poems by, on Fowke's birthday, 153; relationship with Fowke, 15, 17–18, 21, 24, 31–37, 42; response to Fowke's death, 39; verses by, 170–72, 173, 174, 178–90
Hill, Henrietta, Mrs. Aaron, 35, 39
Hill, Mrs. George (sister-in-law of Aaron), 191
Hillarius (pseudonym for Aaron Hill), 151
H———n, Mr., 120–21
Horneck, Philip, 24
Huguenots, 65, 66, 67
Hyde Park, 77
Hyde, Chancellor, 108, 163
Hyde, Lady Frances, 108, 163

Incest, 28, 29, 157
"Inconstant" (Fowke), 26
Injur'd Husband (Haywood), 30
Inner Temple, 38, 164 (2)
"Interview" (Fowke), 15
Ireland: Fowke's brother in, 74, 82, 89–90, 110; Fowke's connections in, 79, 108–9, 152, 155; lovers from, 70–72, 111–12, 114–16
Isaac, Mr. (dancing master), 56, 151
Italy, 25

Jacob, Giles, 15
Jacobitism, 23, 154, 158, 159, 164, 165, 166
James II, King, 60, 152
Jealousy, 26, 30
Jesuit priest, 21, 65–66, 73, 154
Johnson, Samuel, 17
Jointures, 60, 62, 72, 152
Julius Caesar, 151, 170–71

Keightley, Thomas, 108–10, 153, 159, 163
Kensington (London), 106, 162
Ker, Colonel William, 92, 159
King Street, Westminster, 92, 159
Knightley. *See* Keightley
K———r, Colonel. *See* Ker, Colonel William

La Montre, or The Lover's Watch, 43
Latin, 21, 154

Lawrence, Elizabeth (daughter of Mrs. Ryder), 106–7, 163
Leicester, 39
Letters: to Bond, 125; cousin returns Fowke's, 103; to and from Hill, 18, 113, 131, 132; lovers', 72, 78, 91, 115, 121, 128; from merchant, 76, 77, 78; from Oxford, 92; to and from Sansom, 113, 117
Letters from a Lady of Quality, 28
Libertinism, 19, 26–29, 40, 161
Liberty. *See* Freedom
Limehouse, Stepney, 19
Literary circles, 18, 24, 28, 34, 35
London Gazette, 20
Lonsdale, Roger, 17
Lottery tickets, 24, 107, 163
"Louisa" (in Manley's *Memoirs of the New Atalantis*), 42, 153
Louis XIV (King of France), 67, 154
Love in Excess (Haywood), 30
Love-Letters between a Nobleman and his Sister, 43
Lovers, 16–17, 25–26; A——s, Mr., 116–17; B——, Mr. (French Huguenot), 66–67; B——, Mr. (married to friend of Fowke's), 82–85; B——fort (Beaufort), Duke of, 94–96, 103, 104–5; B——l——n, Mr., 69–72; B——s, Mr., 110–12, 114–16; B——y, Sir Harry, 92–93; C——(C——y), Mr., 106–8; C——y, Mr., 123–24; clergyman from Sweden, 121–22; country squire, 120–21; cousin (paternal), 75–76, 93–94, 103–6; cousin-german, 78–79; Crofts, Mr., 120; deaf relation, 67–68; fop at Fulham, 100; friend of Mr. B——s, 112–13; G——Mr., 122–23, 125, 129; gardener, 102–3; gentleman of good estate, engaged to wealthy young lady, 102; gentleman of nineteen, 122–23, 125, 129; gentleman with ring, 91; H——, Mr., 128–31; Hill, Aaron, 31–37, 131–32; H——n, Mr., 120–21; Keightley, Mr., 108–10; M——y——d (Maynard), Sir William, 85–90; merchant, 74–75, 76–78; painter, 106–8; R., Mr., 108–10; relation from Ireland, 108–10; S——, Mr., 96–99; S——, Mr. (Sansom, Arnold), 113–17, 119, 129; Swedish clergyman, 121–22; T——ds, Mr., 125–27; Theobald, Lewis, 125–27; whiner at Fulham, 100; witty young man, 79; Wycherley, William, 91; young man on boat to Richmond, 117–19

Manley, Delariviere, 18, 23, 34, 42, 153, 160, 163
Manuscript, 17, 32, 36, 154; circulation in, 29, 42; coterie traditions of, 35
Marche, Richard (maternal grandfather), 19, 62, 152
Marlborough, Duke of, 62, 101, 152, 162
Marriage: father's views of, 62; Fowke's dislike of, 38, 75, 76, 92, 129; Fowke's to Sansom, 129; proposals of, 75, 87, 92
Mask, 69, 155
Maynard, Sir William, 26, 85–90, 158
Mazarine, Duchess of (Hortense Mancini), 101, 162
Memoirs of a Certain Island, Adjacent to the Kingdom of Utopia (Haywood), 28–31, 191–97
Memoirs of the New Atalantis (Manley), 42, 153
Merchants, 19, 24, 75, 76, 77–78, 152, 156
"Mira" ("Myra") (pseudonym for Fowke), 49, 165, 169
Miscellaneous Poems, Original and Translated by Several Hands (1724), 164
Miscellaneous Poems and Translations, ed. Savage (1726), 159, 165, 167
Money: Fowke's attitudes to, 23–24, 69, 107–8; financial consequences of mother's death, 72; financial situation after marriage, 29, 30, 38; paid out for brother, 107, 108; settlement of, on Fowke, 73, 155
Monmouth, Duke of, 119, 165
Moor, Mrs., 117, 164
Murder of father, 20, 81–82, 150–51, 157
Musgrave, W: annotated copy of *Clio,* 163, 165
Muses, 81, 101, 103, 136, 137, 139, 143, 147–48

Music: education in, 21, 65; Fowke plays for lovers, 67, 86; Fowke's interest in, 94, 151; as entertainment, 90

Needlework, 21, 65
New Miscellany of Original Poems and Translations, ed. Anthony Hammond, 32, 149–51
Nussbaum, Felicity, 17

Oculist, 85, 158
Oldmixon, John, 160
Oronooko (Behn, adapted by Southerne), 23, 69, 155
Ovid, 21, 154
Oxford, 92, 159

P——, Mrs. (lady who lodged at Fulham), 123–24, 165–66
Pack, Colonel Richardson, 24, 34, 164
Painter, 26, 106–8, 116, 162–63
Pall Mall, London, 97, 154
Parson's Green, Middlesex, 120, 121
Patriarchy, 37
Periodicals, 15, 40; *Barbados Gazette,* 15, 166; *Censor,* 166; *Delights for the Ingenious,* 15, 162; *Plain Dealer,* 34; *Spectator,* 166
Philips, John, 24
Philips, Katherine, 17
Phillips, Teresa Constantia, 17
Picture, 32. *See also* Portrait
"Picture of Love" (Hill), 34
Pilkington, Laetitia, 17, 21
Plain Dealer (Bond and Hill), 34
Platonic love, 26, 37, 94, 160, 165
Playhouse. *See* Theater
Poetical Register, 15
Pope, Alexander, 17, 26, 31, 34, 42
Porter, John, 15
Portraits: frontispiece, 32, 149; of Fowke, by C——y, 106, 162–63; of Fowke, by Dyer, 25, 167; of Fowke's brother, 110; returned by cousin, 103
Price, Mrs., 165–66
Publishers, 24, 42, 149, 193–94
Putney, 122, 165

Queens: Anne, 151, 155; Mary (wife of James II), 125; Caroline (wife of George II), 164; Henrietta Maria, 166; Mary II (wife of William III), 76

R——, Mr., 109, 163. *See also* Keightley
Rakes. *See* Libertinism
Read, Sir William, 158
Reading: complexity of, 35; of Cowley, 65, 66; Fowke's passion for, 18, 64, 70, 74, 92, 101, 110; of French romances, 21, 64; instruction in, 157; oral, 86; of Ovid, 65–66; restriction of, 21, 65; of Shakespeare, 100–101, 102, 111
Red-Lyon-Square, London, 88, 158
Rench (Wrench) family (gardeners at Fulham), 162
Richardson, Samuel, 27, 36, 161
Richmond, Duke of, 160
Richmond, Surrey, 117, 158, 164
"Riverius" (Haywood's pseudonym for Richard Savage), 195–97
Rowe, Nicholas, 21, 161
Rumbold, Valerie, 26
"Rutho" (Haywood's pseudonym for Arnold Sansom), 29, 192
Ryder, Dudley, 163
Ryder, Mrs. (mother of Elizabeth Lawrence), 163

S., Mr. *See* Sansom, Arnold
S., Mr. (partner at dance), 22, 96–99
Sackville-West, Vita, 43
St. James, London, 67, 73, 94
St. James's Park, 157
St. James's Square, 92, 159
St. James's Street, 94, 155, 159
Sansom, Arnold, 17, 24; legal connections of, 24, 163; marriage of Fowke to, 129, 164, 167; relationship with Fowke, 26–27, 29, 37–38, 113–20; 123; residence in Inner Temple, 164
Sappho, 15, 149
Savage, Richard, 17, 21, 24 (2), 26, 30, 39; *Miscellaneous Poems and Translations* (1726), 159, 165; plays by, 165–66; verses on Fowke's portrait by Dyer, 167
Scandal memoir, 17
Scarborough Anthology for the Year 1733, 160
Sewell, George, 24, 34
Sexuality, 25–28
Shakespeare, William: allusions to, 31, 32, 92, 115; Fowke's passion for, 17,

21, 32 (2), 100–101, 111; gardener and, 102; Hill's interest in, 32; imitation of, 15, 17, 31; performance of *Julius Caesar,* 151, 170; popularity of, 161; Theobald and, 166
Sincerity, 35, 113, 138
Smith, Edmund, 94, 160
South, Bishop, 20
South Sea Bubble, 23, 29, 38, 167
Southerne, Thomas, 23
Spain, 110, 150
Spectator, 166
Spring Garden, Westminster, 74, 156
Spy upon the Conjurer (Haywood), 28
Stafford, Lord, 125, 155, 166
Staffordshire: family connections in, 19, 28, 39, 60, 99, 152, 153; Fowke's childhood in, 64, 66; friends from, 157, 165
Steele, Sir Richard; connections with Fowke's circle, 34, 153, 158, 160, 166; lodges in same street as Fowke, 159; rents lodgings from Cenny family, 23, 157; praises Fowke, 15
Stone, Lawrence, 27
"Strephon," 125, 166. *See also* Bond, William
Swedish clergyman, 121–22, 165
Sydenham, Thomas, 19, 158
Sydenham, William, 158

T——ds, Mr. *See* Theobald, Lewis
Theater, 23, 69, 131, 166, 167
Theobald, Lewis, 24, 125–27, 166
Thomas, Elizabeth, 42
Thomson, James, 34, 37, 164
Tracy, Clarence, 17, 166
Tracy family of Stanway, 163
Turkey, 24, 156, 158
Turner, James, 27

Vanderput, Lady, 159
Vane, Lady, 17
Verrio, Antonio, 164
Victor, Benjamin, 34
Vincent, Sir Antony; 19, 62, 152; Anne, widow of, (Thomas Fowke's first wife), 19, 62, 152
Virginia, 24, 156

Walker, Mary, 156
Walpole, Lady, 41
Walpole, Sir Robert, 38
Whores, 29, 30, 162
Windsor, 26, 75, 116, 156, 164
Winter (Thomson), 37
Wit: Fowke as a, 15, 20, 66; and love, 87, 140, 146; lovers with, 79, 100, 107, 112, 129; as social characteristic, 25, 60, 90; women friends with, 101, 106, 119, 123
Writing: for family, by Fowke, 20, 66; forbidden by mother, 21–22, 65; learning of, 21, 65–66; by lovers, 100, 109; physicality of, 32, 36; of verses, 66. *See also* Muses
Wroth: Dorothy, 156; Joyce, 156; Thomas, 156
Wycherley, William, 18, 91, 158, 166